MAJESTIC

Meanwhile, Back on Earth...

MAJESTIC: MEANWHILE, BACK ON EARTH... Published by WildStorm
Productions, an imprint of DC Comics. 888 Prospect St. #240, La Jolla, CA 92037.
Compilation © 2006 DC Comics. All Rights Reserved. Originally published in
single magazine form as MAJESTIC #8-12 copyright © 2005, 2006. All Rights
Reserved. Majestic, WildStorm Universe Series and its logo, all characters, the
distinctive likenesses thereof and all related elements are trademarks of DC
Comics. The stories, characters, and incidents mentioned in this magazine are
entirely fictional. Printed on recyclable paper. WildStorm does not read or
accept unsolicited submissions of ideas, stories or artwork.

PRINTED IN CANADA
DC Comics, a Warner Bros. Entertainment Company.

ISBN: 1-4012-0989-0
ISBN-13: 978-1-4012-0989-6

Written by
Dan Abnett
Andy Lanning

Penciled by
Neil Googe (#8, 12)
Georges Jeanty (#9-11)

Inked by
Trevor Scott with Neil Googe (#8)
Trevor Scott (#9)
Scott with Richard Friend and Sandra Hope (#10)
Scott with Carlos D'Anda (#11)
Neil Googe (#12)

Additional art by: Scott Iwahashi (#11)

Colored by
Carrie Strachan (#8-10,12)
Strachan with Jonny Rench (#11)
Lettered by
Phil Balsman

Original series covers by Neil Googe

Loose Ends

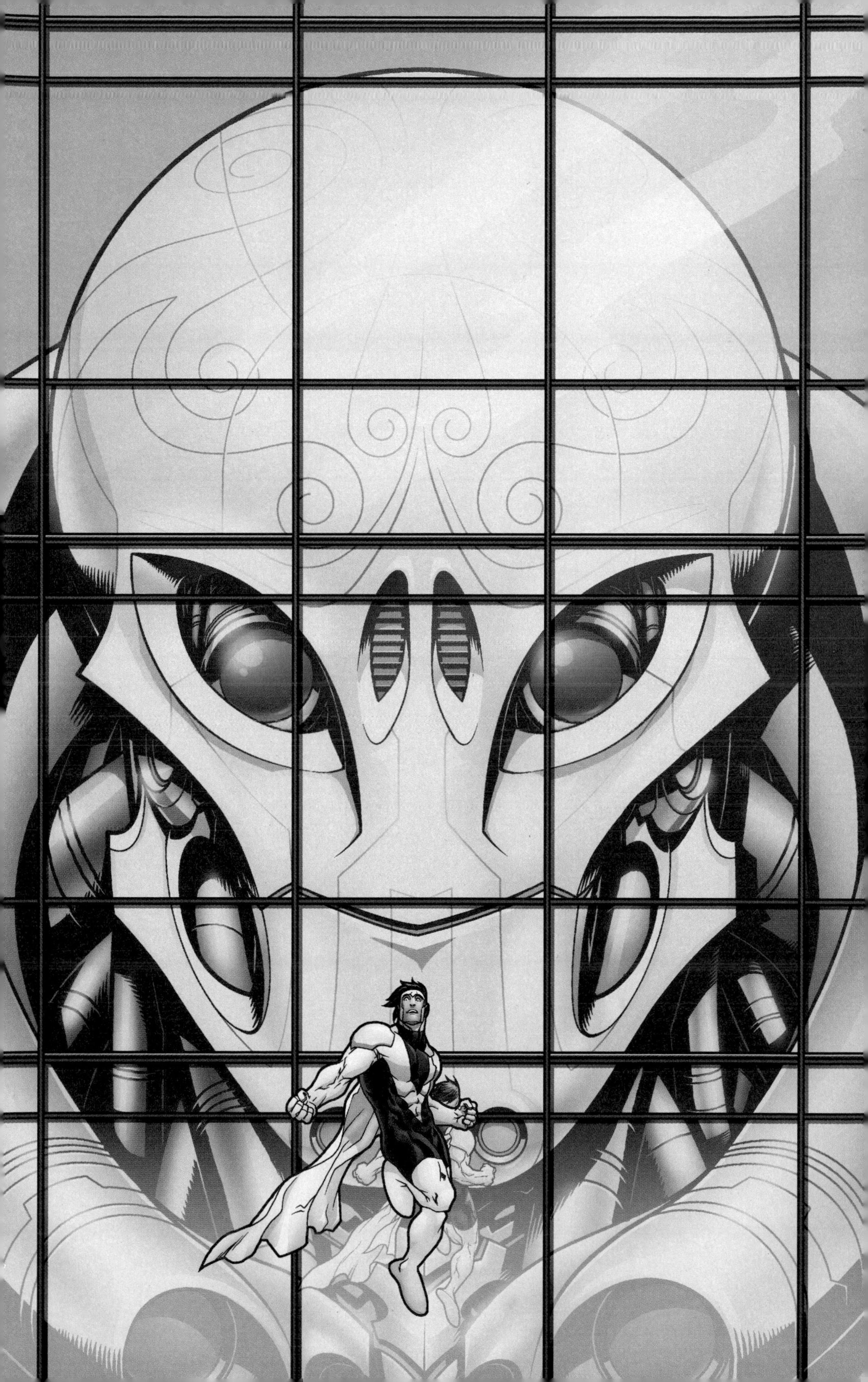

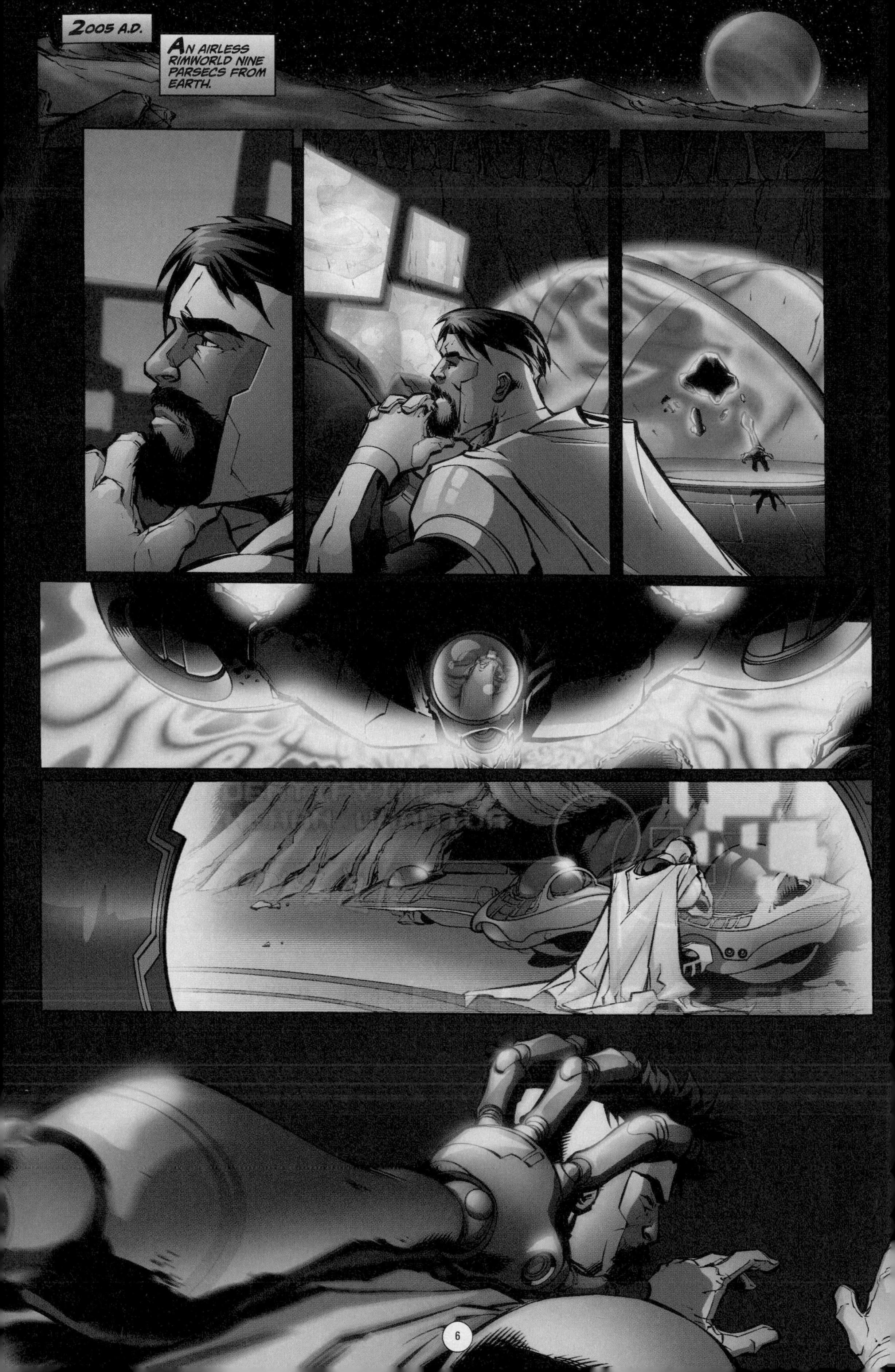
2005 A.D.
An airless rimworld nine parsecs from Earth.

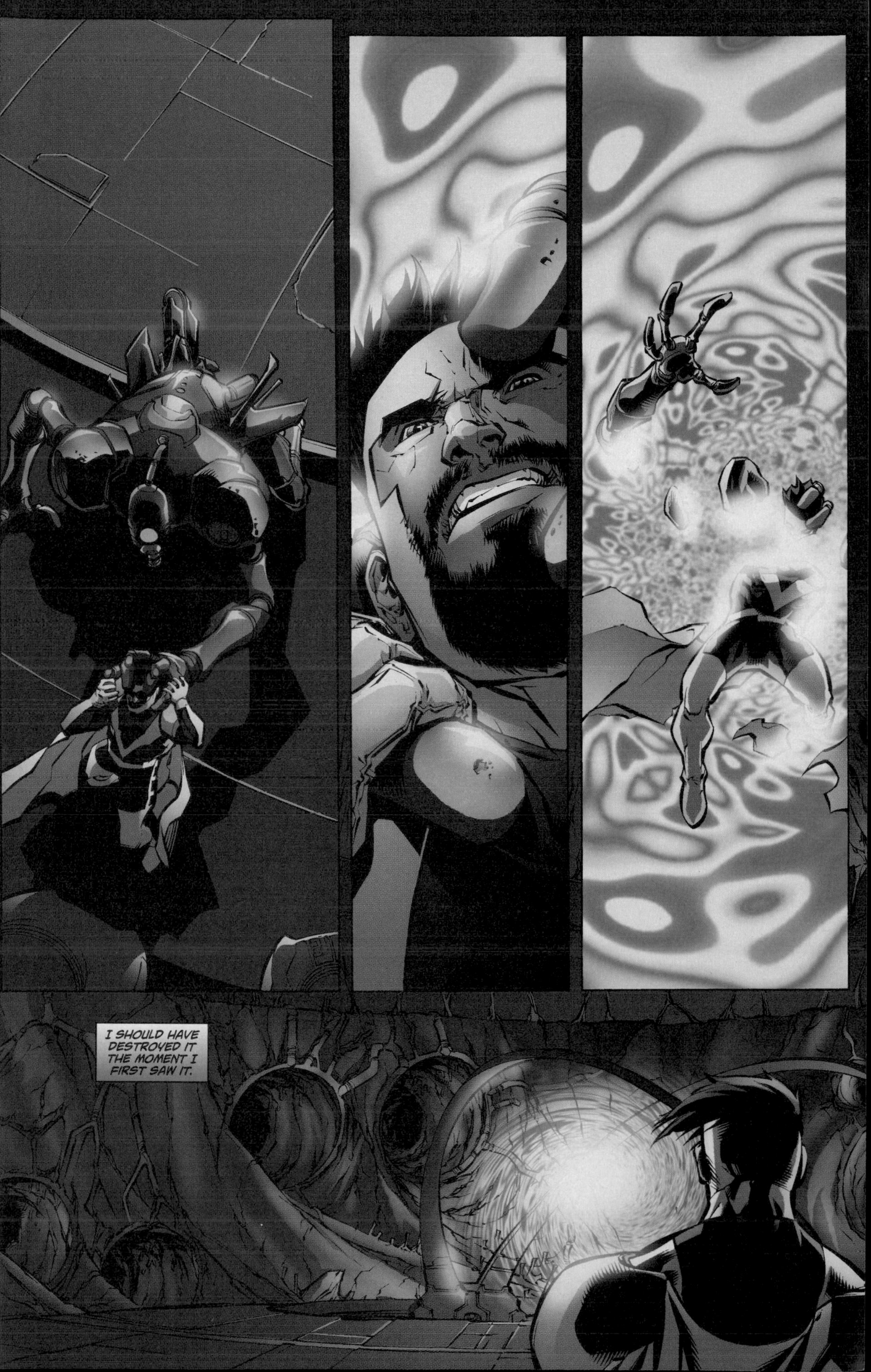
I SHOULD HAVE DESTROYED IT THE MOMENT I FIRST SAW IT.

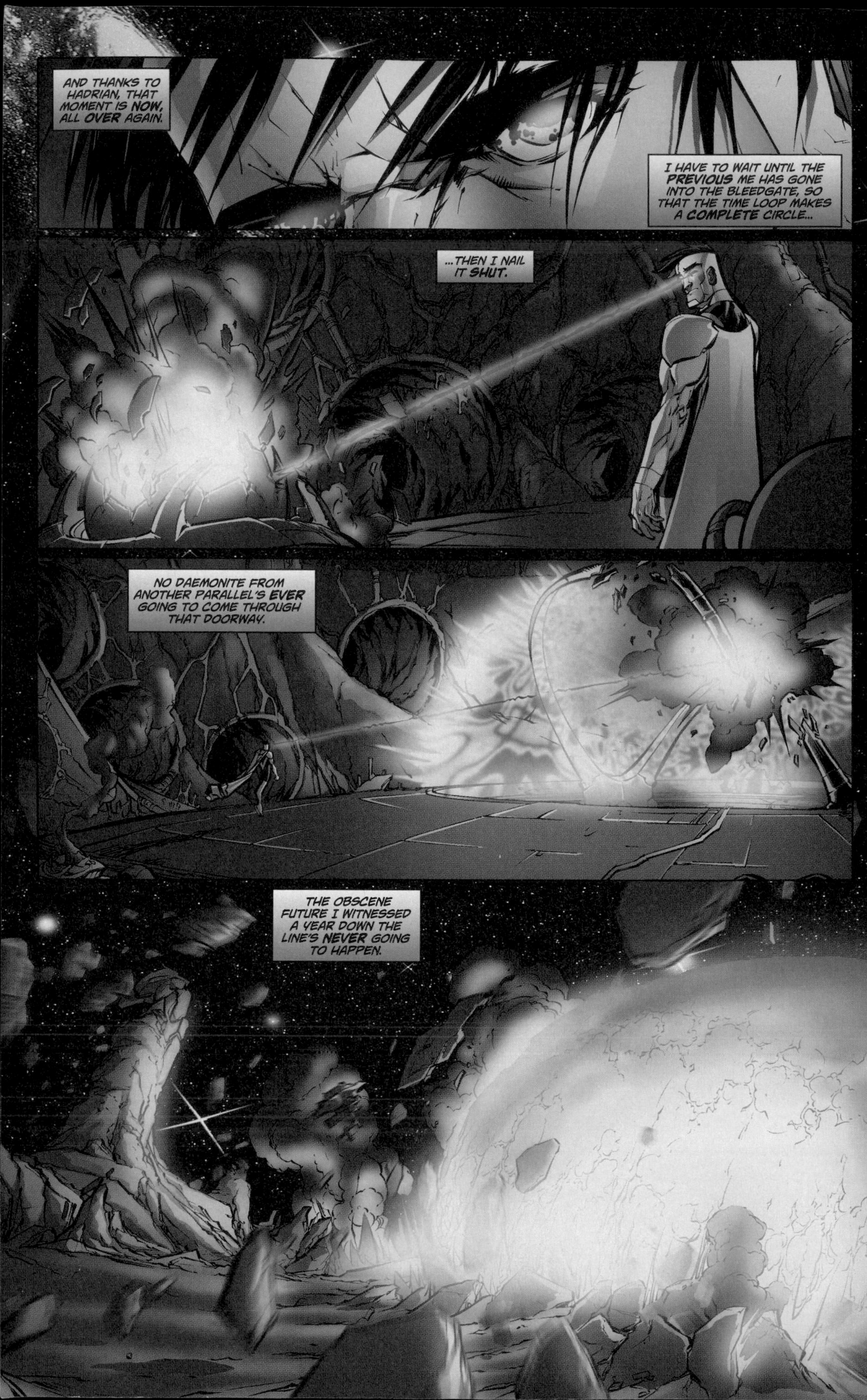
AND THANKS TO HADRIAN, THAT MOMENT IS NOW, ALL OVER AGAIN.
I HAVE TO WAIT UNTIL THE PREVIOUS ME HAS GONE INTO THE BLEEDGATE, SO THAT THE TIME LOOP MAKES A COMPLETE CIRCLE...
...THEN I NAIL IT SHUT.
NO DAEMONITE FROM ANOTHER PARALLEL'S EVER GOING TO COME THROUGH THAT DOORWAY.
THE OBSCENE FUTURE I WITNESSED A YEAR DOWN THE LINE'S NEVER GOING TO HAPPEN.

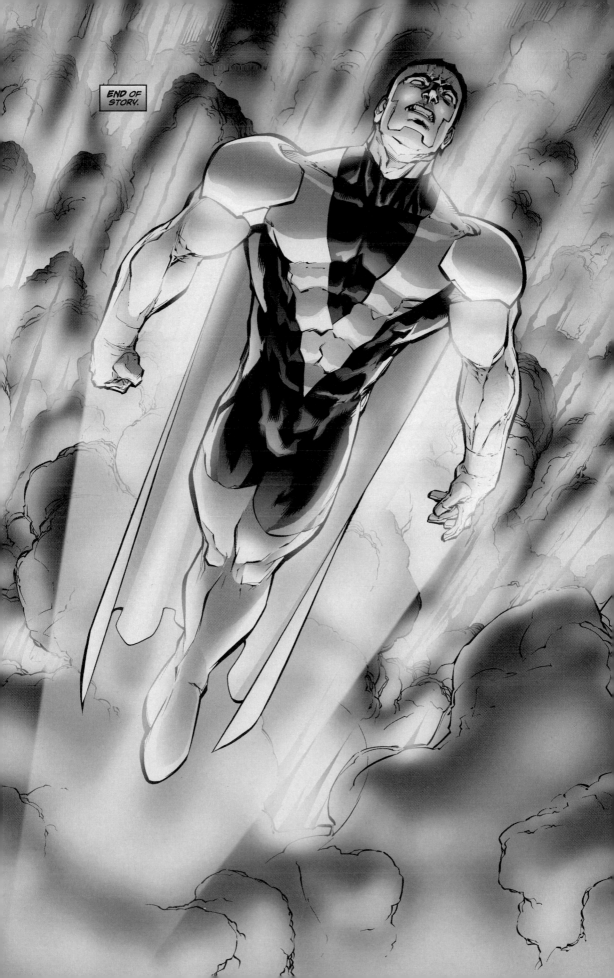

END OF STORY.

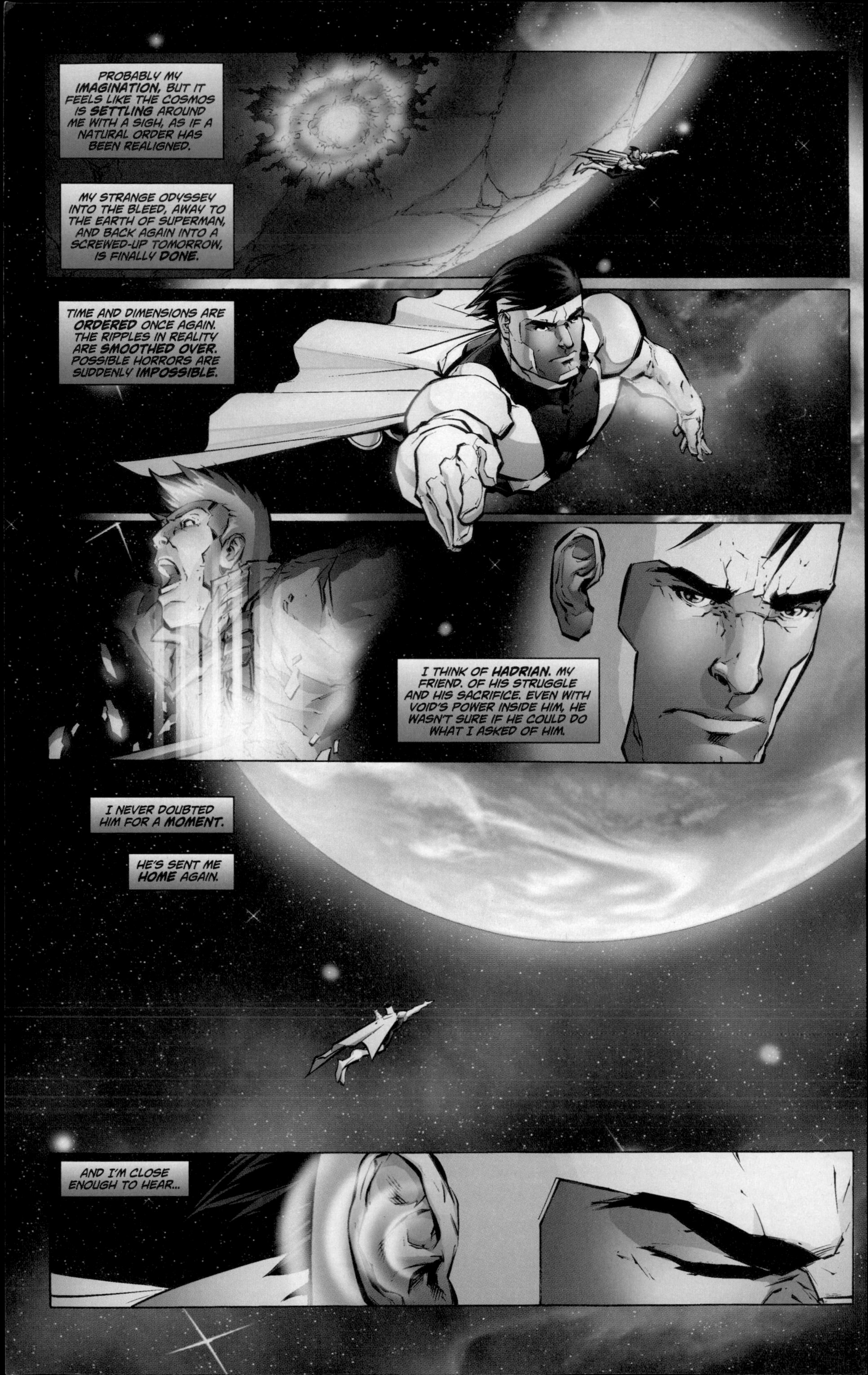
PROBABLY MY IMAGINATION, BUT IT FEELS LIKE THE COSMOS IS SETTLING AROUND ME WITH A SIGH, AS IF A NATURAL ORDER HAS BEEN REALIGNED.
MY STRANGE ODYSSEY INTO THE BLEED, AWAY TO THE EARTH OF SUPERMAN, AND BACK AGAIN INTO A SCREWED-UP TOMORROW, IS FINALLY DONE.
TIME AND DIMENSIONS ARE ORDERED ONCE AGAIN. THE RIPPLES IN REALITY ARE SMOOTHED OVER. POSSIBLE HORRORS ARE SUDDENLY IMPOSSIBLE.
I THINK OF HADRIAN. MY FRIEND. OF HIS STRUGGLE AND HIS SACRIFICE. EVEN WITH VOID'S POWER INSIDE HIM, HE WASN'T SURE IF HE COULD DO WHAT I ASKED OF HIM.
I NEVER DOUBTED HIM FOR A MOMENT.
HE'S SENT ME HOME AGAIN.
AND I'M CLOSE ENOUGH TO HEAR...

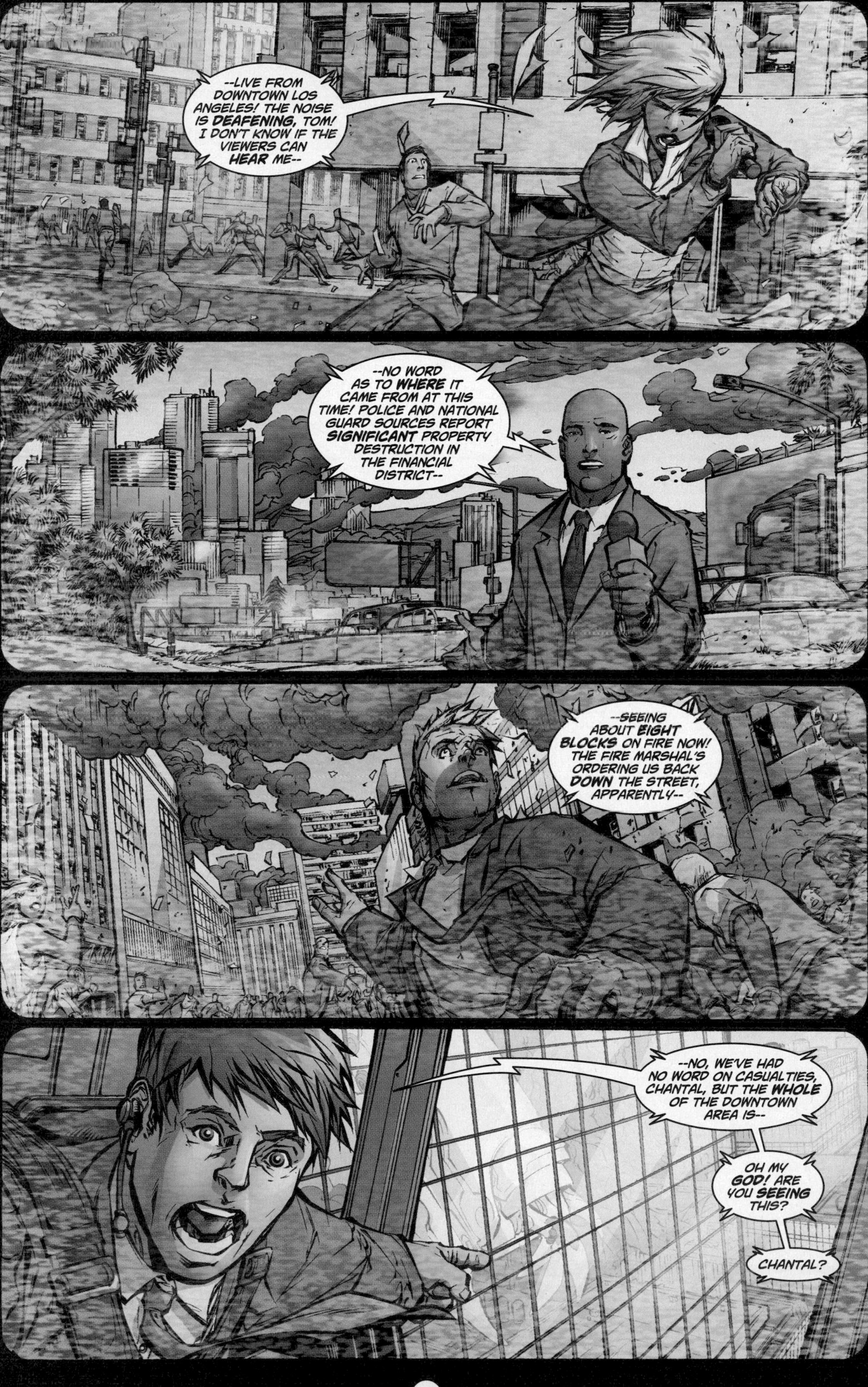
--LIVE FROM DOWNTOWN LOS ANGELES! THE NOISE IS DEAFENING, TOM! I DON'T KNOW IF THE VIEWERS CAN HEAR ME--
--NO WORD AS TO WHERE IT CAME FROM AT THIS TIME! POLICE AND NATIONAL GUARD SOURCES REPORT SIGNIFICANT PROPERTY DESTRUCTION IN THE FINANCIAL DISTRICT--
--SEEING ABOUT EIGHT BLOCKS ON FIRE NOW! THE FIRE MARSHAL'S ORDERING US BACK DOWN THE STREET, APPARENTLY--
--NO, WE'VE HAD NO WORD ON CASUALTIES, CHANTAL, BUT THE WHOLE OF THE DOWNTOWN AREA IS--
OH MY GOD! ARE YOU SEEING THIS?
CHANTAL?

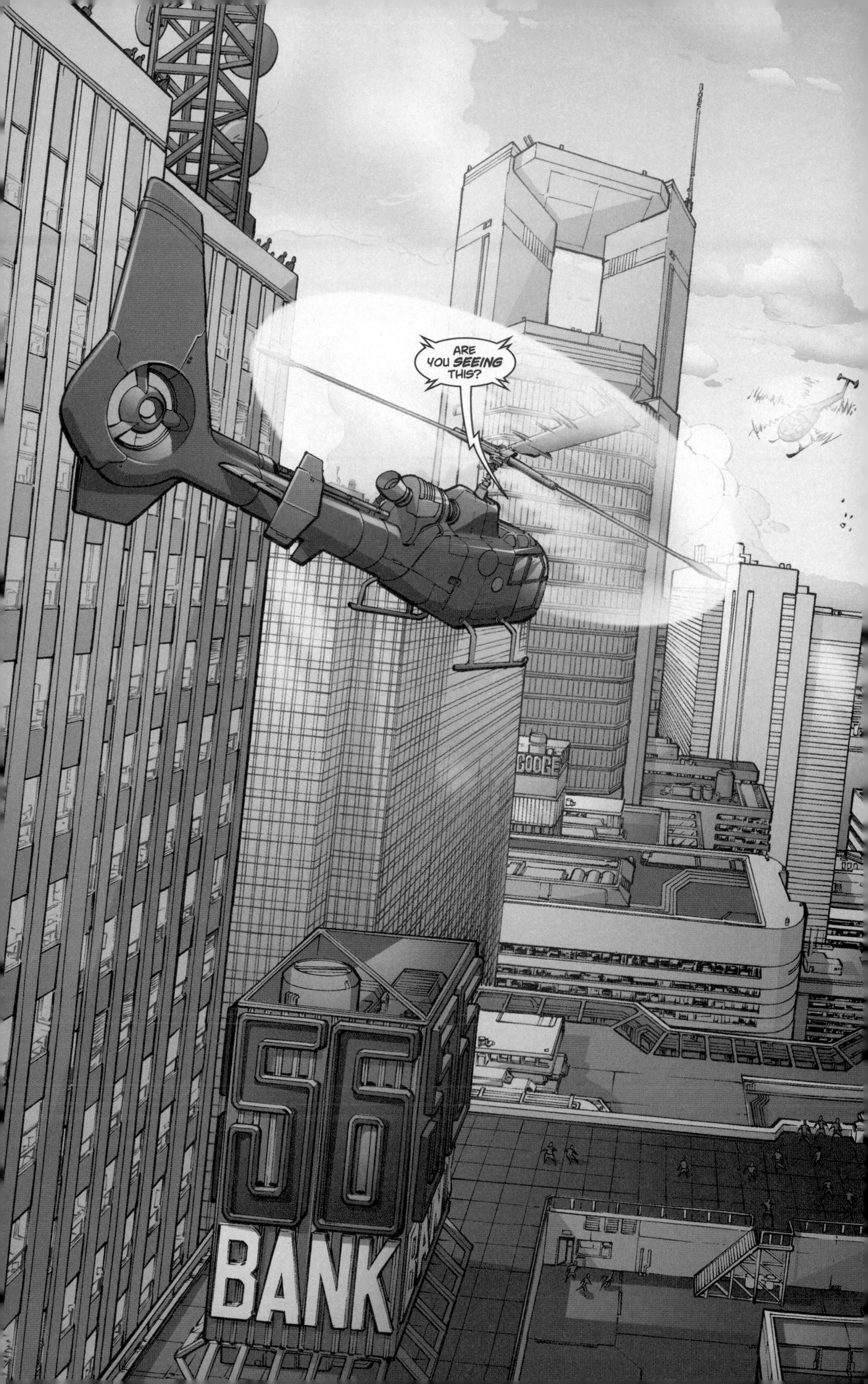
ARE YOU SEEING THIS?
56
BANK

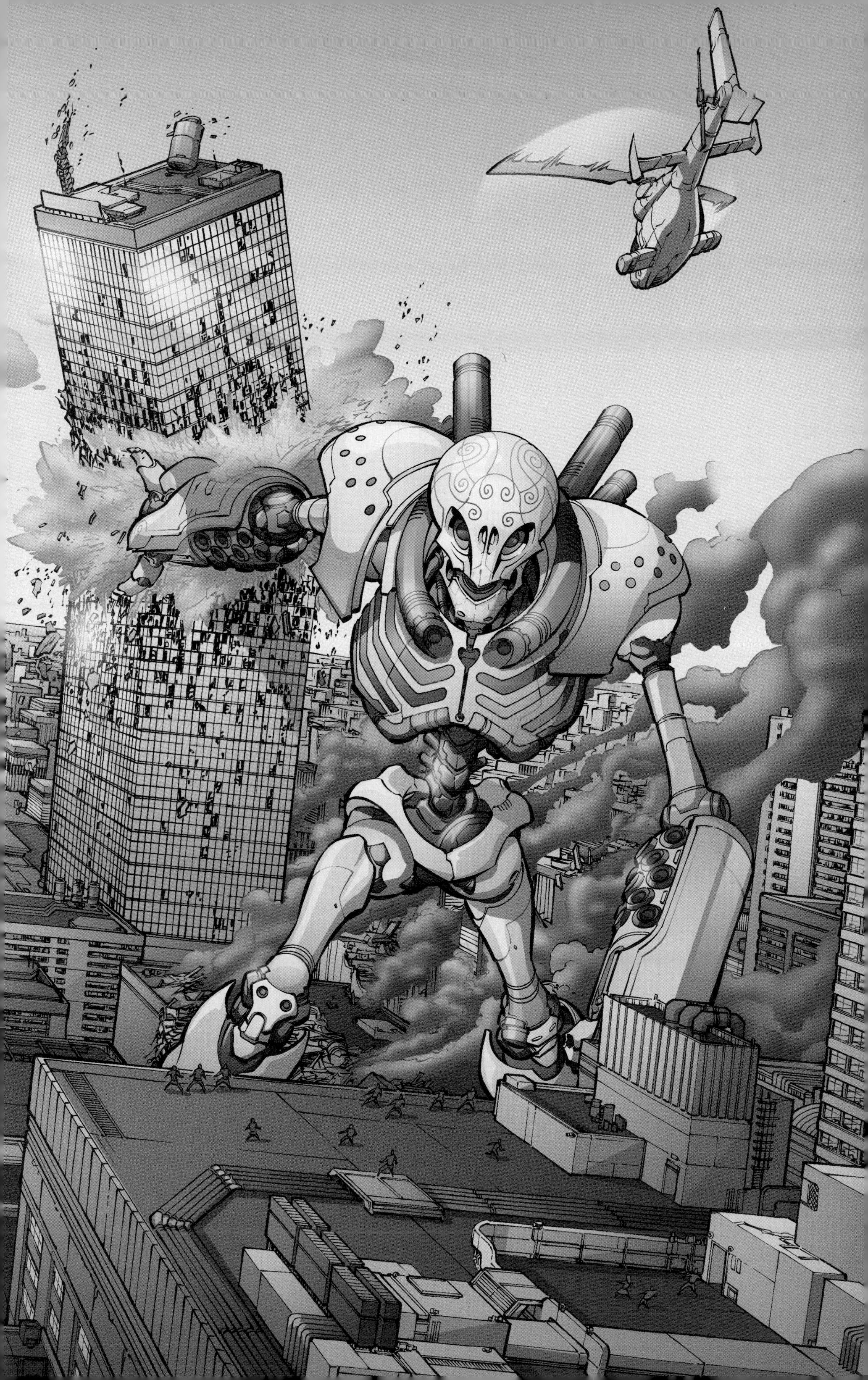

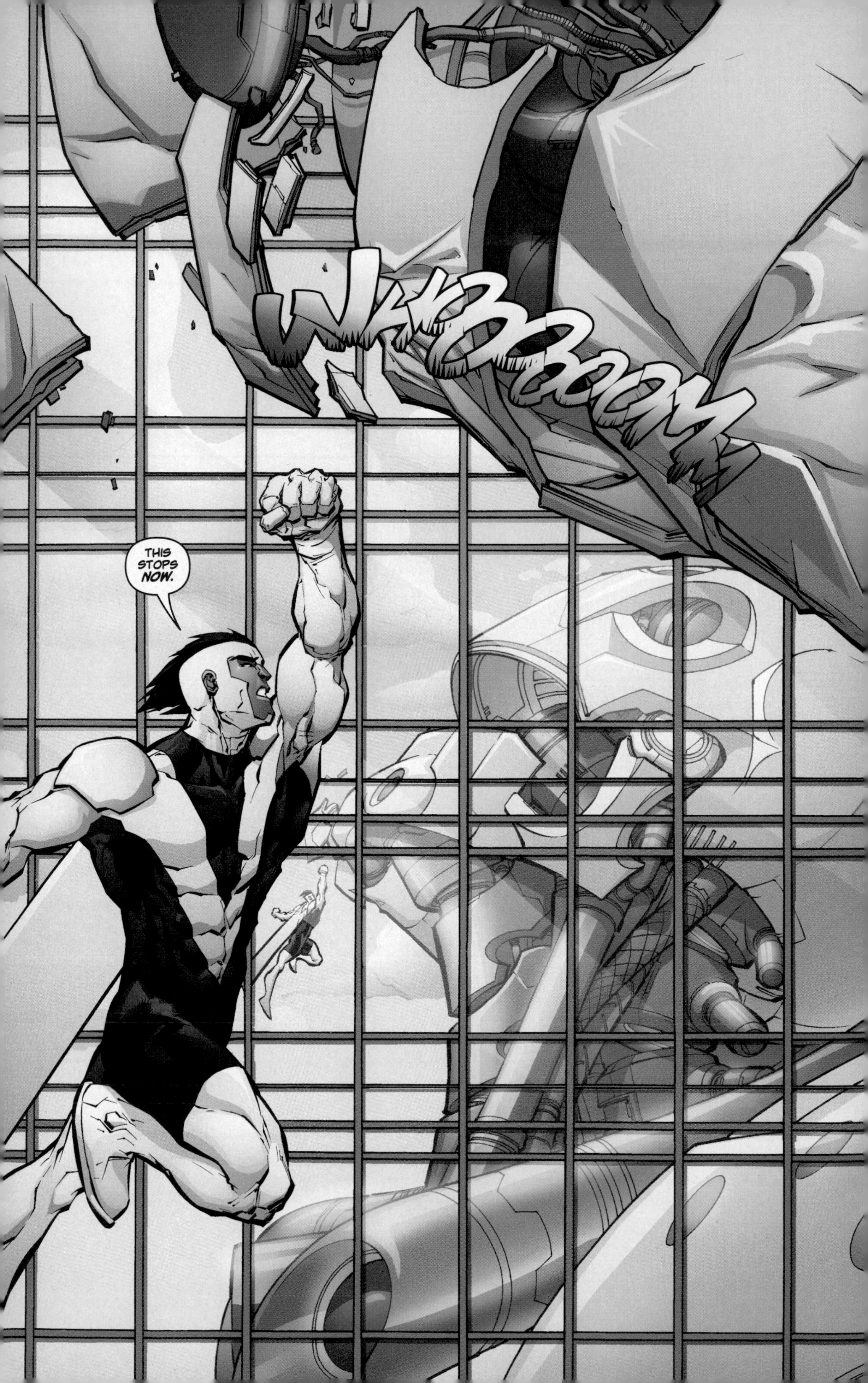
WHOOOOM
THIS STOPS NOW.

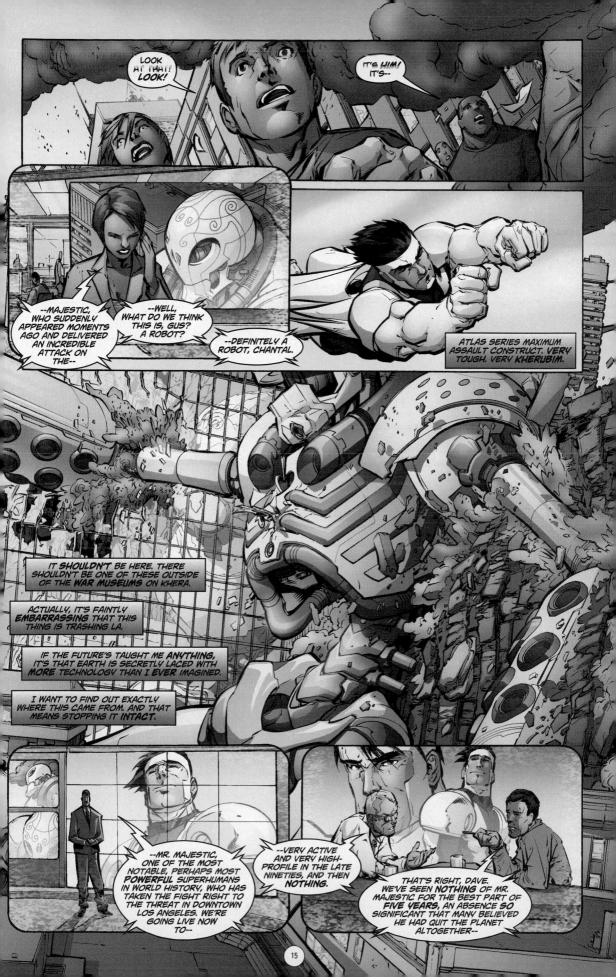

LOOK AT THAT! LOOK!

IT'S HIM! IT'S--

--MAJESTIC, WHO SUDDENLY APPEARED MOMENTS AGO AND DELIVERED AN INCREDIBLE ATTACK ON THE--

--WELL, WHAT DO WE THINK THIS IS, GUS? A ROBOT?

--DEFINITELY A ROBOT, CHANTAL.

ATLAS SERIES MAXIMUM ASSAULT CONSTRUCT. VERY TOUGH. VERY KHERUBIM.

IT SHOULDN'T BE HERE. THERE SHOULDN'T BE ONE OF THESE OUTSIDE OF THE WAR MUSEUMS ON KHERA.

ACTUALLY, IT'S FAINTLY EMBARRASSING THAT THIS THING IS TRASHING LA.

IF THE FUTURE'S TAUGHT ME ANYTHING, IT'S THAT EARTH IS SECRETLY LACED WITH MORE TECHNOLOGY THAN I EVER IMAGINED.

I WANT TO FIND OUT EXACTLY WHERE THIS CAME FROM. AND THAT MEANS STOPPING IT INTACT.

--MR. MAJESTIC, ONE OF THE MOST NOTABLE, PERHAPS MOST POWERFUL SUPERHUMANS IN WORLD HISTORY, WHO HAS TAKEN THE FIGHT RIGHT TO THE THREAT IN DOWNTOWN LOS ANGELES. WE'RE GOING LIVE NOW TO--

--VERY ACTIVE AND VERY HIGH-PROFILE IN THE LATE NINETIES, AND THEN NOTHING.

THAT'S RIGHT, DAVE. WE'VE SEEN NOTHING OF MR. MAJESTIC FOR THE BEST PART OF FIVE YEARS, AN ABSENCE SO SIGNIFICANT THAT MANY BELIEVED HE HAD QUIT THE PLANET ALTOGETHER--

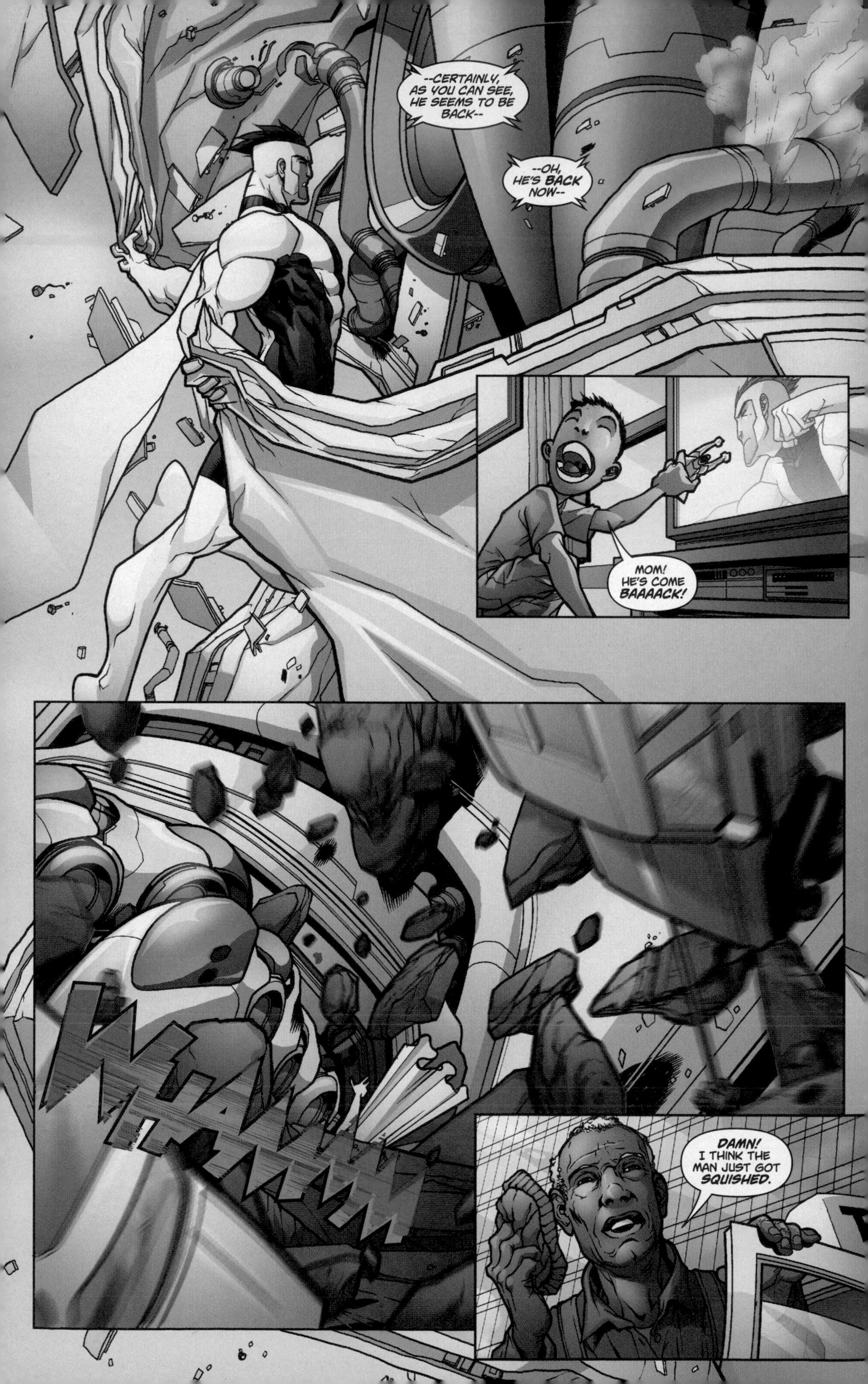
--CERTAINLY, AS YOU CAN SEE, HE SEEMS TO BE BACK--
--OH, HE'S BACK NOW--
MOM! HE'S COME BAAAACK!
WHAAAMM
DAMN! I THINK THE MAN JUST GOT SQUISHED.

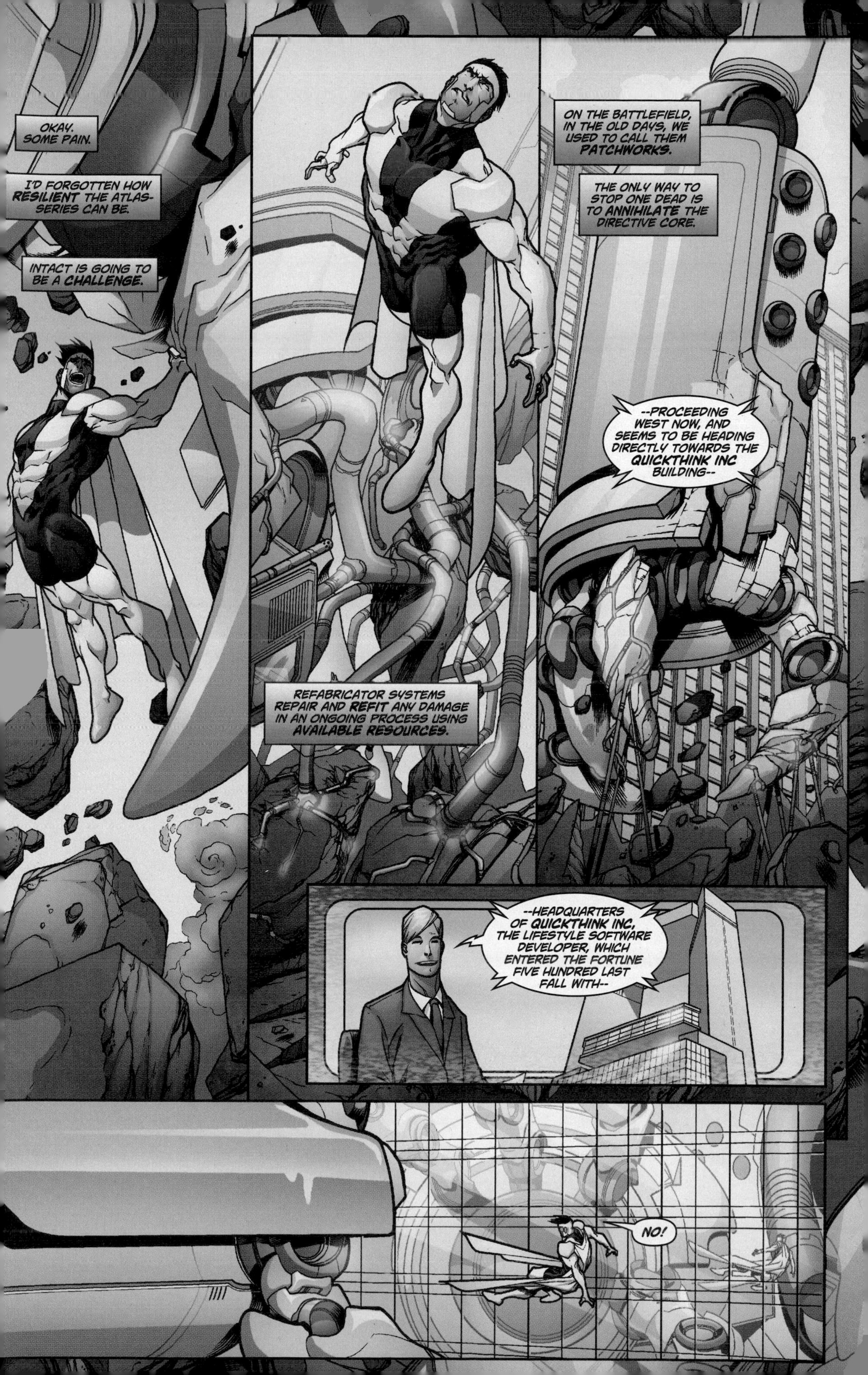
OKAY. SOME PAIN.
I'D FORGOTTEN HOW RESILIENT THE ATLAS-SERIES CAN BE.
INTACT IS GOING TO BE A CHALLENGE.
REFABRICATOR SYSTEMS REPAIR AND REFIT ANY DAMAGE IN AN ONGOING PROCESS USING AVAILABLE RESOURCES.
ON THE BATTLEFIELD, IN THE OLD DAYS, WE USED TO CALL THEM PATCHWORKS.
THE ONLY WAY TO STOP ONE DEAD IS TO ANNIHILATE THE DIRECTIVE CORE.
--PROCEEDING WEST NOW, AND SEEMS TO BE HEADING DIRECTLY TOWARDS THE QUICKTHINK INC BUILDING--
--HEADQUARTERS OF QUICKTHINK INC, THE LIFESTYLE SOFTWARE DEVELOPER, WHICH ENTERED THE FORTUNE FIVE HUNDRED LAST FALL WITH--
NO!

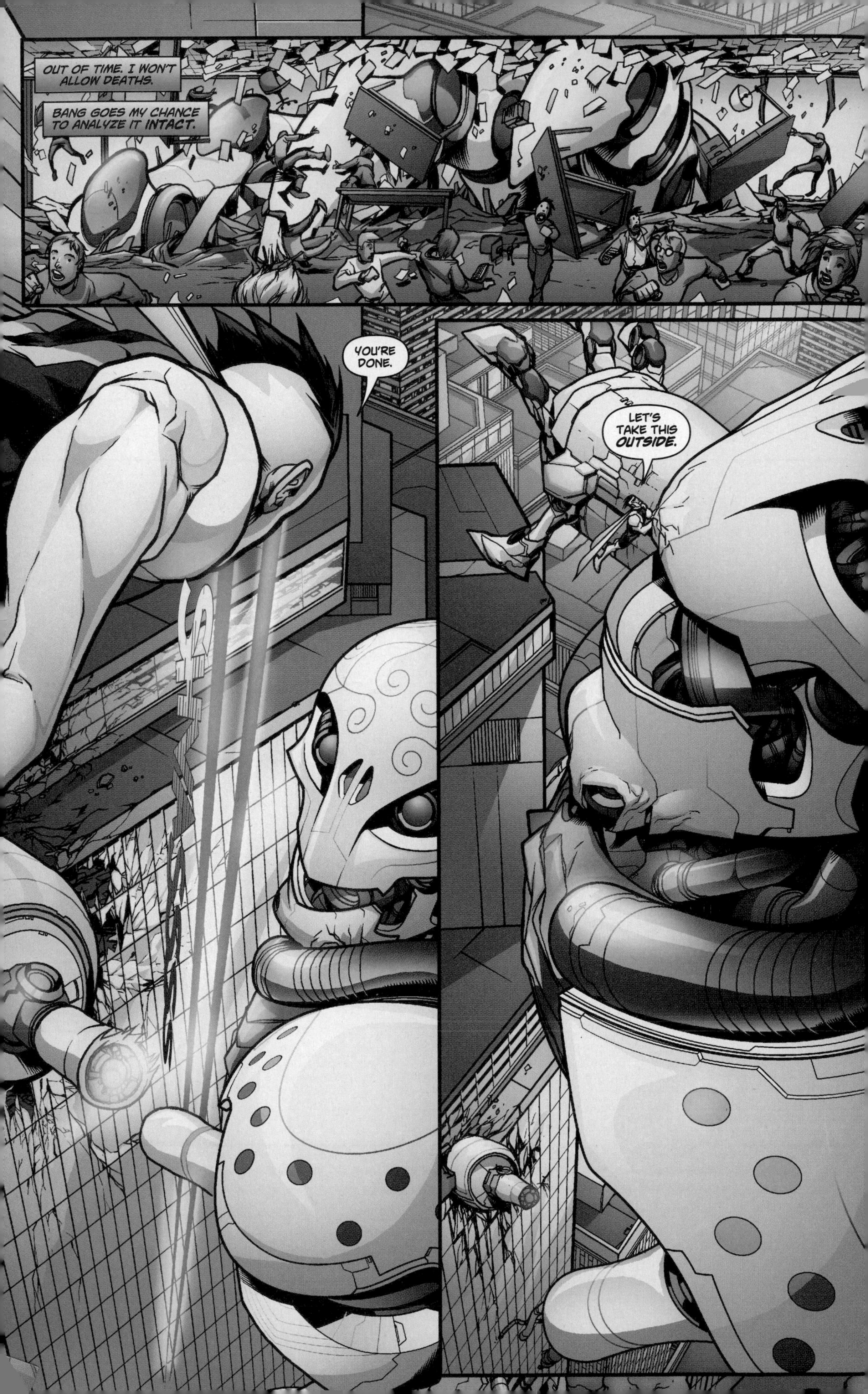
OUT OF TIME. I WON'T ALLOW DEATHS.
BANG GOES MY CHANCE TO ANALYZE IT INTACT.
YOU'RE DONE.
LET'S TAKE THIS OUTSIDE.

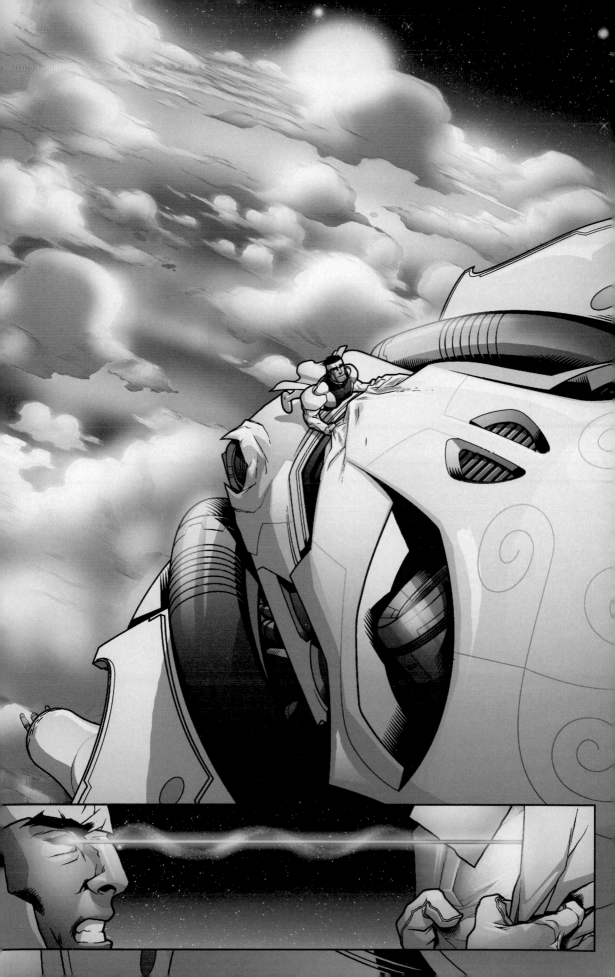

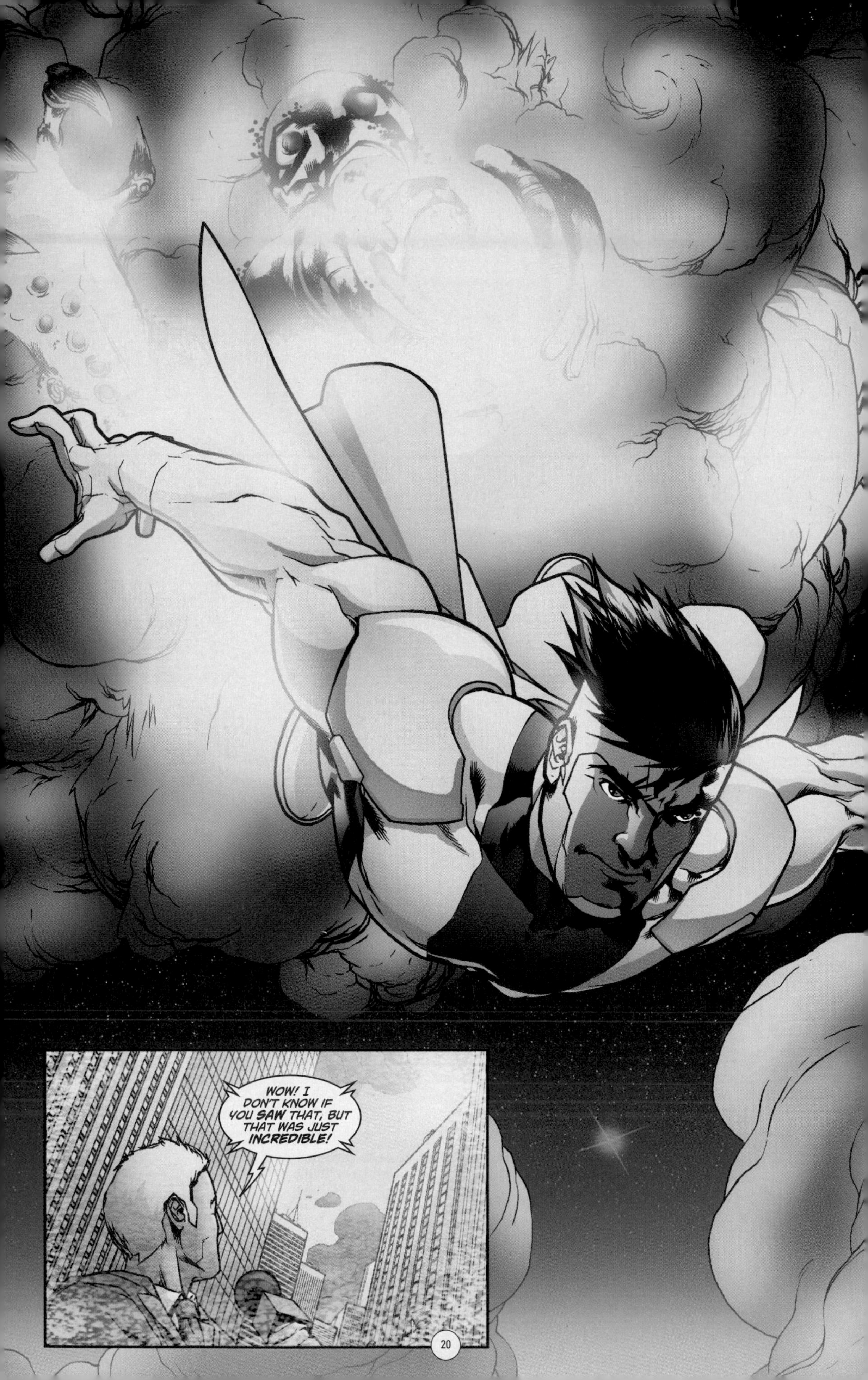
WOW! I DON'T KNOW IF YOU SAW THAT, BUT THAT WAS JUST INCREDIBLE!

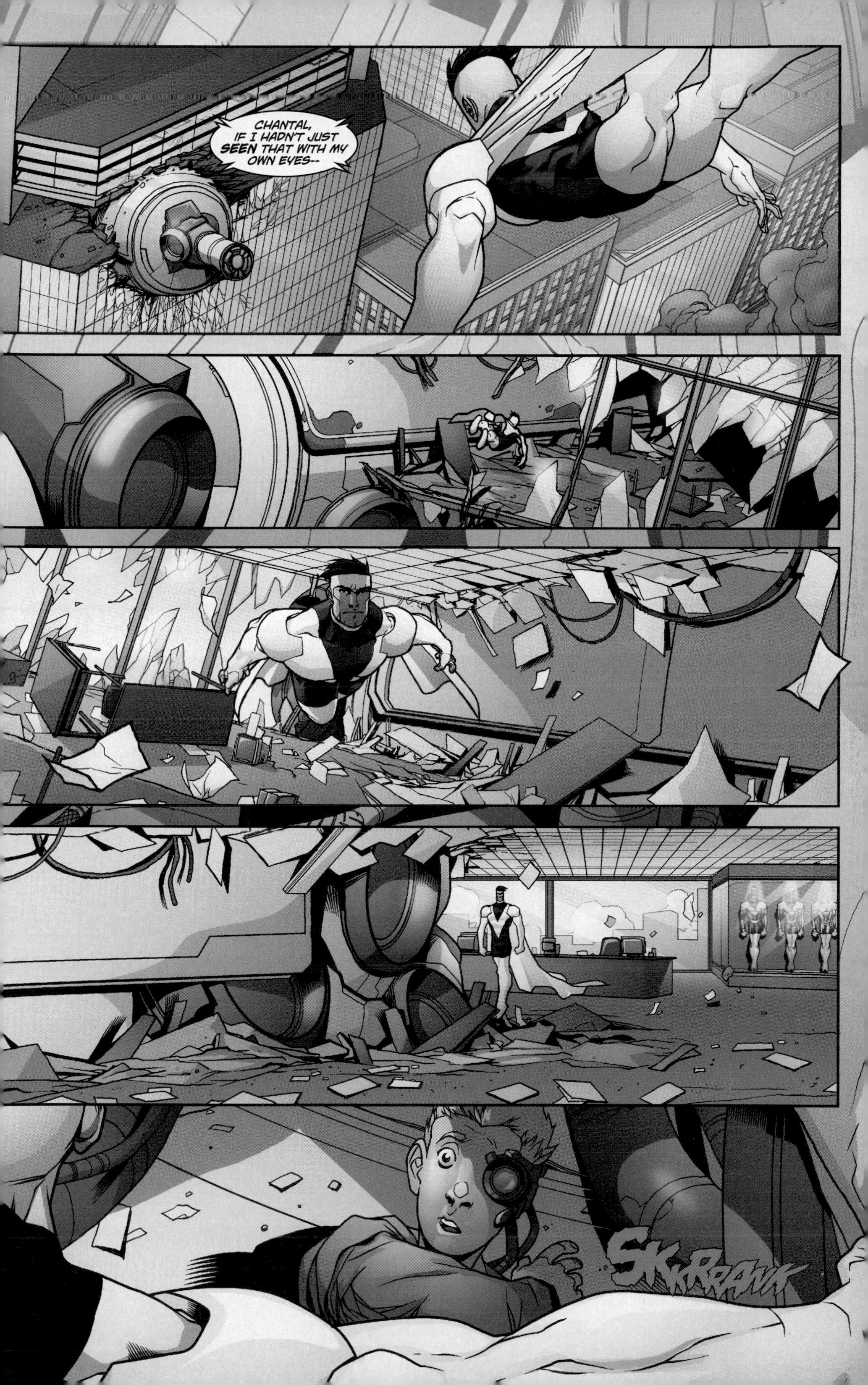
CHANTAL, IF I HADN'T JUST SEEN THAT WITH MY OWN EYES--
SKKRRANK

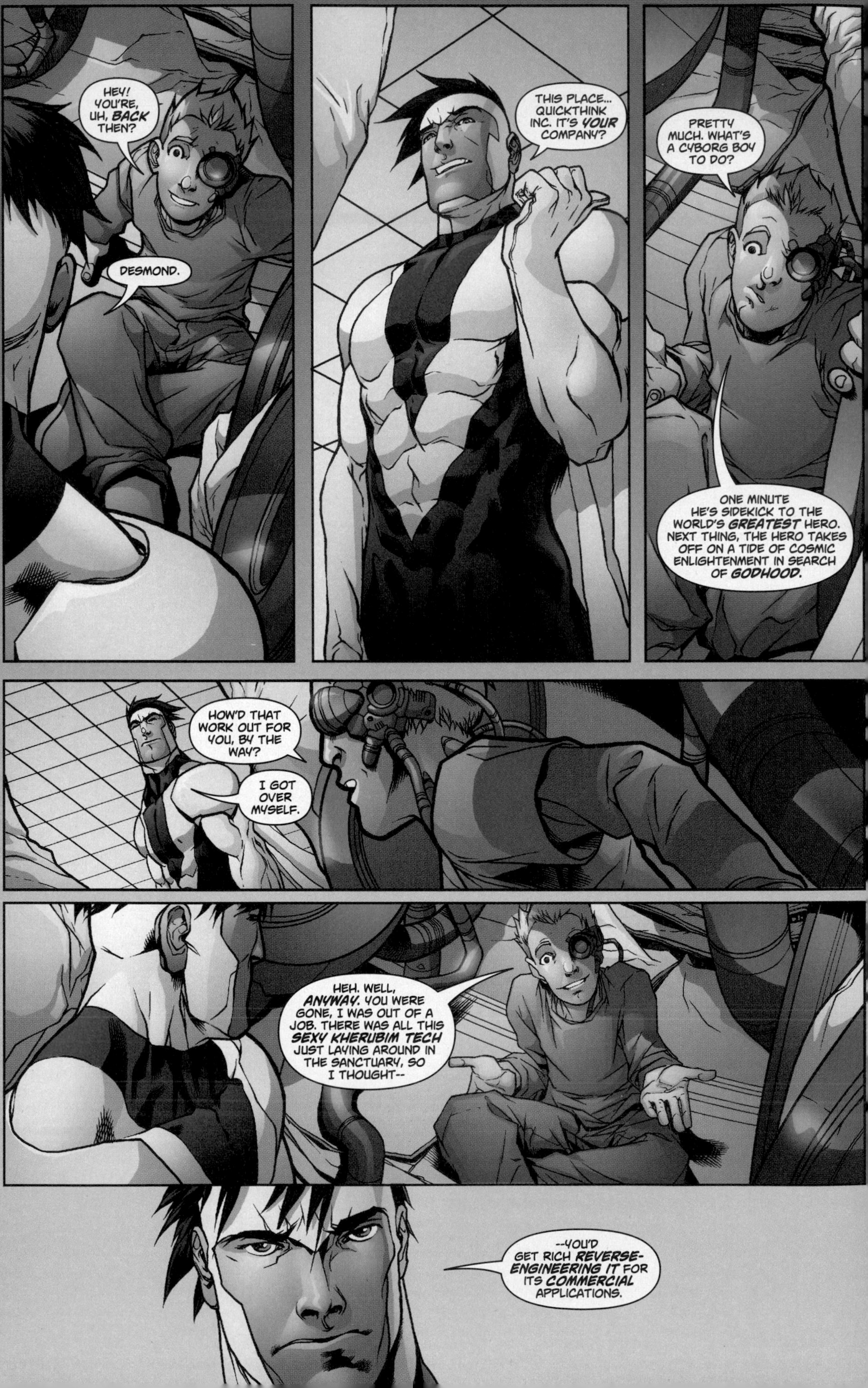
HEY! YOU'RE, UH, BACK THEN?
DESMOND.
THIS PLACE... QUICKTHINK INC. IT'S YOUR COMPANY?
PRETTY MUCH. WHAT'S A CYBORG BOY TO DO?
ONE MINUTE HE'S SIDEKICK TO THE WORLD'S GREATEST HERO. NEXT THING, THE HERO TAKES OFF ON A TIDE OF COSMIC ENLIGHTENMENT IN SEARCH OF GODHOOD.
HOW'D THAT WORK OUT FOR YOU, BY THE WAY?
I GOT OVER MYSELF.
HEH. WELL, ANYWAY. YOU WERE GONE, I WAS OUT OF A JOB. THERE WAS ALL THIS SEXY KHERUBIM TECH JUST LAYING AROUND IN THE SANCTUARY, SO I THOUGHT--
--YOU'D GET RICH REVERSE-ENGINEERING IT FOR ITS COMMERCIAL APPLICATIONS.

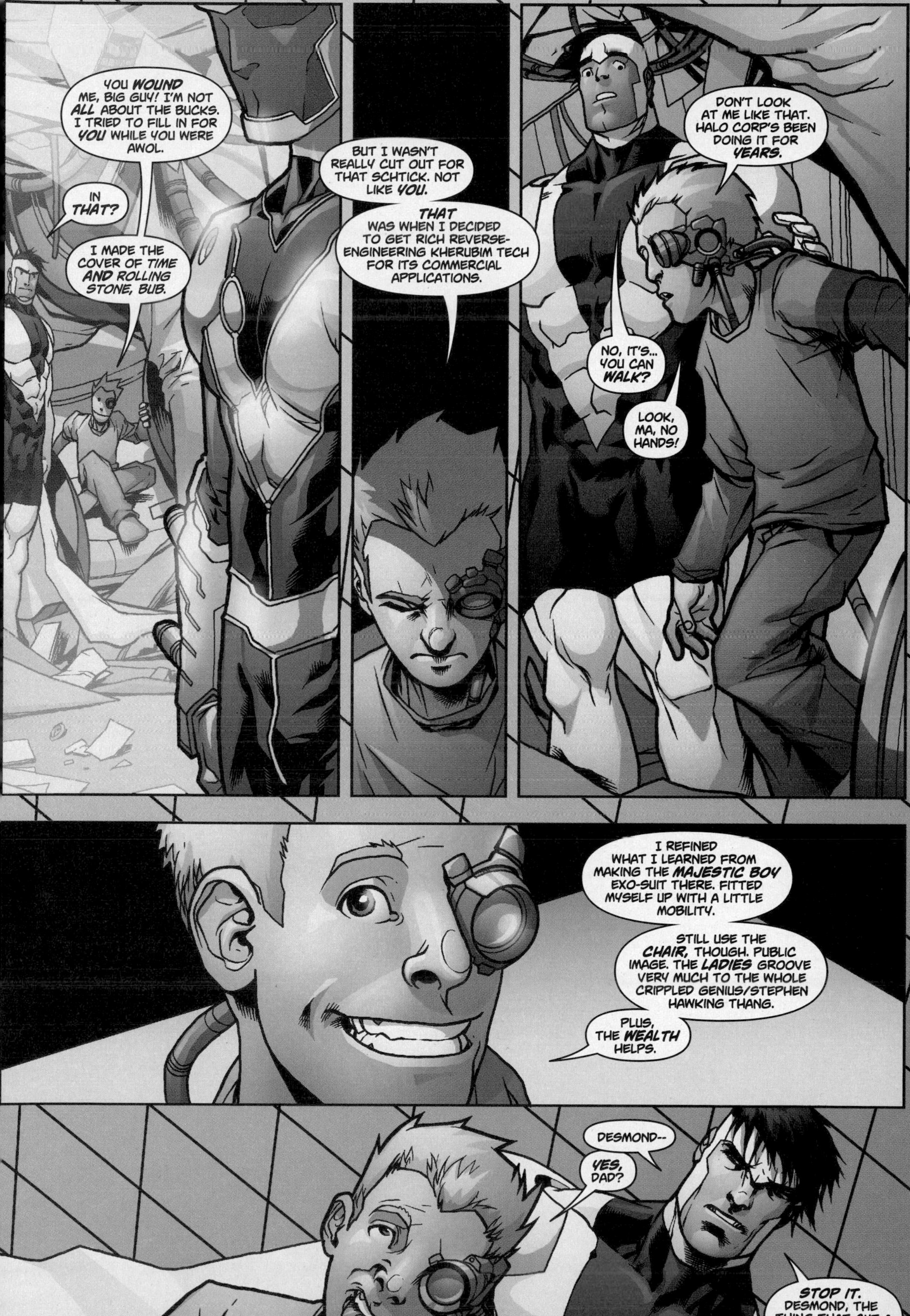
YOU WOUND ME, BIG GUY! I'M NOT ALL ABOUT THE BUCKS. I TRIED TO FILL IN FOR YOU WHILE YOU WERE AWOL.
IN THAT?
I MADE THE COVER OF TIME AND ROLLING STONE, BUB.
BUT I WASN'T REALLY CUT OUT FOR THAT SCHTICK. NOT LIKE YOU.
THAT WAS WHEN I DECIDED TO GET RICH REVERSE-ENGINEERING KHERUBIM TECH FOR ITS COMMERCIAL APPLICATIONS.
DON'T LOOK AT ME LIKE THAT. HALO CORP'S BEEN DOING IT FOR YEARS.
NO, IT'S... YOU CAN WALK?
LOOK, MA, NO HANDS!
I REFINED WHAT I LEARNED FROM MAKING THE MAJESTIC BOY EXO-SUIT THERE. FITTED MYSELF UP WITH A LITTLE MOBILITY.
STILL USE THE CHAIR, THOUGH. PUBLIC IMAGE. THE LADIES GROOVE VERY MUCH TO THE WHOLE CRIPPLED GENIUS/STEPHEN HAWKING THANG.
PLUS, THE WEALTH HELPS.
DESMOND--
YES, DAD?
STOP IT. DESMOND, THE THING THAT CUT A PATH THROUGH LA TODAY--

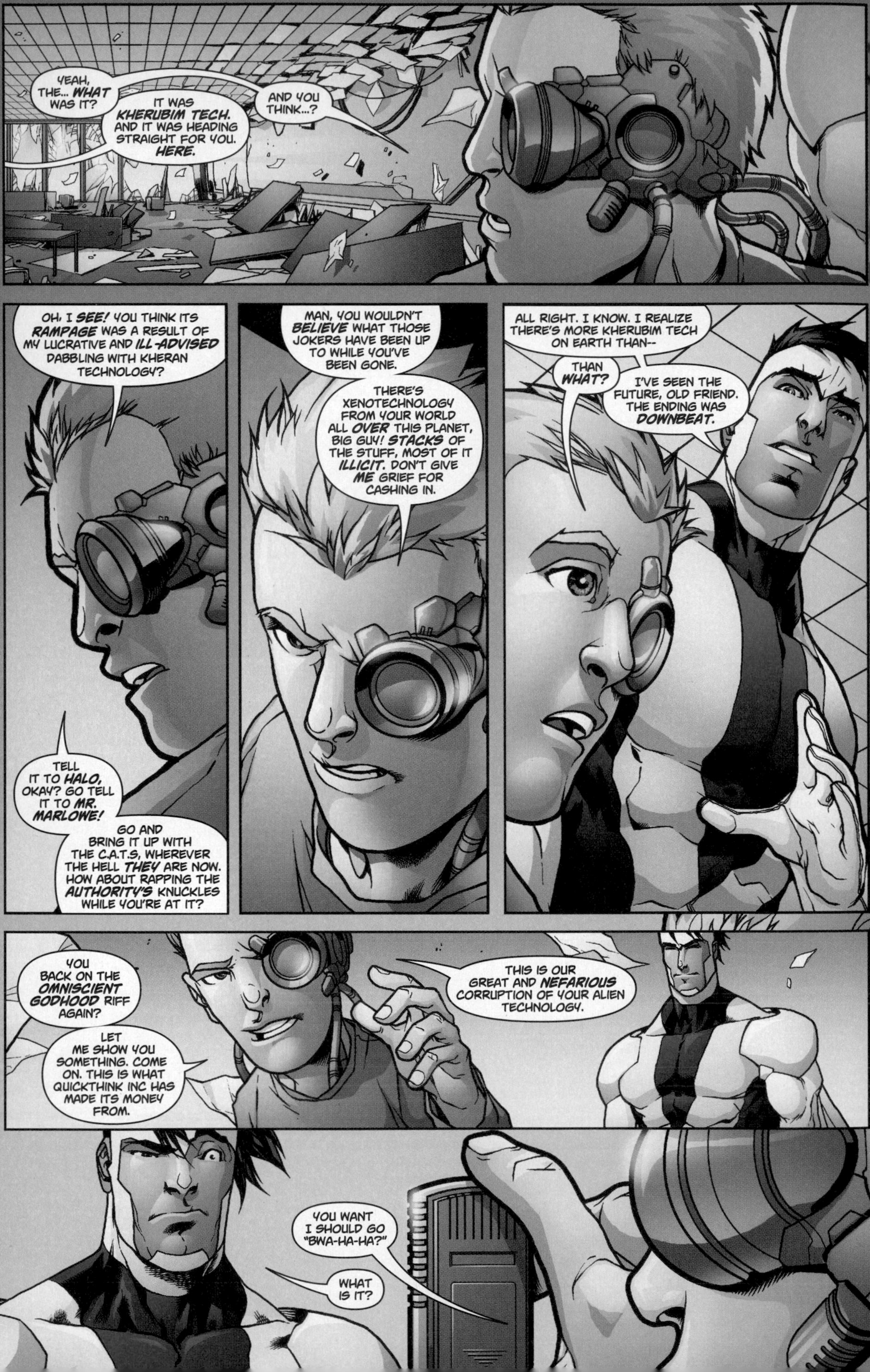
YEAH, THE... WHAT WAS IT?
IT WAS KHERUBIM TECH. AND IT WAS HEADING STRAIGHT FOR YOU. HERE.
AND YOU THINK...?
OH, I SEE! YOU THINK ITS RAMPAGE WAS A RESULT OF MY LUCRATIVE AND ILL-ADVISED DABBLING WITH KHERAN TECHNOLOGY?
TELL IT TO HALO, OKAY? GO TELL IT TO MR. MARLOWE!
GO AND BRING IT UP WITH THE C.A.T.S, WHEREVER THE HELL THEY ARE NOW. HOW ABOUT RAPPING THE AUTHORITY'S KNUCKLES WHILE YOU'RE AT IT?
MAN, YOU WOULDN'T BELIEVE WHAT THOSE JOKERS HAVE BEEN UP TO WHILE YOU'VE BEEN GONE.
THERE'S XENOTECHNOLOGY FROM YOUR WORLD ALL OVER THIS PLANET, BIG GUY! STACKS OF THE STUFF, MOST OF IT ILLICIT. DON'T GIVE ME GRIEF FOR CASHING IN.
ALL RIGHT. I KNOW. I REALIZE THERE'S MORE KHERUBIM TECH ON EARTH THAN--
THAN WHAT?
I'VE SEEN THE FUTURE, OLD FRIEND. THE ENDING WAS DOWNBEAT.
YOU BACK ON THE OMNISCIENT GODHOOD RIFF AGAIN?
LET ME SHOW YOU SOMETHING. COME ON. THIS IS WHAT QUICKTHINK INC HAS MADE ITS MONEY FROM.
THIS IS OUR GREAT AND NEFARIOUS CORRUPTION OF YOUR ALIEN TECHNOLOGY.
YOU WANT I SHOULD GO "BWA-HA-HA?"
WHAT IS IT?

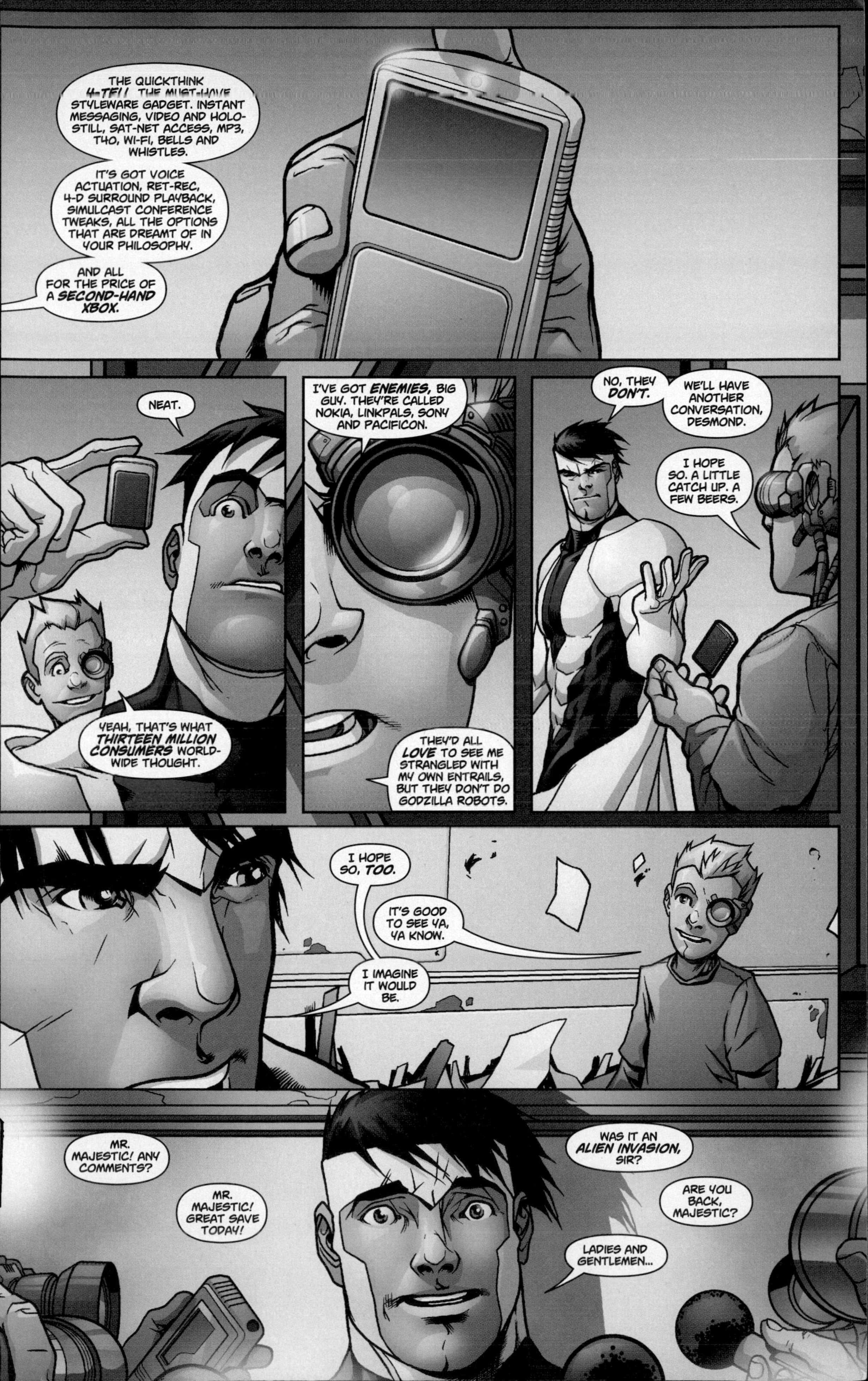
THE QUICKTHINK 4-TF! THE MUST-HAVE STYLEWARE GADGET. INSTANT MESSAGING, VIDEO AND HOLO-STILL, SAT-NET ACCESS, MP3, T4O, WI-FI, BELLS AND WHISTLES.
IT'S GOT VOICE ACTUATION, RET-REC, 4-D SURROUND PLAYBACK, SIMULCAST CONFERENCE TWEAKS, ALL THE OPTIONS THAT ARE DREAMT OF IN YOUR PHILOSOPHY.
AND ALL FOR THE PRICE OF A SECOND-HAND XBOX.
NEAT.
YEAH, THAT'S WHAT THIRTEEN MILLION CONSUMERS WORLD-WIDE THOUGHT.
I'VE GOT ENEMIES, BIG GUY. THEY'RE CALLED NOKIA, LINKPALS, SONY AND PACIFICON.
THEY'D ALL LOVE TO SEE ME STRANGLED WITH MY OWN ENTRAILS, BUT THEY DON'T DO GODZILLA ROBOTS.
NO, THEY DON'T.
WE'LL HAVE ANOTHER CONVERSATION, DESMOND.
I HOPE SO. A LITTLE CATCH UP. A FEW BEERS.
I HOPE SO, TOO.
IT'S GOOD TO SEE YA, YA KNOW.
I IMAGINE IT WOULD BE.
MR. MAJESTIC! ANY COMMENTS?
MR. MAJESTIC! GREAT SAVE TODAY!
WAS IT AN ALIEN INVASION, SIR?
ARE YOU BACK, MAJESTIC?
LADIES AND GENTLEMEN...

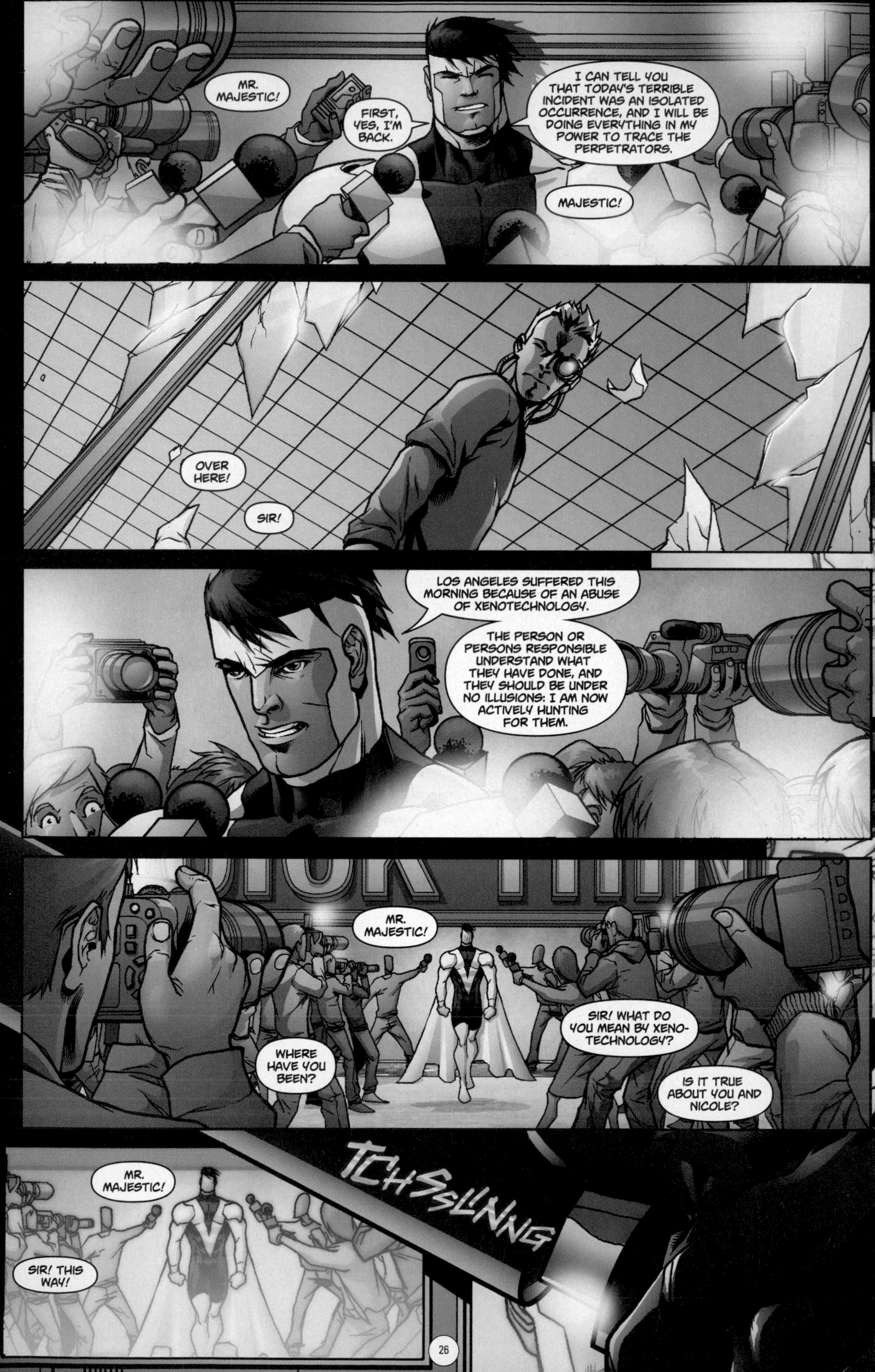

MR. MAJESTIC!
FIRST, YES, I'M BACK.
I CAN TELL YOU THAT TODAY'S TERRIBLE INCIDENT WAS AN ISOLATED OCCURRENCE, AND I WILL BE DOING EVERYTHING IN MY POWER TO TRACE THE PERPETRATORS.
MAJESTIC!
OVER HERE!
SIR!
LOS ANGELES SUFFERED THIS MORNING BECAUSE OF AN ABUSE OF XENOTECHNOLOGY.
THE PERSON OR PERSONS RESPONSIBLE UNDERSTAND WHAT THEY HAVE DONE, AND THEY SHOULD BE UNDER NO ILLUSIONS: I AM NOW ACTIVELY HUNTING FOR THEM.
MR. MAJESTIC!
WHERE HAVE YOU BEEN?
SIR! WHAT DO YOU MEAN BY XENO-TECHNOLOGY?
IS IT TRUE ABOUT YOU AND NICOLE?
TCHSSLINNG
MR. MAJESTIC!
SIR! THIS WAY!

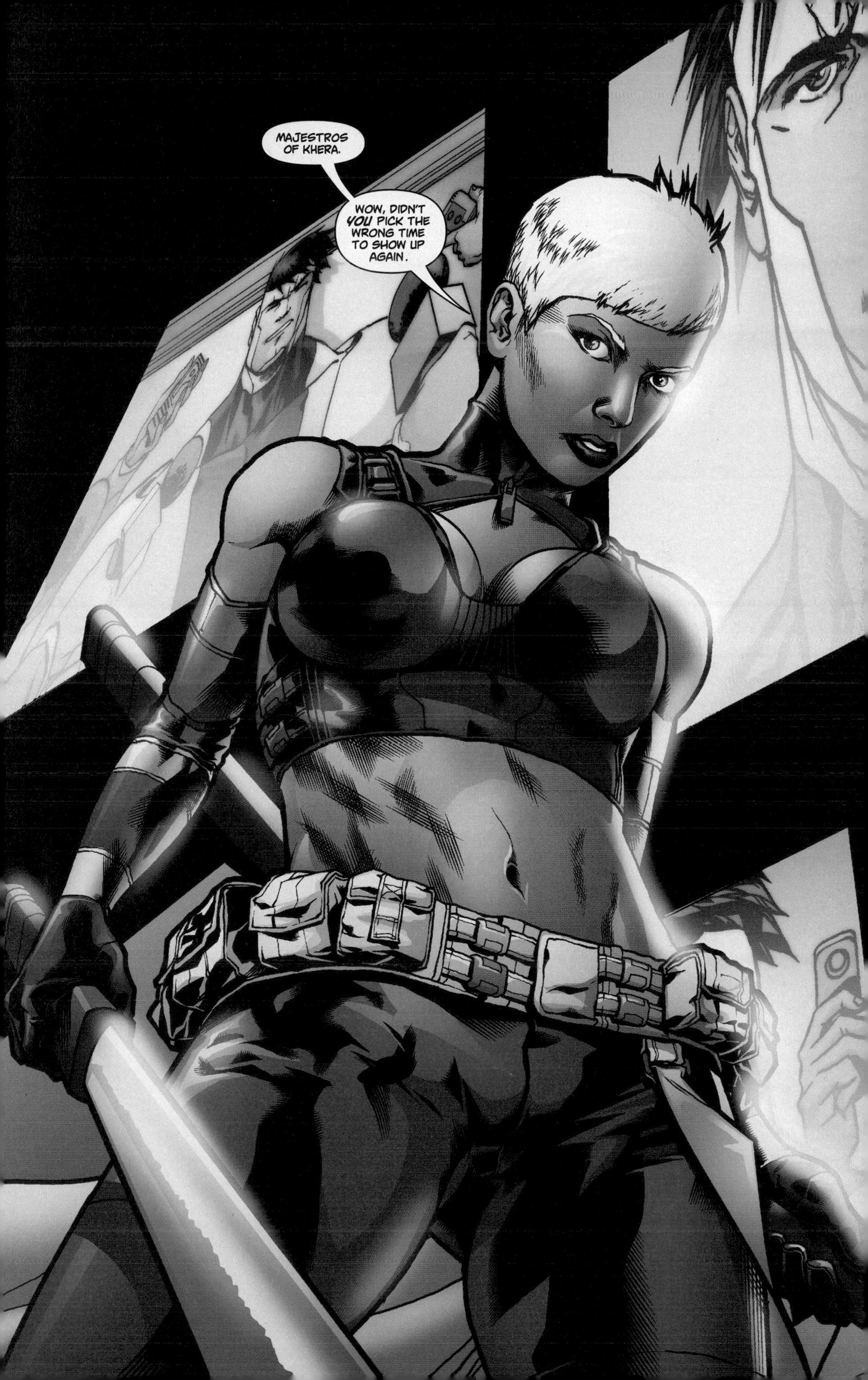
MAJESTROS OF KHERA.
WOW, DIDN'T YOU PICK THE WRONG TIME TO SHOW UP AGAIN.

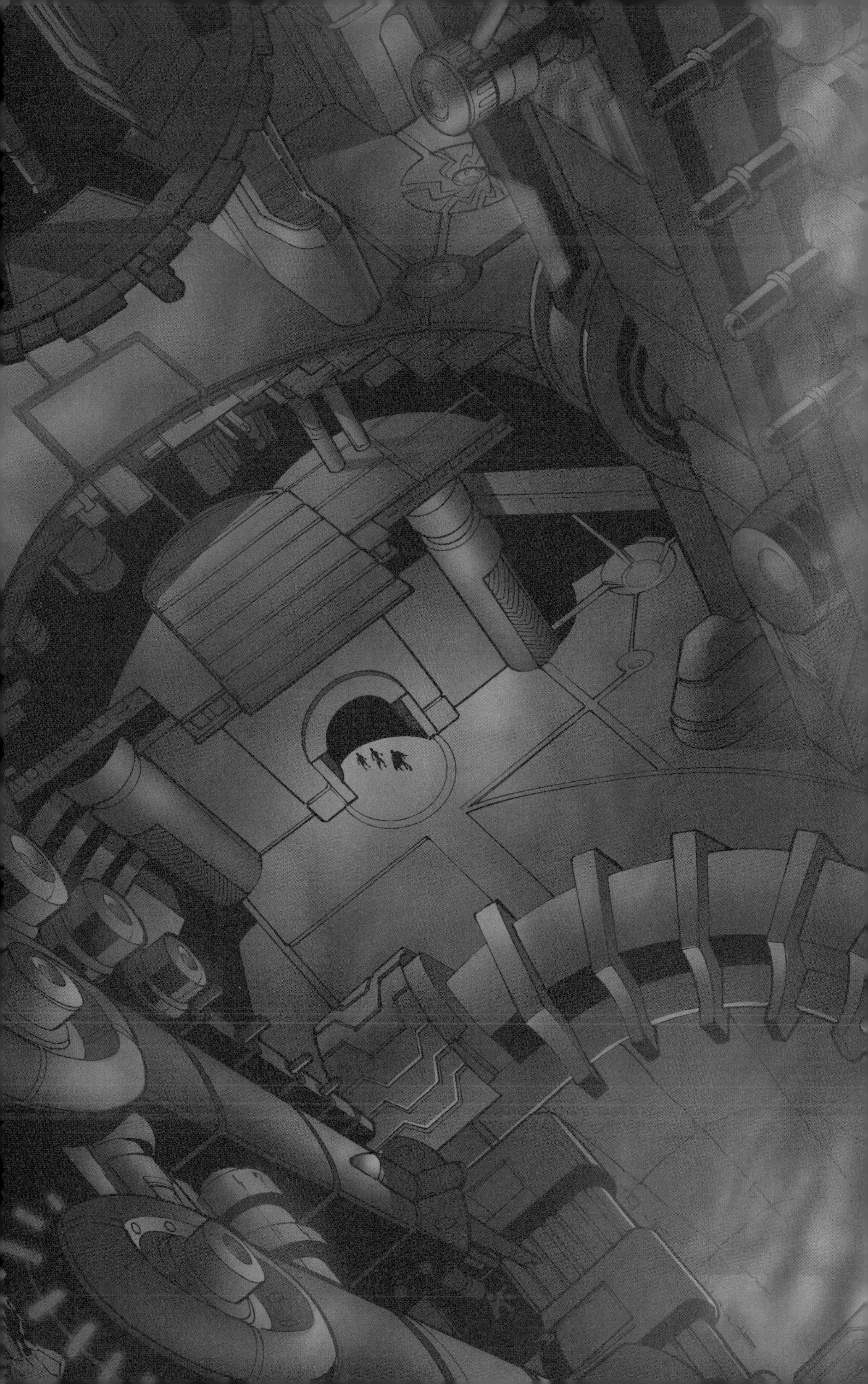

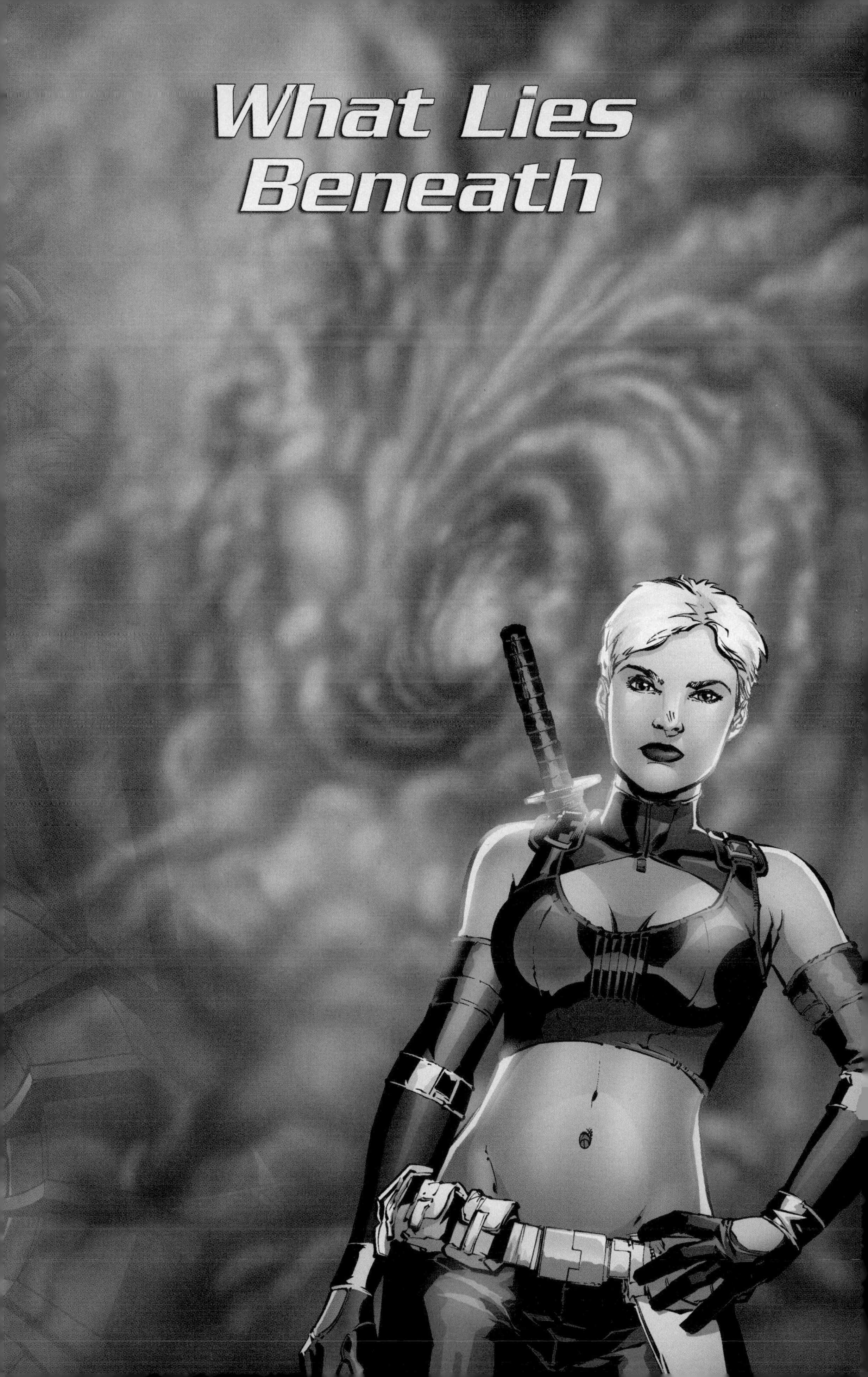
What Lies
Beneath

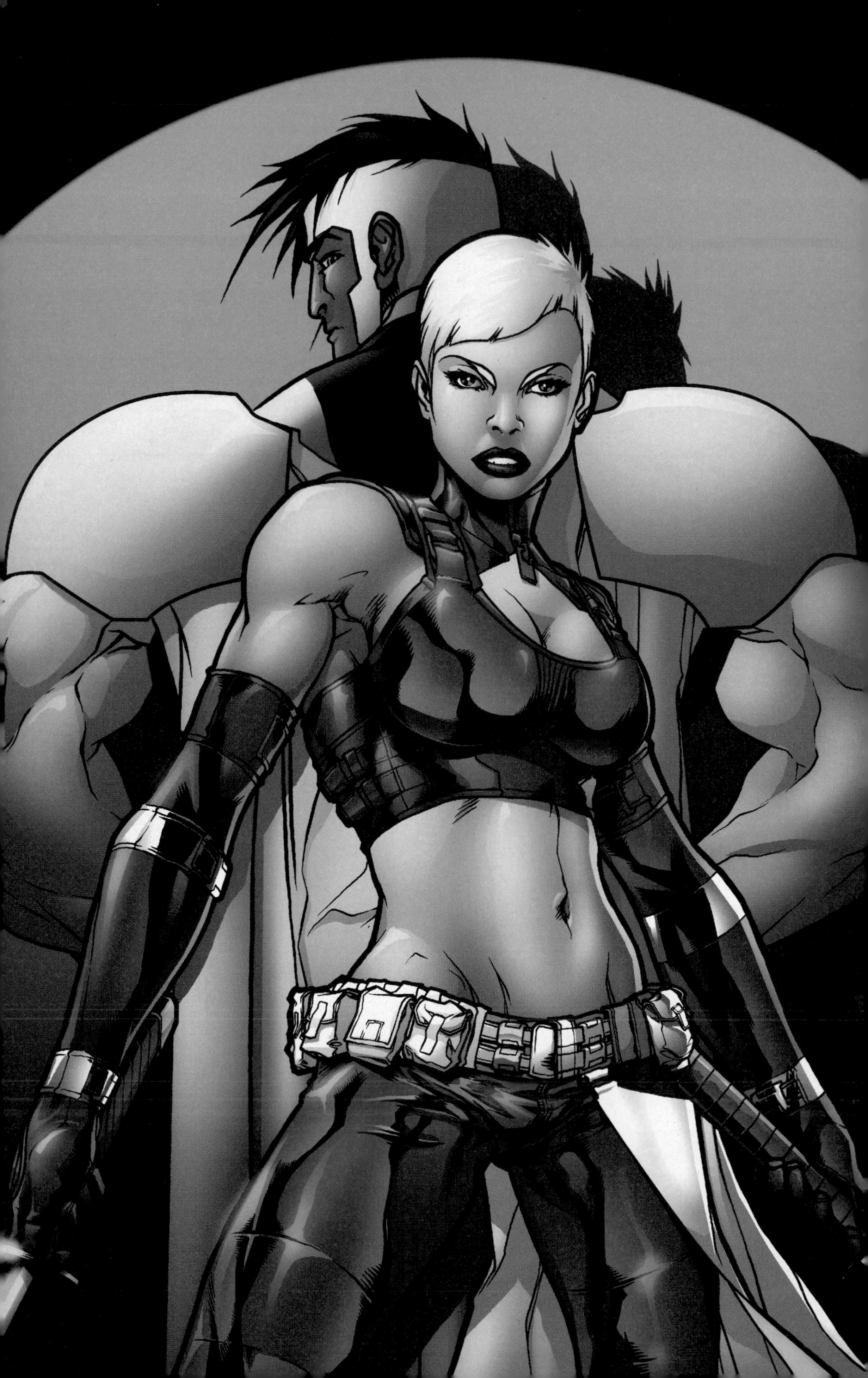

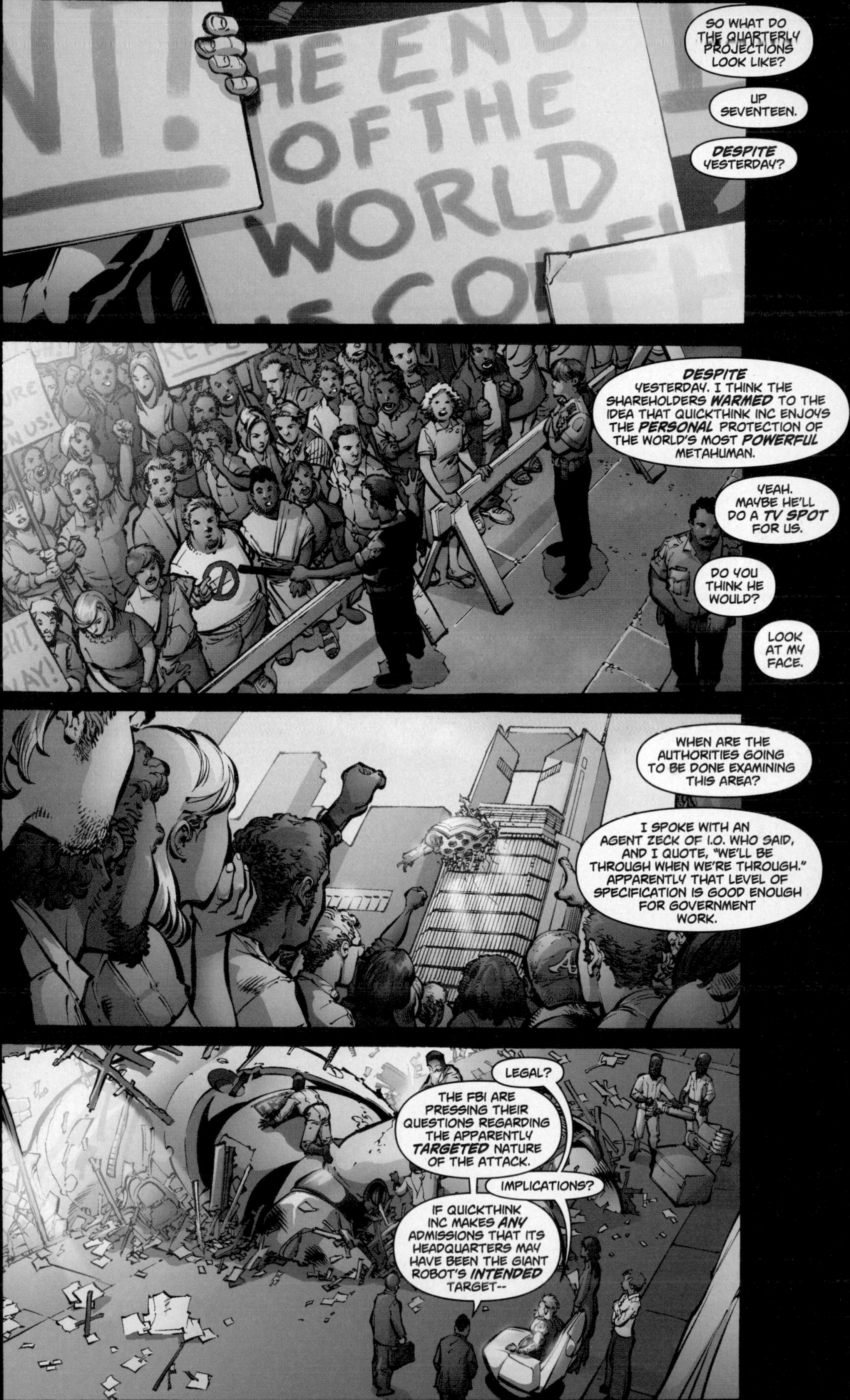
HE END OF THE WORLD
SO WHAT DO THE QUARTERLY PROJECTIONS LOOK LIKE?
UP SEVENTEEN.
DESPITE YESTERDAY?
DESPITE YESTERDAY. I THINK THE SHAREHOLDERS *WARMED* TO THE IDEA THAT QUICKTHINK INC ENJOYS THE *PERSONAL* PROTECTION OF THE WORLD'S MOST *POWERFUL* METAHUMAN.
YEAH. MAYBE HE'LL DO A *TV SPOT* FOR US.
DO YOU THINK HE WOULD?
LOOK AT MY FACE.
WHEN ARE THE AUTHORITIES GOING TO BE DONE EXAMINING THIS AREA?
I SPOKE WITH AN AGENT ZECK OF I.O. WHO SAID, AND I QUOTE, "WE'LL BE THROUGH WHEN WE'RE THROUGH." APPARENTLY THAT LEVEL OF SPECIFICATION IS GOOD ENOUGH FOR GOVERNMENT WORK.
LEGAL?
THE FBI ARE PRESSING THEIR QUESTIONS REGARDING THE APPARENTLY *TARGETED* NATURE OF THE ATTACK.
IMPLICATIONS?
IF QUICKTHINK INC MAKES *ANY* ADMISSIONS THAT ITS HEADQUARTERS MAY HAVE BEEN THE GIANT ROBOT'S *INTENDED* TARGET--

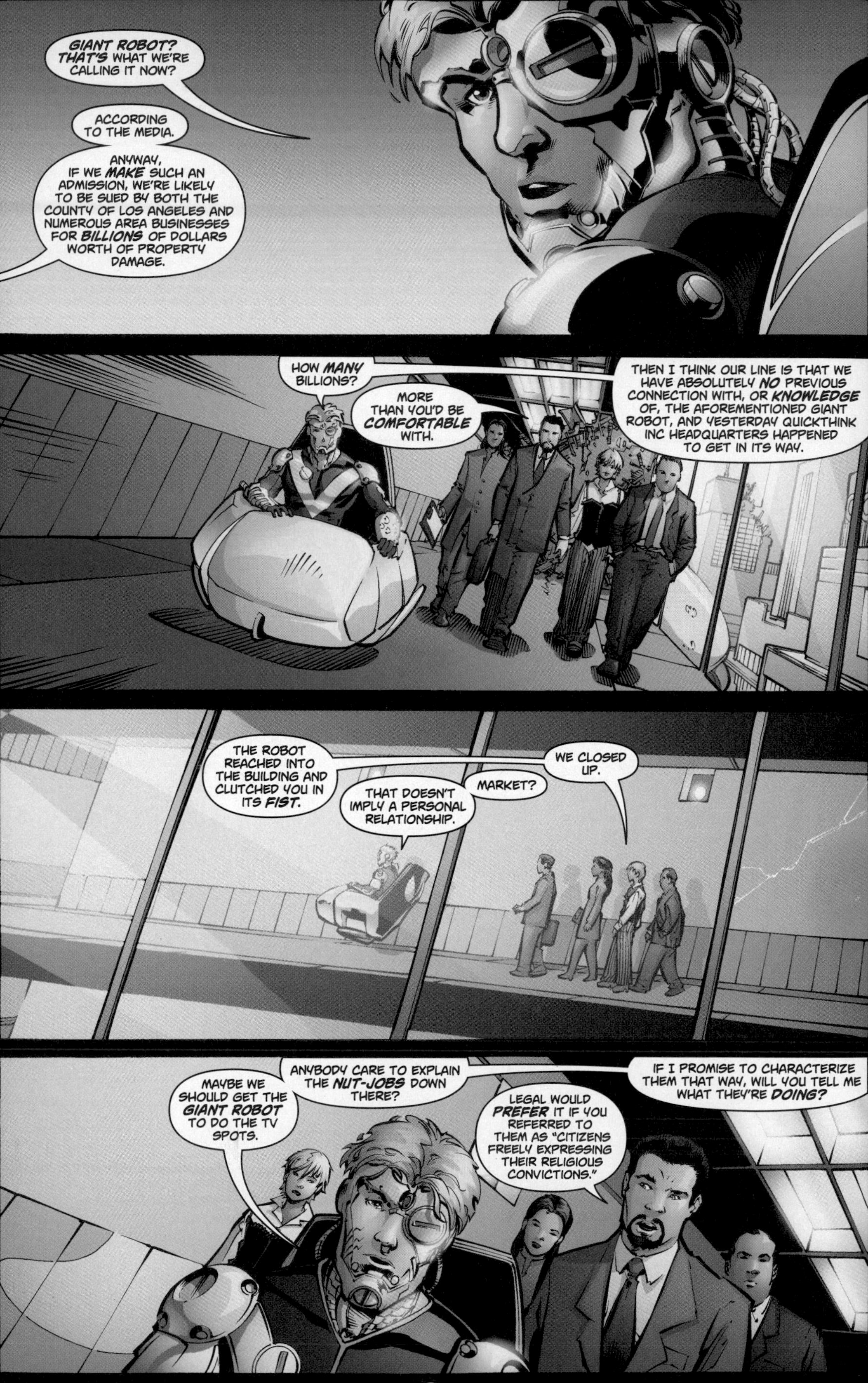
GIANT ROBOT? THAT'S WHAT WE'RE CALLING IT NOW?
ACCORDING TO THE MEDIA.
ANYWAY, IF WE MAKE SUCH AN ADMISSION, WE'RE LIKELY TO BE SUED BY BOTH THE COUNTY OF LOS ANGELES AND NUMEROUS AREA BUSINESSES FOR BILLIONS OF DOLLARS WORTH OF PROPERTY DAMAGE.
HOW MANY BILLIONS?
MORE THAN YOU'D BE COMFORTABLE WITH.
THEN I THINK OUR LINE IS THAT WE HAVE ABSOLUTELY NO PREVIOUS CONNECTION WITH, OR KNOWLEDGE OF, THE AFOREMENTIONED GIANT ROBOT, AND YESTERDAY QUICKTHINK INC HEADQUARTERS HAPPENED TO GET IN ITS WAY.
THE ROBOT REACHED INTO THE BUILDING AND CLUTCHED YOU IN ITS FIST.
WE CLOSED UP.
THAT DOESN'T IMPLY A PERSONAL RELATIONSHIP.
MARKET?
MAYBE WE SHOULD GET THE GIANT ROBOT TO DO THE TV SPOTS.
ANYBODY CARE TO EXPLAIN THE NUT-JOBS DOWN THERE?
LEGAL WOULD PREFER IT IF YOU REFERRED TO THEM AS "CITIZENS FREELY EXPRESSING THEIR RELIGIOUS CONVICTIONS."
IF I PROMISE TO CHARACTERIZE THEM THAT WAY, WILL YOU TELL ME WHAT THEY'RE DOING?

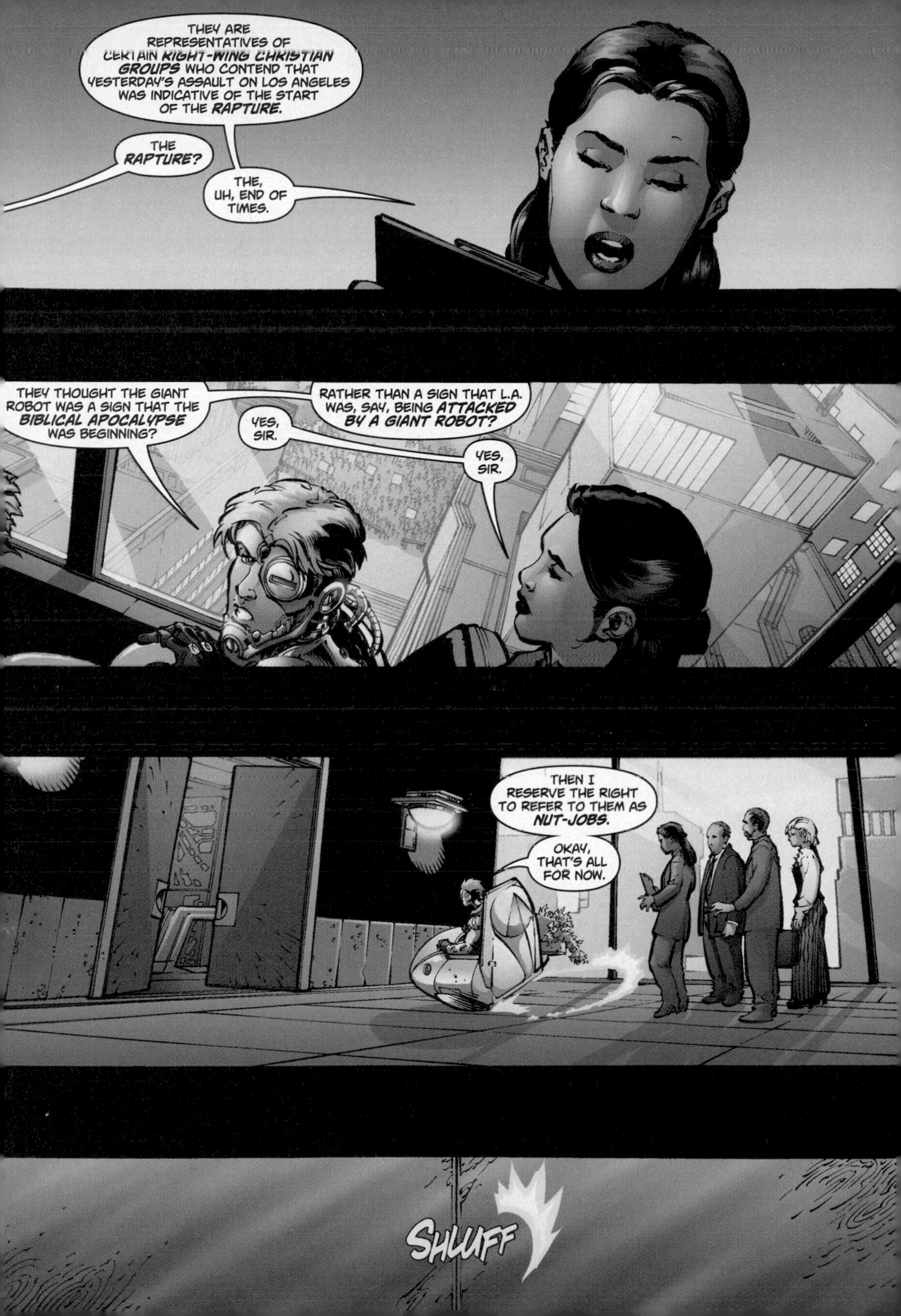
THEY ARE REPRESENTATIVES OF CERTAIN RIGHT-WING CHRISTIAN GROUPS WHO CONTEND THAT YESTERDAY'S ASSAULT ON LOS ANGELES WAS INDICATIVE OF THE START OF THE RAPTURE.
THE RAPTURE?
THE, UH, END OF TIMES.
THEY THOUGHT THE GIANT ROBOT WAS A SIGN THAT THE BIBLICAL APOCALYPSE WAS BEGINNING?
YES, SIR.
RATHER THAN A SIGN THAT L.A. WAS, SAY, BEING ATTACKED BY A GIANT ROBOT?
YES, SIR.
THEN I RESERVE THE RIGHT TO REFER TO THEM AS NUT-JOBS.
OKAY, THAT'S ALL FOR NOW.
SHLUFF

AHHHHH.

SPY-LINK.
RUSHMORE ONE.

RUSHMORE
TWO.

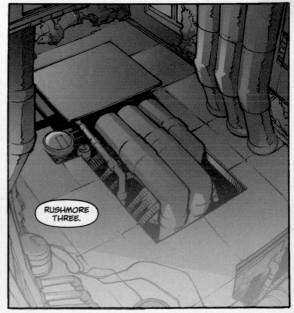

RUSHMORE
THREE.

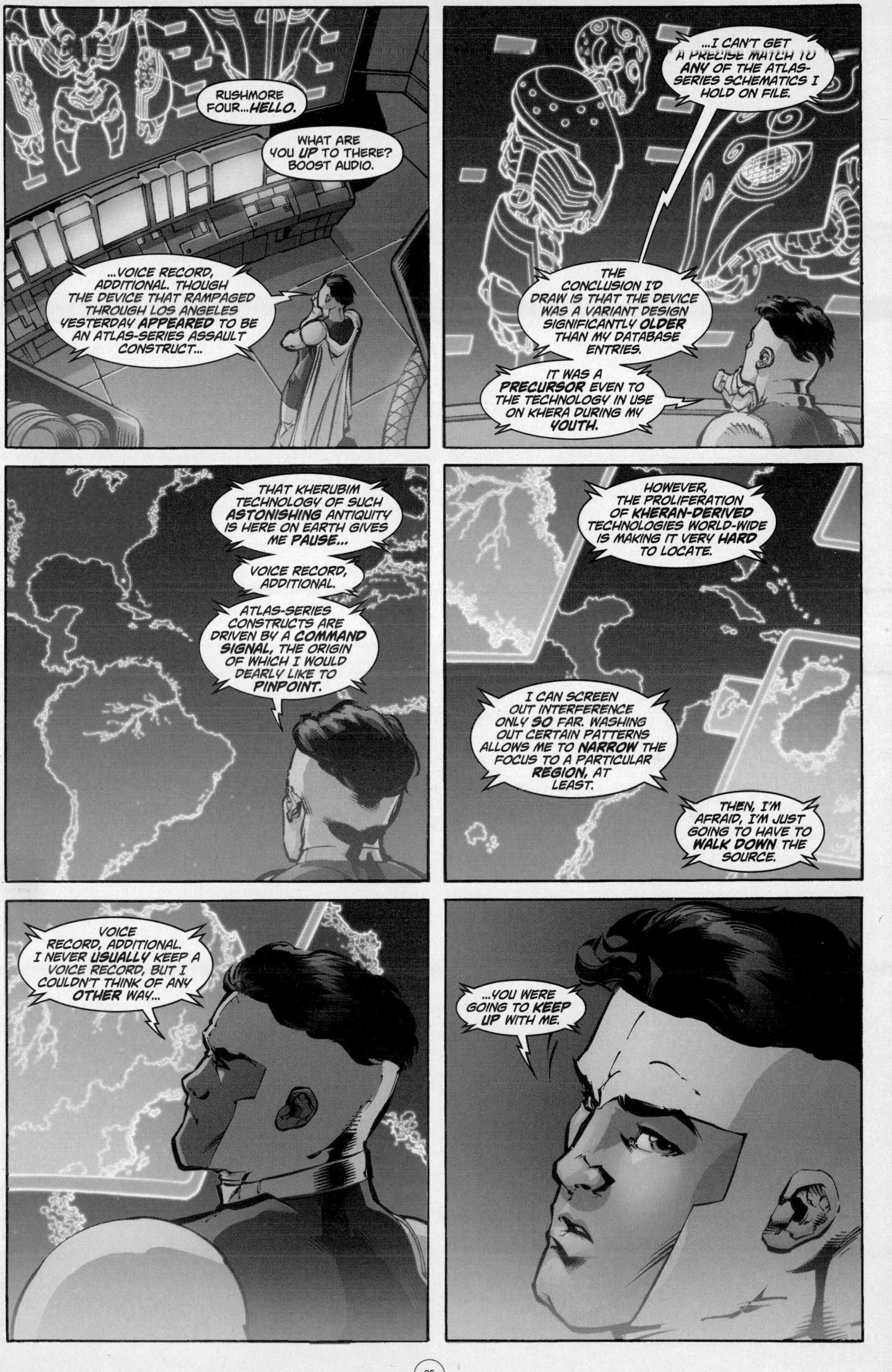
RUSHMORE FOUR...HELLO.
WHAT ARE YOU UP TO THERE? BOOST AUDIO.
...VOICE RECORD, ADDITIONAL. THOUGH THE DEVICE THAT RAMPAGED THROUGH LOS ANGELES YESTERDAY APPEARED TO BE AN ATLAS-SERIES ASSAULT CONSTRUCT...
...I CAN'T GET A PRECISE MATCH TO ANY OF THE ATLAS-SERIES SCHEMATICS I HOLD ON FILE.
THE CONCLUSION I'D DRAW IS THAT THE DEVICE WAS A VARIANT DESIGN SIGNIFICANTLY OLDER THAN MY DATABASE ENTRIES.
IT WAS A PRECURSOR EVEN TO THE TECHNOLOGY IN USE ON KHERA DURING MY YOUTH.
THAT KHERUBIM TECHNOLOGY OF SUCH ASTONISHING ANTIQUITY IS HERE ON EARTH GIVES ME PAUSE...
VOICE RECORD, ADDITIONAL.
ATLAS-SERIES CONSTRUCTS ARE DRIVEN BY A COMMAND SIGNAL, THE ORIGIN OF WHICH I WOULD DEARLY LIKE TO PINPOINT.
HOWEVER, THE PROLIFERATION OF KHERAN-DERIVED TECHNOLOGIES WORLD-WIDE IS MAKING IT VERY HARD TO LOCATE.
I CAN SCREEN OUT INTERFERENCE ONLY SO FAR. WASHING OUT CERTAIN PATTERNS ALLOWS ME TO NARROW THE FOCUS TO A PARTICULAR REGION, AT LEAST.
THEN, I'M AFRAID, I'M JUST GOING TO HAVE TO WALK DOWN THE SOURCE.
VOICE RECORD, ADDITIONAL. I NEVER USUALLY KEEP A VOICE RECORD, BUT I COULDN'T THINK OF ANY OTHER WAY...
...YOU WERE GOING TO KEEP UP WITH ME.

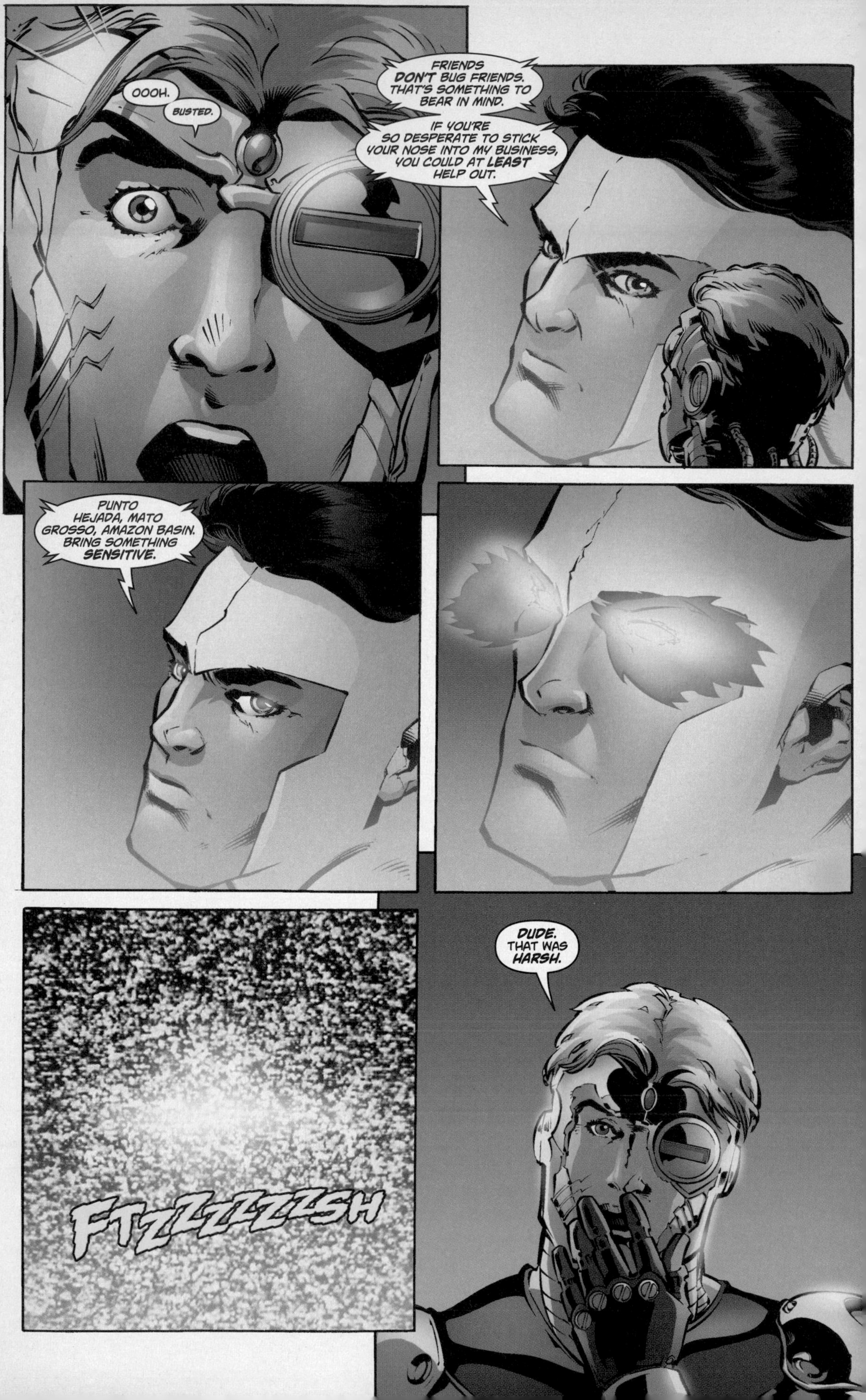
OOOH.
BUSTED.
FRIENDS DON'T BUG FRIENDS. THAT'S SOMETHING TO BEAR IN MIND.
IF YOU'RE SO DESPERATE TO STICK YOUR NOSE INTO MY BUSINESS, YOU COULD AT LEAST HELP OUT.
PUNTO HEJADA, MATO GROSSO, AMAZON BASIN. BRING SOMETHING SENSITIVE.
FTZZZZZZZSH
DUDE. THAT WAS HARSH.

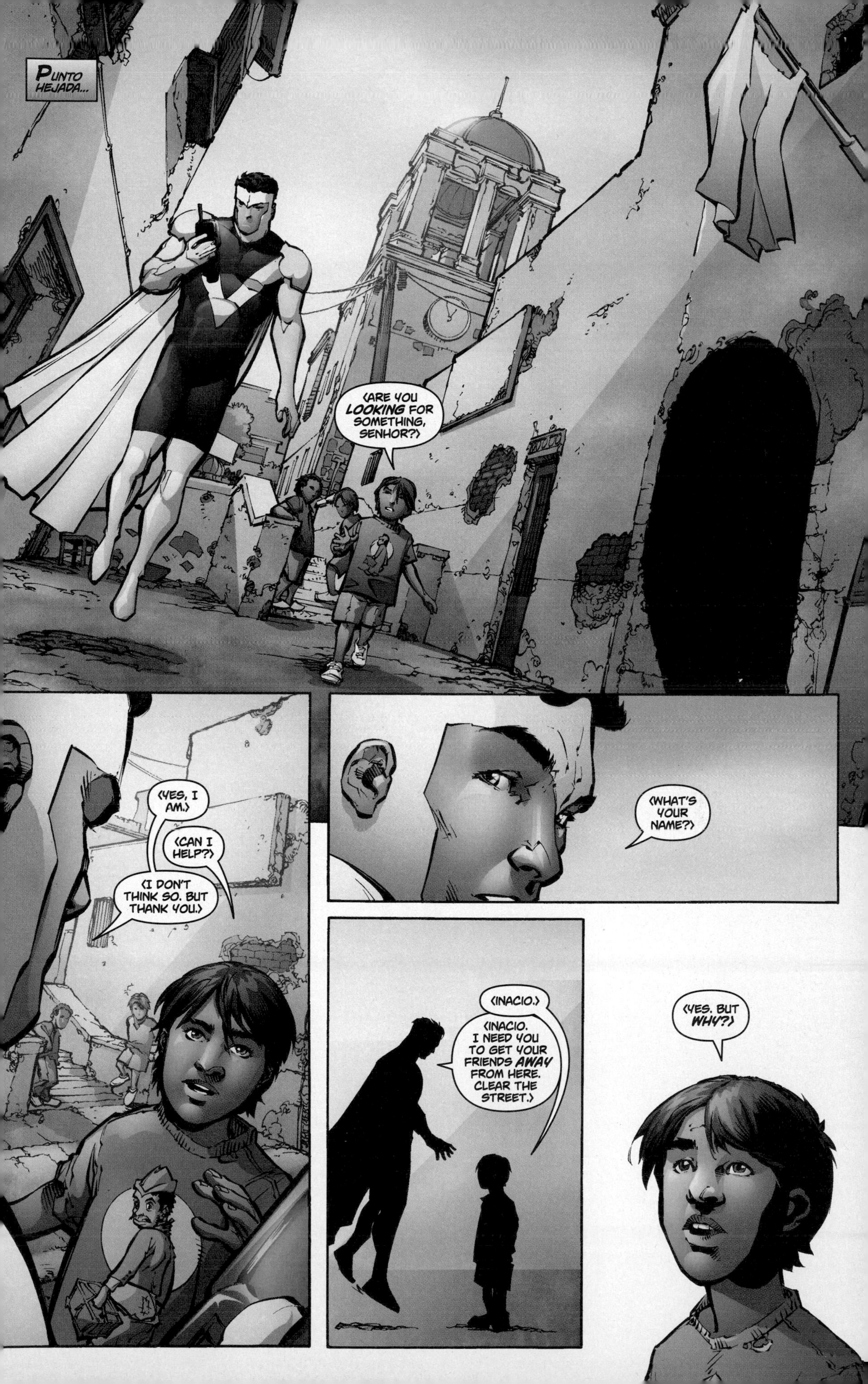
PUNTO HEJADA...
(ARE YOU LOOKING FOR SOMETHING, SENHOR?)
(YES, I AM.)
(CAN I HELP?)
(I DON'T THINK SO. BUT THANK YOU.)
(WHAT'S YOUR NAME?)
(INACIO.)
(INACIO. I NEED YOU TO GET YOUR FRIENDS AWAY FROM HERE. CLEAR THE STREET.)
(YES. BUT WHY?)

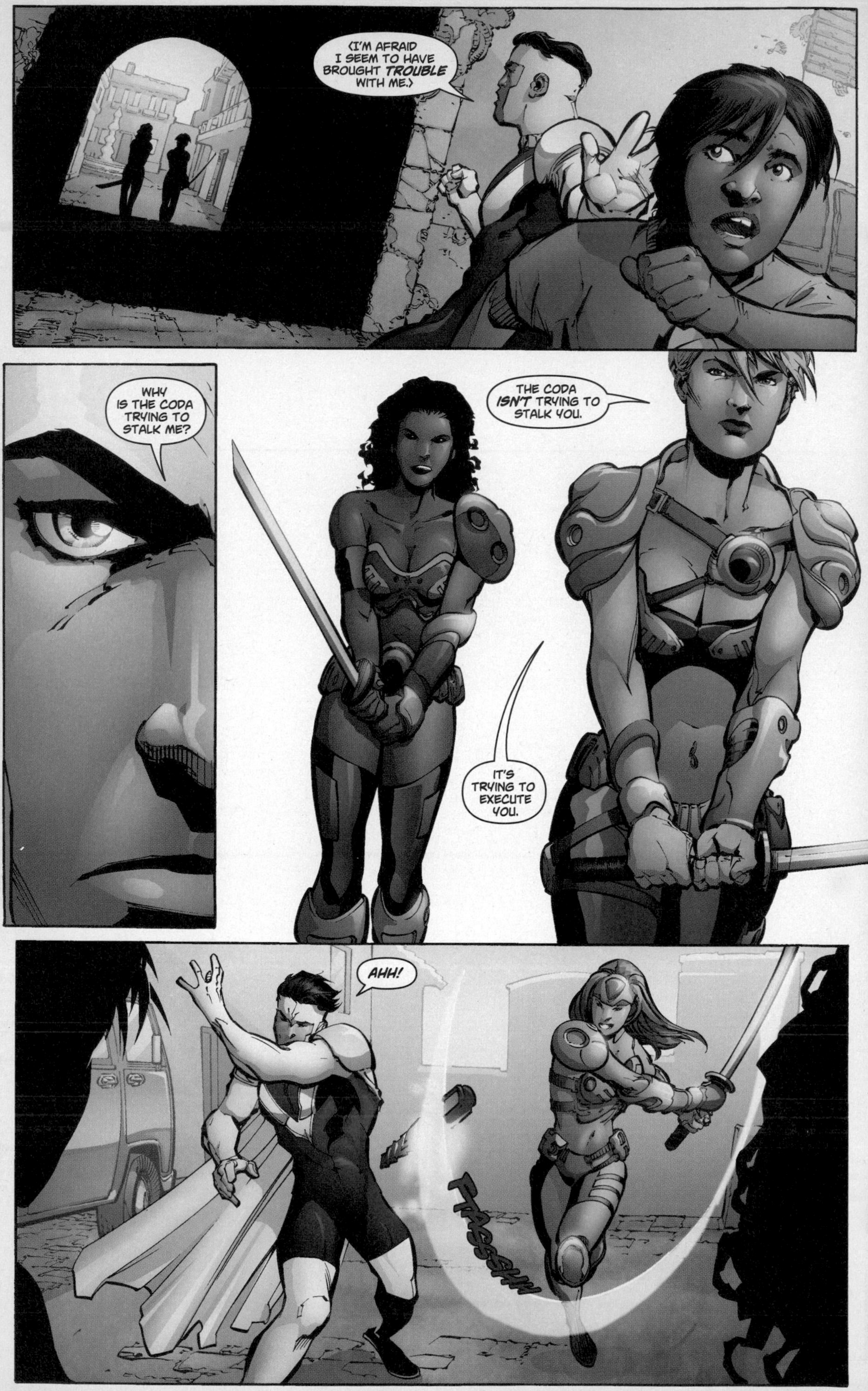
‹I'M AFRAID I SEEM TO HAVE BROUGHT *TROUBLE* WITH ME.›
WHY IS THE CODA TRYING TO STALK ME?
THE CODA *ISN'T* TRYING TO STALK YOU.
IT'S TRYING TO EXECUTE YOU.
AHH!
FRSSHH

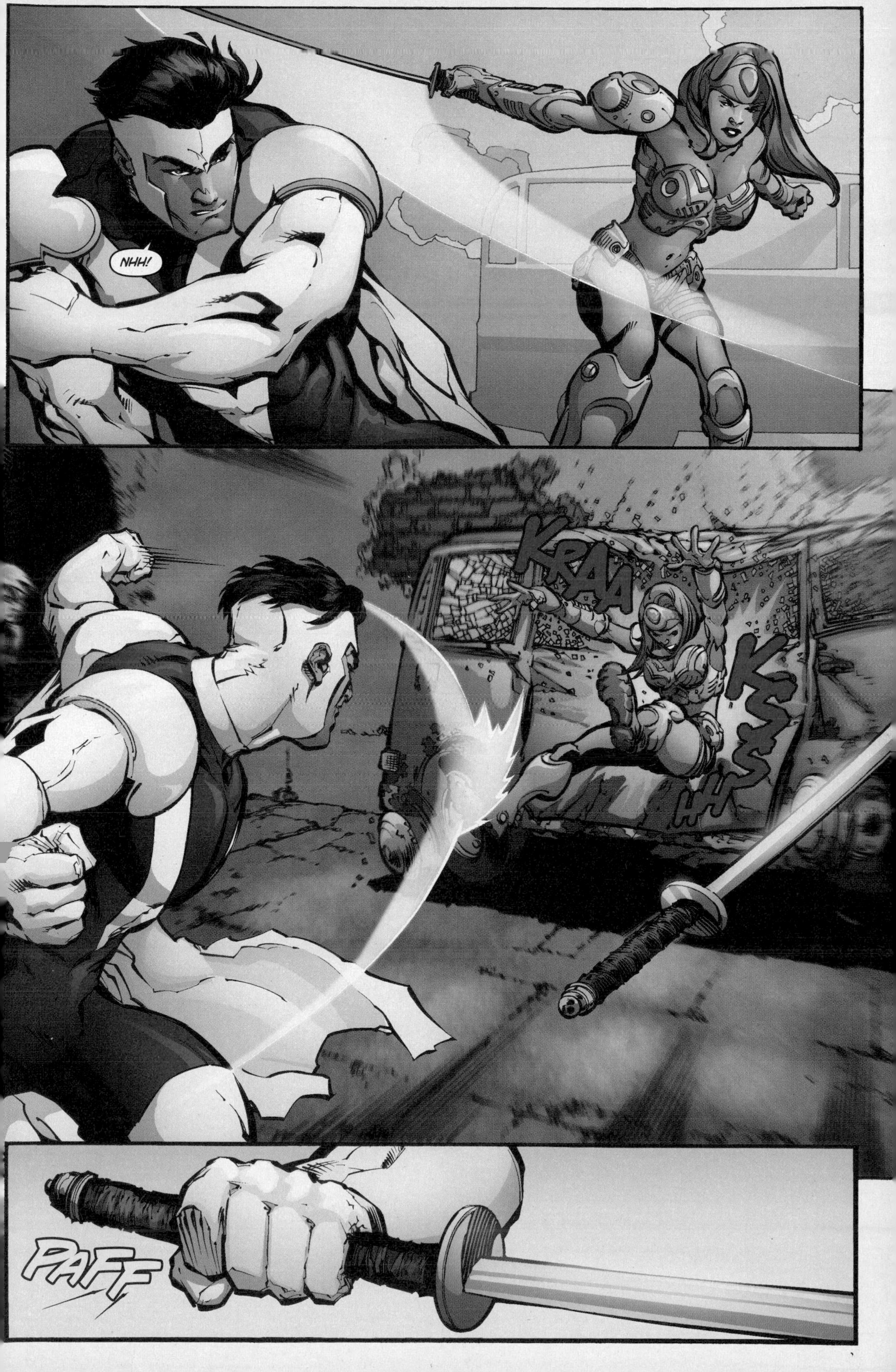
NHH!
KRAAA
KSSSHH
PAFF

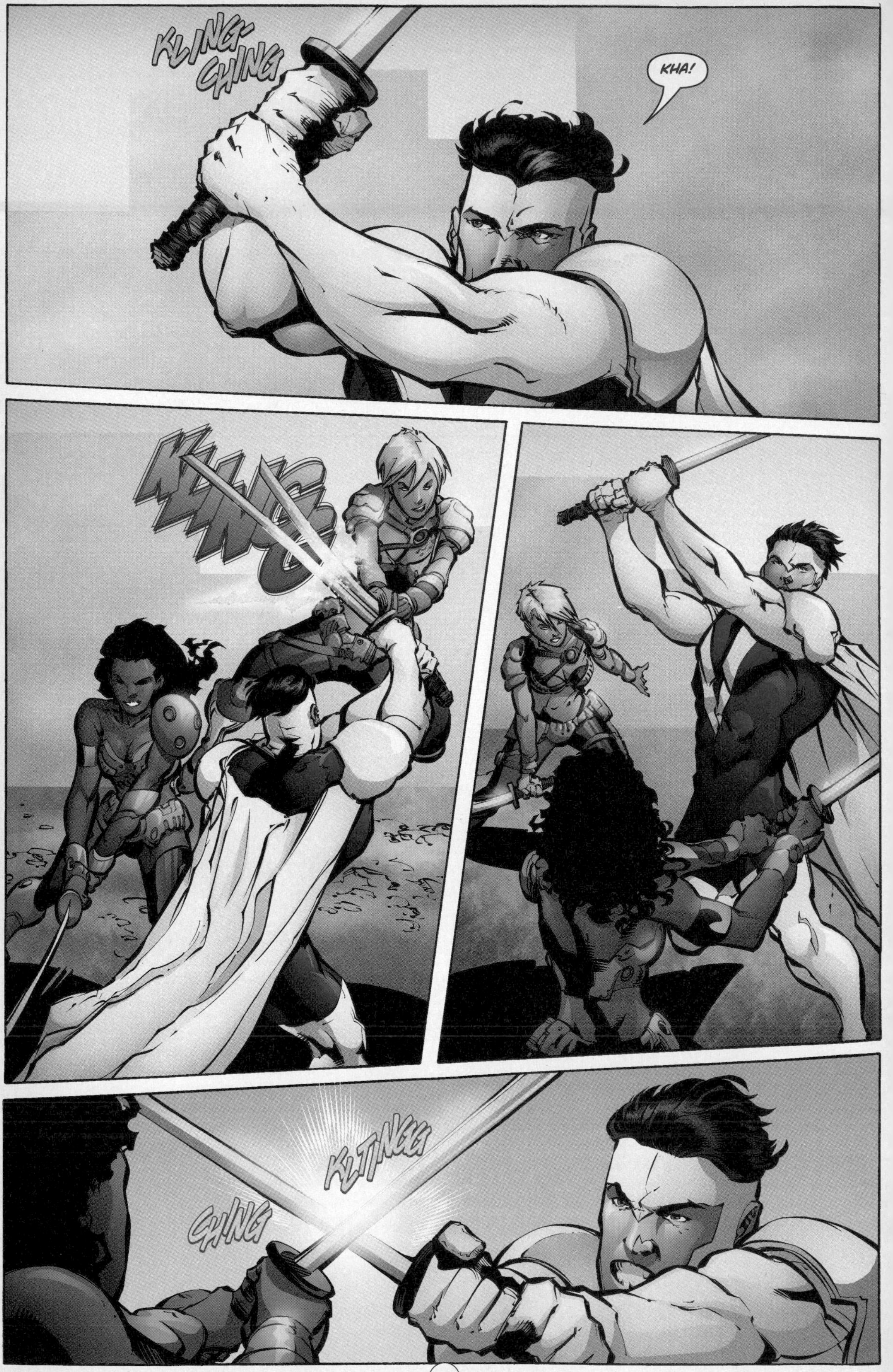
KLING-CHING
KHA!
KLING
KLTINGG
CHING

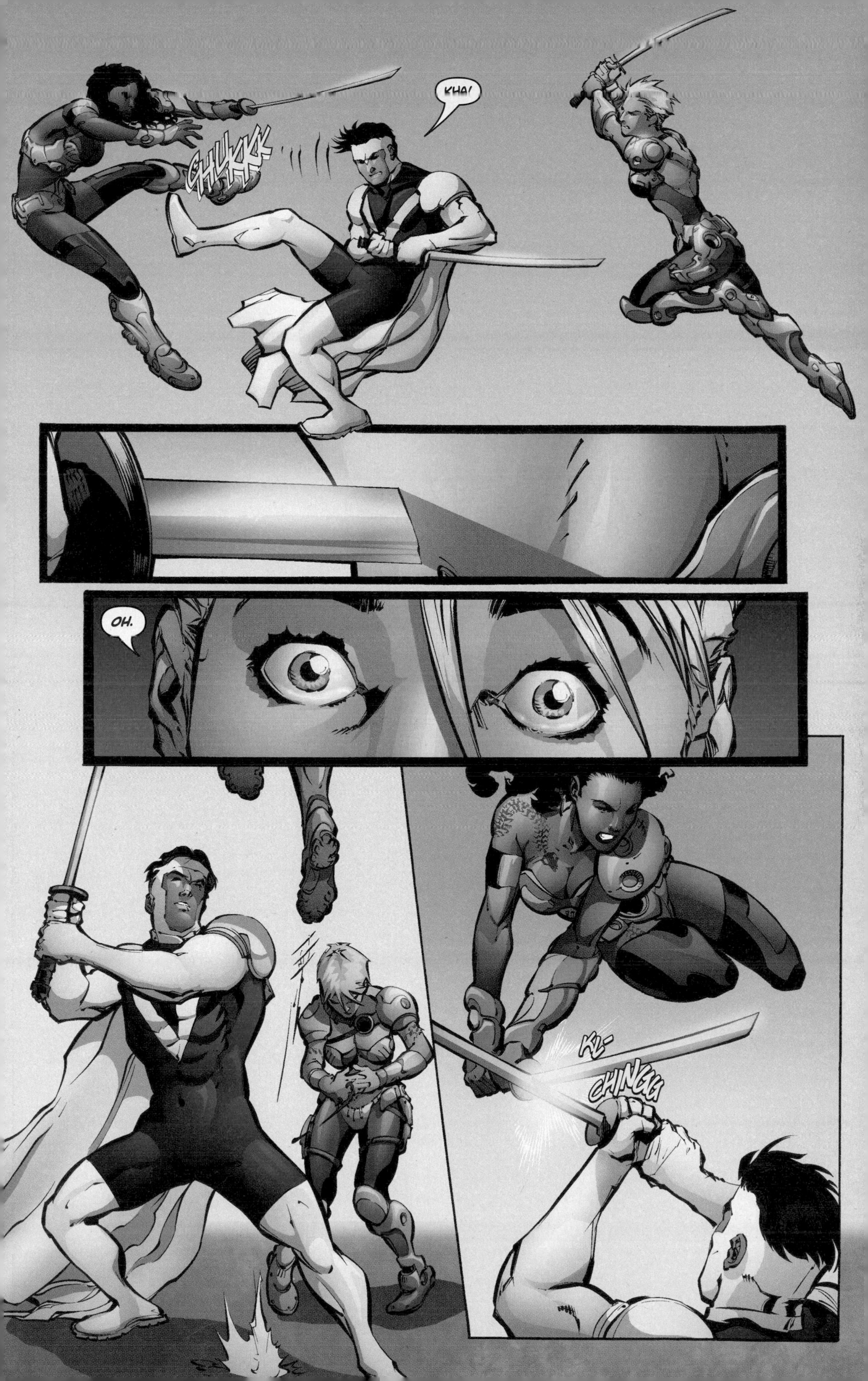
KHA!
CHUKKK
OH.
KL-
CHINGG

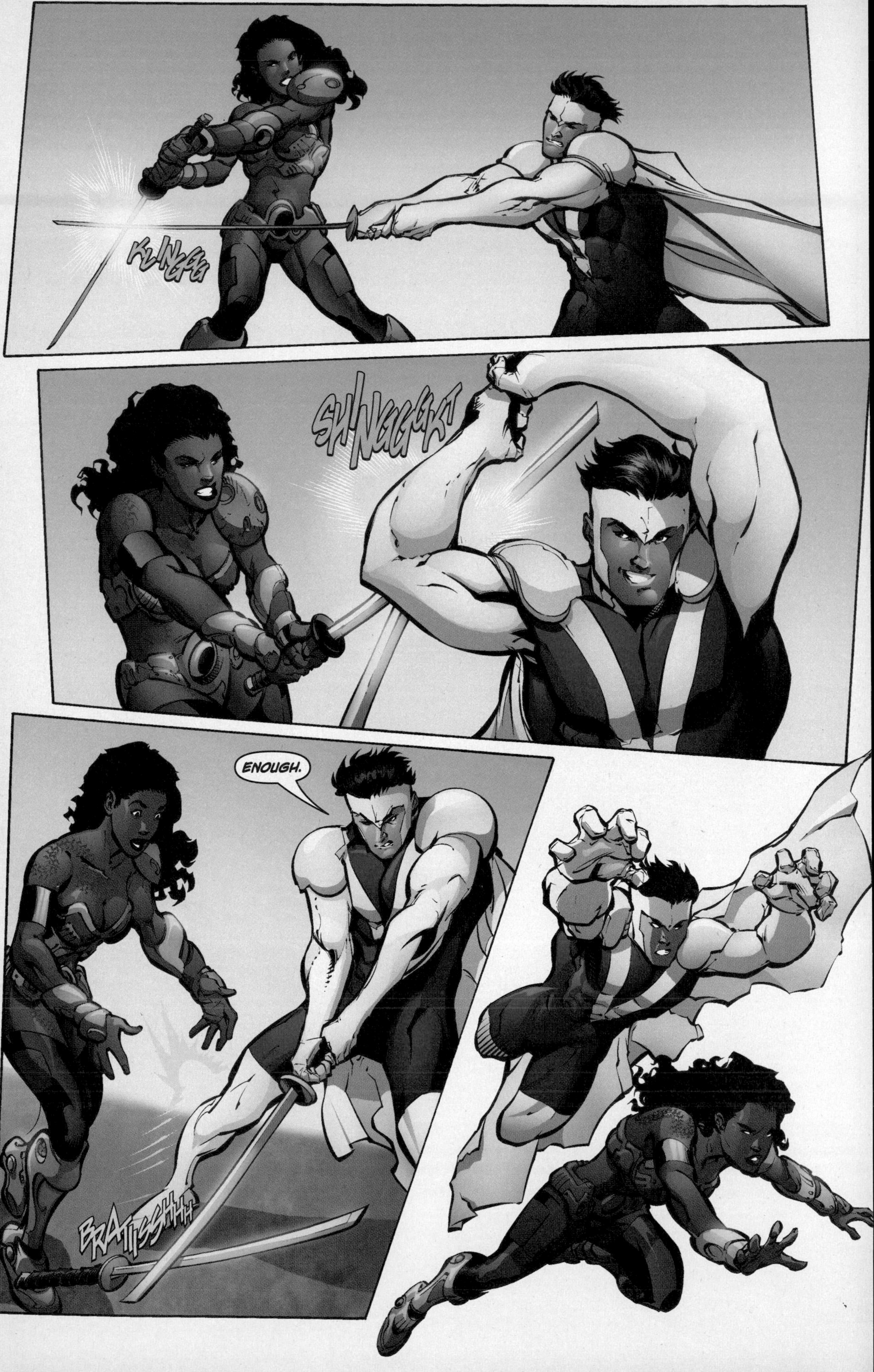
KLINGGG
SHINGGGKT
ENOUGH.
BRATISSHHH

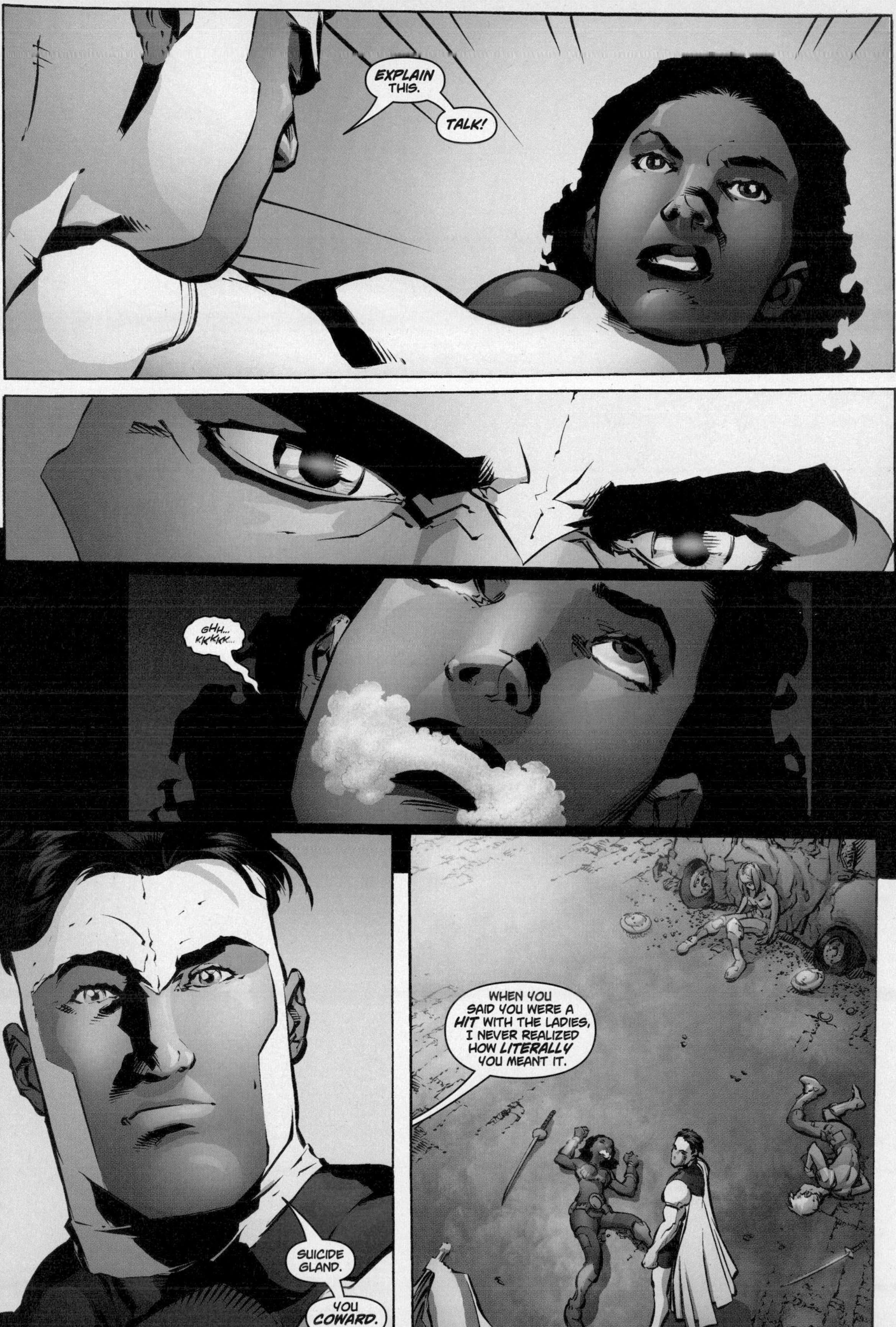
EXPLAIN THIS.
TALK!
GHH... KKKKK...
SUICIDE GLAND.
YOU COWARD.
WHEN YOU SAID YOU WERE A HIT WITH THE LADIES, I NEVER REALIZED HOW LITERALLY YOU MEANT IT.

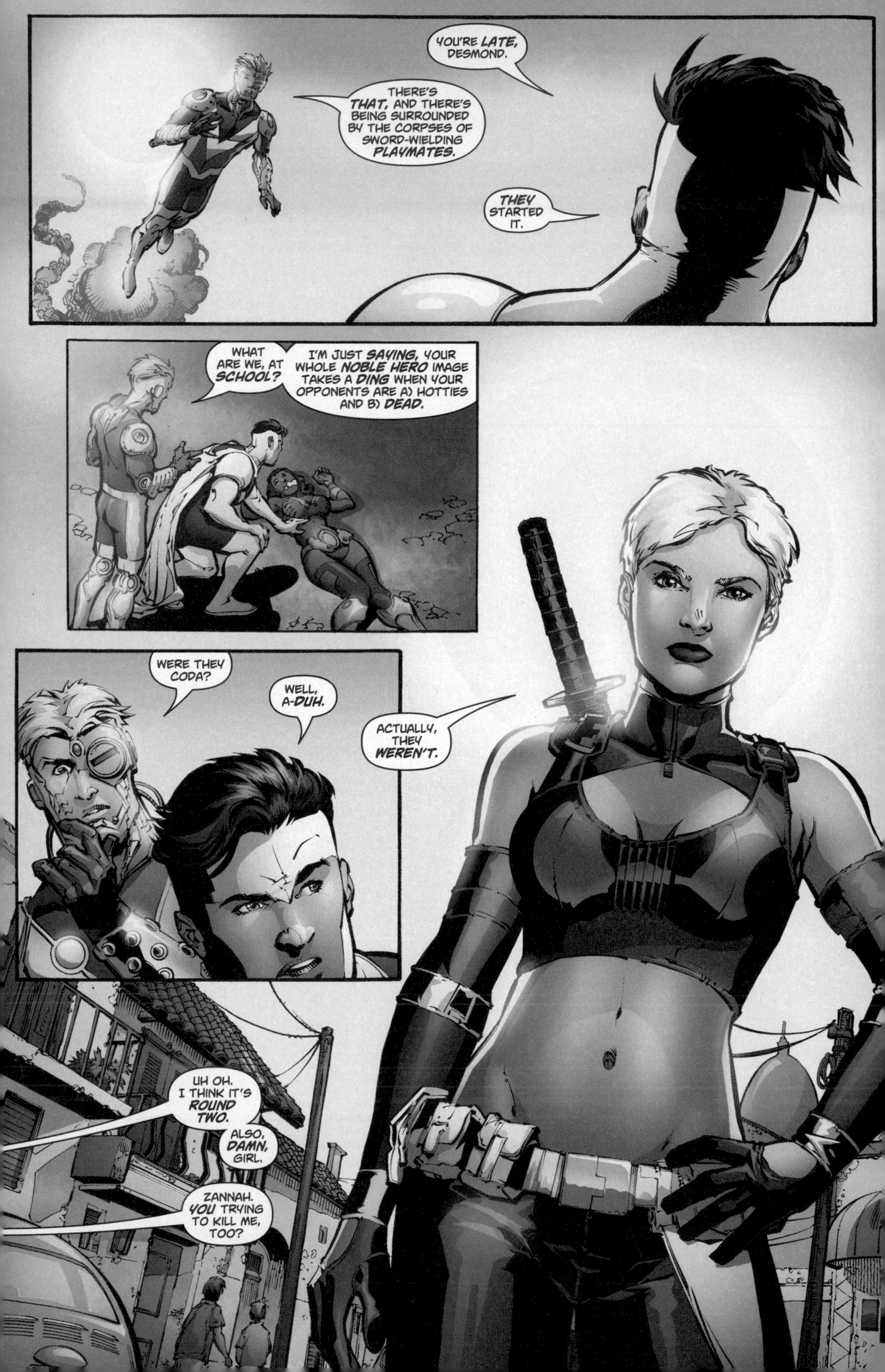
YOU'RE LATE, DESMOND.
THERE'S THAT, AND THERE'S BEING SURROUNDED BY THE CORPSES OF SWORD-WIELDING PLAYMATES.
THEY STARTED IT.
WHAT ARE WE, AT SCHOOL?
I'M JUST SAYING, YOUR WHOLE NOBLE HERO IMAGE TAKES A DING WHEN YOUR OPPONENTS ARE A) HOTTIES AND B) DEAD.
WERE THEY CODA?
WELL, A-DUH.
ACTUALLY, THEY WEREN'T.
UH OH. I THINK IT'S ROUND TWO.
ALSO, DAMN, GIRL.
ZANNAH. YOU TRYING TO KILL ME, TOO?

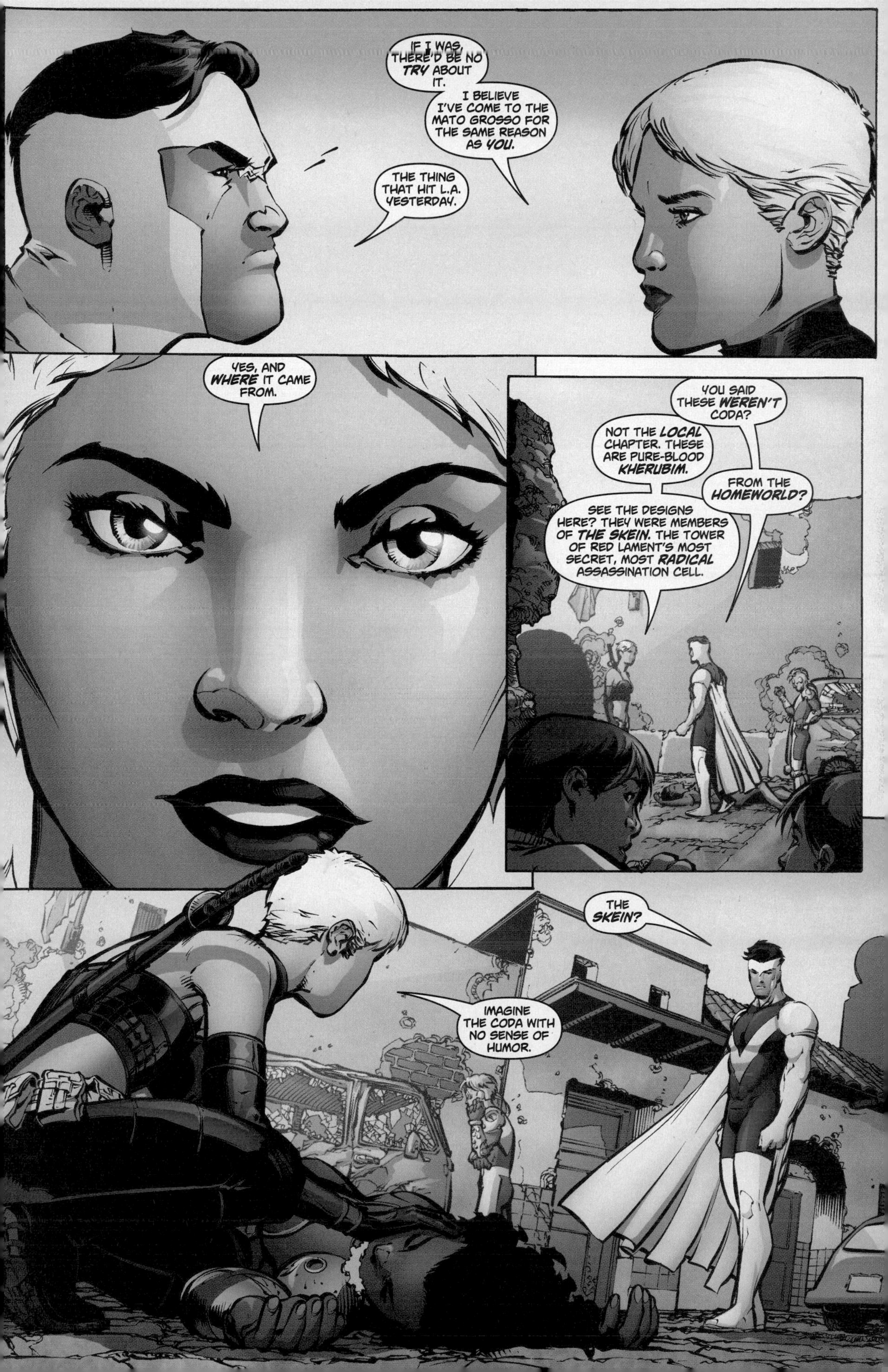
IF I WAS, THERE'D BE NO TRY ABOUT IT.
I BELIEVE I'VE COME TO THE MATO GROSSO FOR THE SAME REASON AS YOU.
THE THING THAT HIT L.A. YESTERDAY.
YES, AND WHERE IT CAME FROM.
YOU SAID THESE WEREN'T CODA?
NOT THE LOCAL CHAPTER. THESE ARE PURE-BLOOD KHERUBIM.
FROM THE HOMEWORLD?
SEE THE DESIGNS HERE? THEY WERE MEMBERS OF THE SKEIN. THE TOWER OF RED LAMENT'S MOST SECRET, MOST RADICAL ASSASSINATION CELL.
THE SKEIN?
IMAGINE THE CODA WITH NO SENSE OF HUMOR.

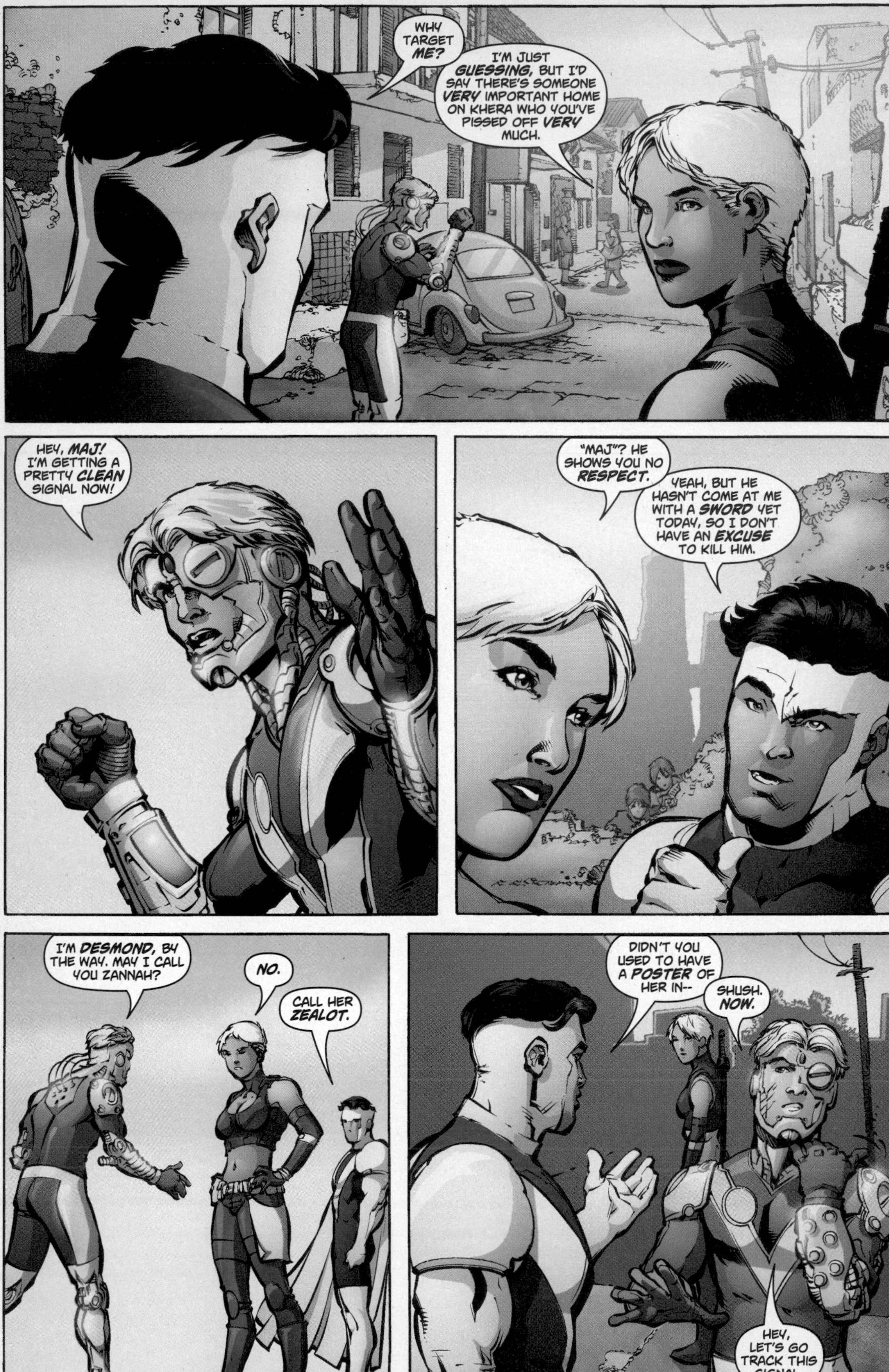
WHY TARGET ME?
I'M JUST GUESSING, BUT I'D SAY THERE'S SOMEONE VERY IMPORTANT HOME ON KHERA WHO YOU'VE PISSED OFF VERY MUCH.
HEY, MAJ! I'M GETTING A PRETTY CLEAN SIGNAL NOW!
"MAJ"? HE SHOWS YOU NO RESPECT.
YEAH, BUT HE HASN'T COME AT ME WITH A SWORD YET TODAY, SO I DON'T HAVE AN EXCUSE TO KILL HIM.
I'M DESMOND, BY THE WAY. MAY I CALL YOU ZANNAH?
NO.
CALL HER ZEALOT.
DIDN'T YOU USED TO HAVE A POSTER OF HER IN--
SHUSH. NOW.
HEY, LET'S GO TRACK THIS SIGNAL.

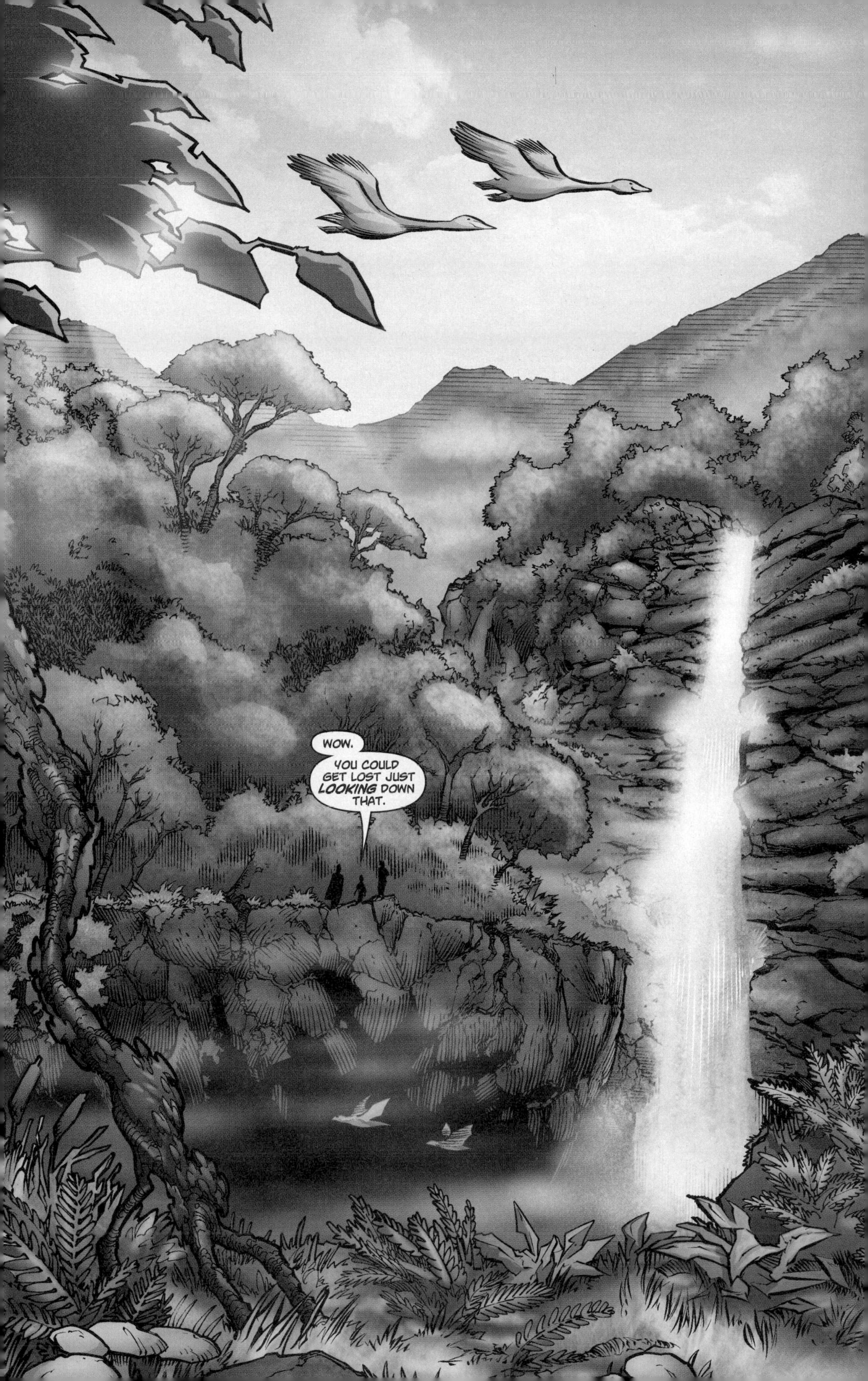
WOW.
YOU COULD GET LOST JUST LOOKING DOWN THAT.

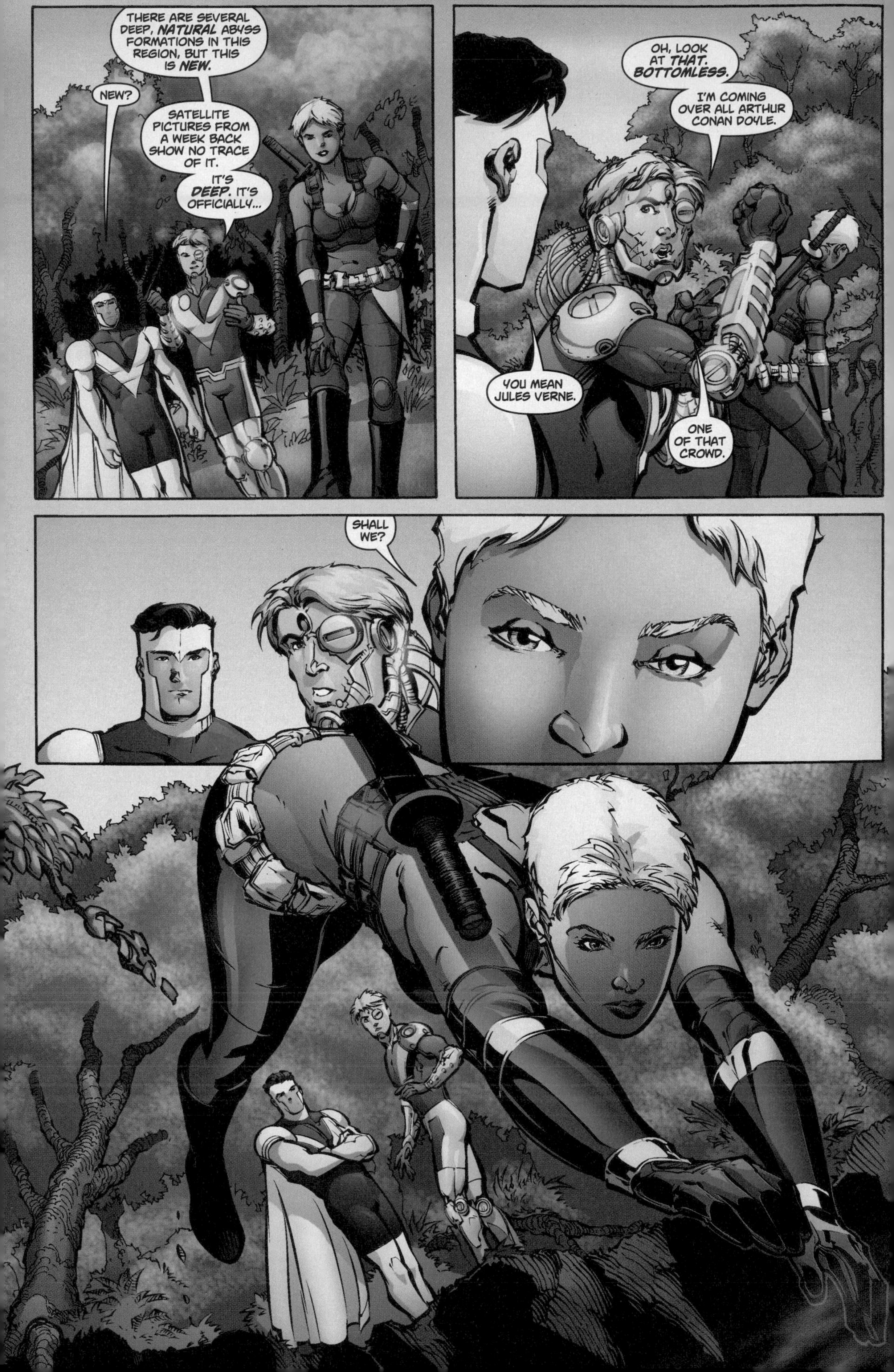
THERE ARE SEVERAL DEEP, NATURAL ABYSS FORMATIONS IN THIS REGION, BUT THIS IS NEW.
NEW?
SATELLITE PICTURES FROM A WEEK BACK SHOW NO TRACE OF IT.
IT'S DEEP. IT'S OFFICIALLY...
OH, LOOK AT THAT. BOTTOMLESS.
I'M COMING OVER ALL ARTHUR CONAN DOYLE.
YOU MEAN JULES VERNE.
ONE OF THAT CROWD.
SHALL WE?

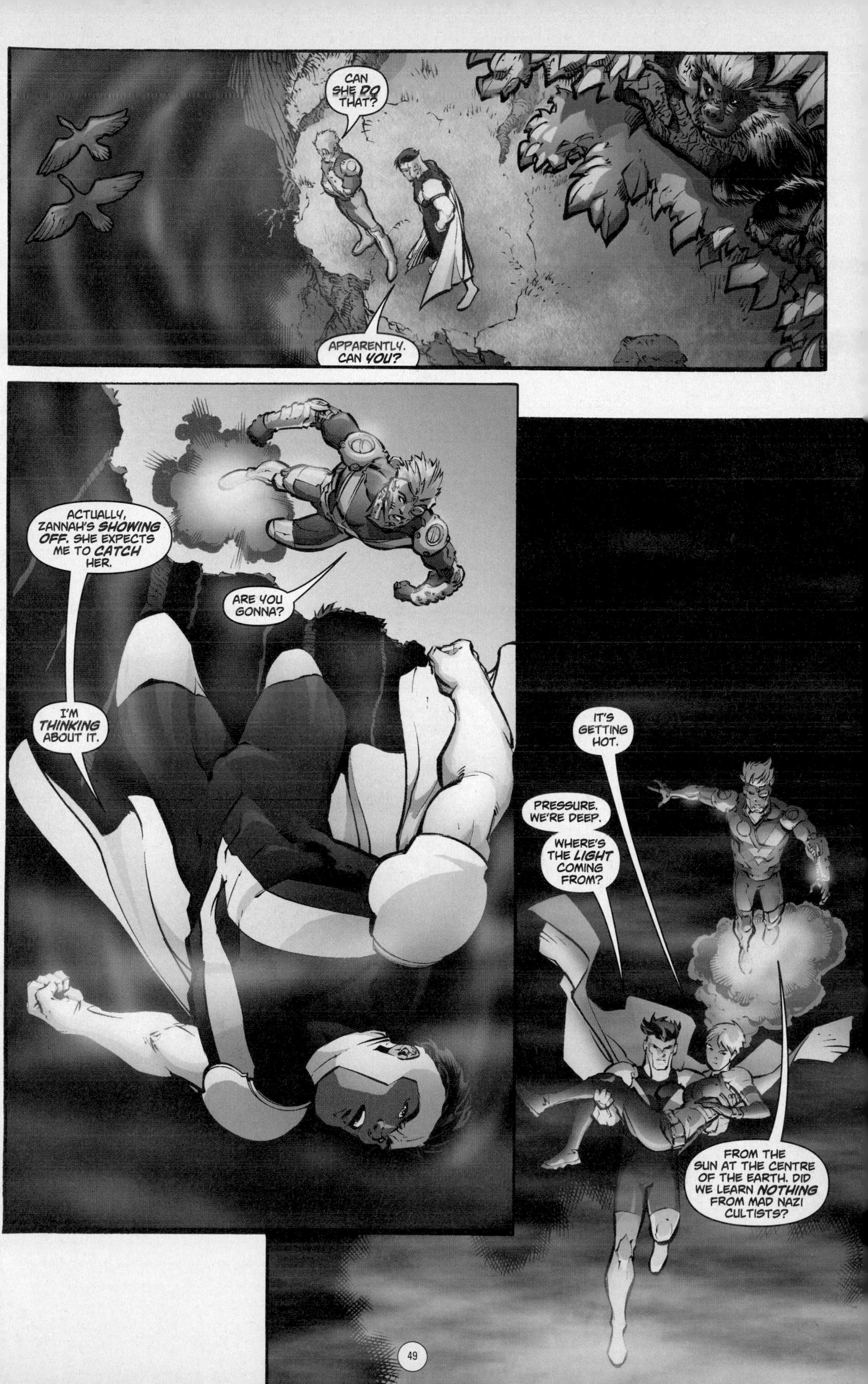
CAN SHE DO THAT?
APPARENTLY. CAN YOU?
ACTUALLY, ZANNAH'S SHOWING OFF. SHE EXPECTS ME TO CATCH HER.
ARE YOU GONNA?
I'M THINKING ABOUT IT.
IT'S GETTING HOT.
PRESSURE. WE'RE DEEP.
WHERE'S THE LIGHT COMING FROM?
FROM THE SUN AT THE CENTRE OF THE EARTH. DID WE LEARN NOTHING FROM MAD NAZI CULTISTS?

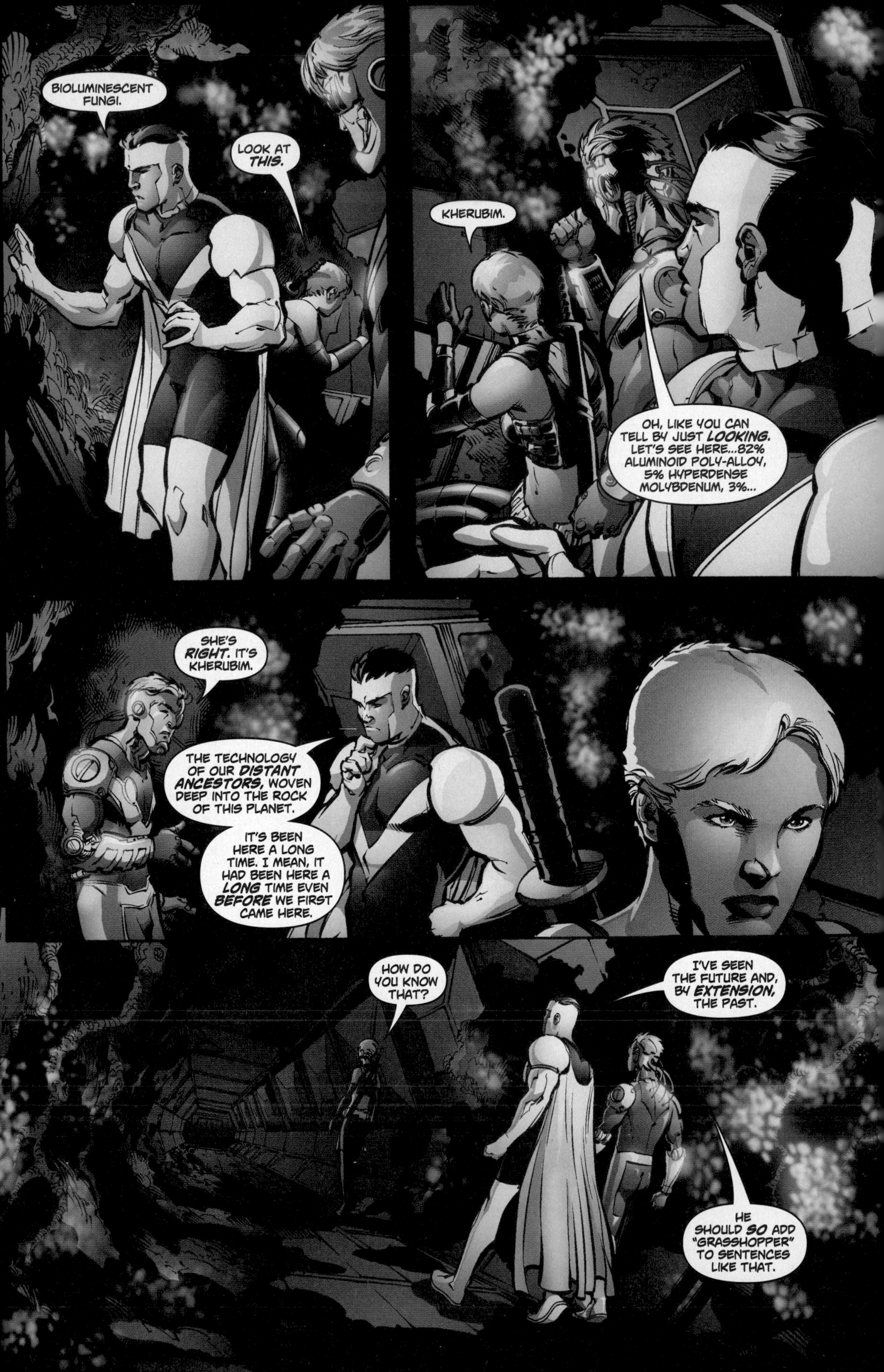
BIOLUMINESCENT FUNGI.
LOOK AT THIS.
KHERUBIM.
OH, LIKE YOU CAN TELL BY JUST LOOKING. LET'S SEE HERE...82% ALUMINOID POLY-ALLOY, 5% HYPERDENSE MOLYBDENUM, 3%...
SHE'S RIGHT. IT'S KHERUBIM.
THE TECHNOLOGY OF OUR DISTANT ANCESTORS, WOVEN DEEP INTO THE ROCK OF THIS PLANET.
IT'S BEEN HERE A LONG TIME. I MEAN, IT HAD BEEN HERE A LONG TIME EVEN BEFORE WE FIRST CAME HERE.
HOW DO YOU KNOW THAT?
I'VE SEEN THE FUTURE AND, BY EXTENSION, THE PAST.
HE SHOULD SO ADD "GRASSHOPPER" TO SENTENCES LIKE THAT.

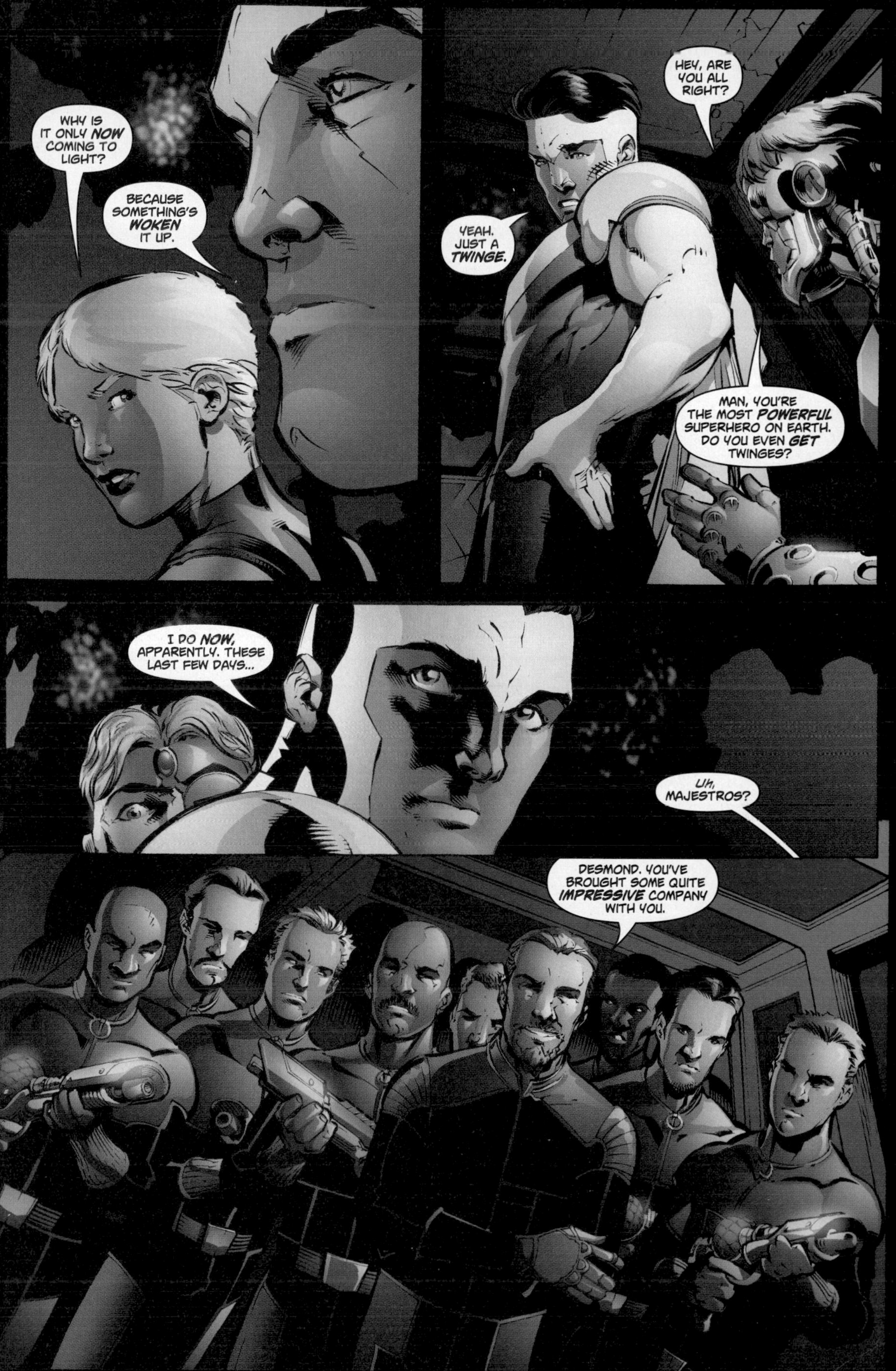
WHY IS IT ONLY NOW COMING TO LIGHT?
BECAUSE SOMETHING'S WOKEN IT UP.
HEY, ARE YOU ALL RIGHT?
YEAH. JUST A TWINGE.
MAN, YOU'RE THE MOST POWERFUL SUPERHERO ON EARTH. DO YOU EVEN GET TWINGES?
I DO NOW, APPARENTLY. THESE LAST FEW DAYS...
UH, MAJESTROS?
DESMOND. YOU'VE BROUGHT SOME QUITE IMPRESSIVE COMPANY WITH YOU.

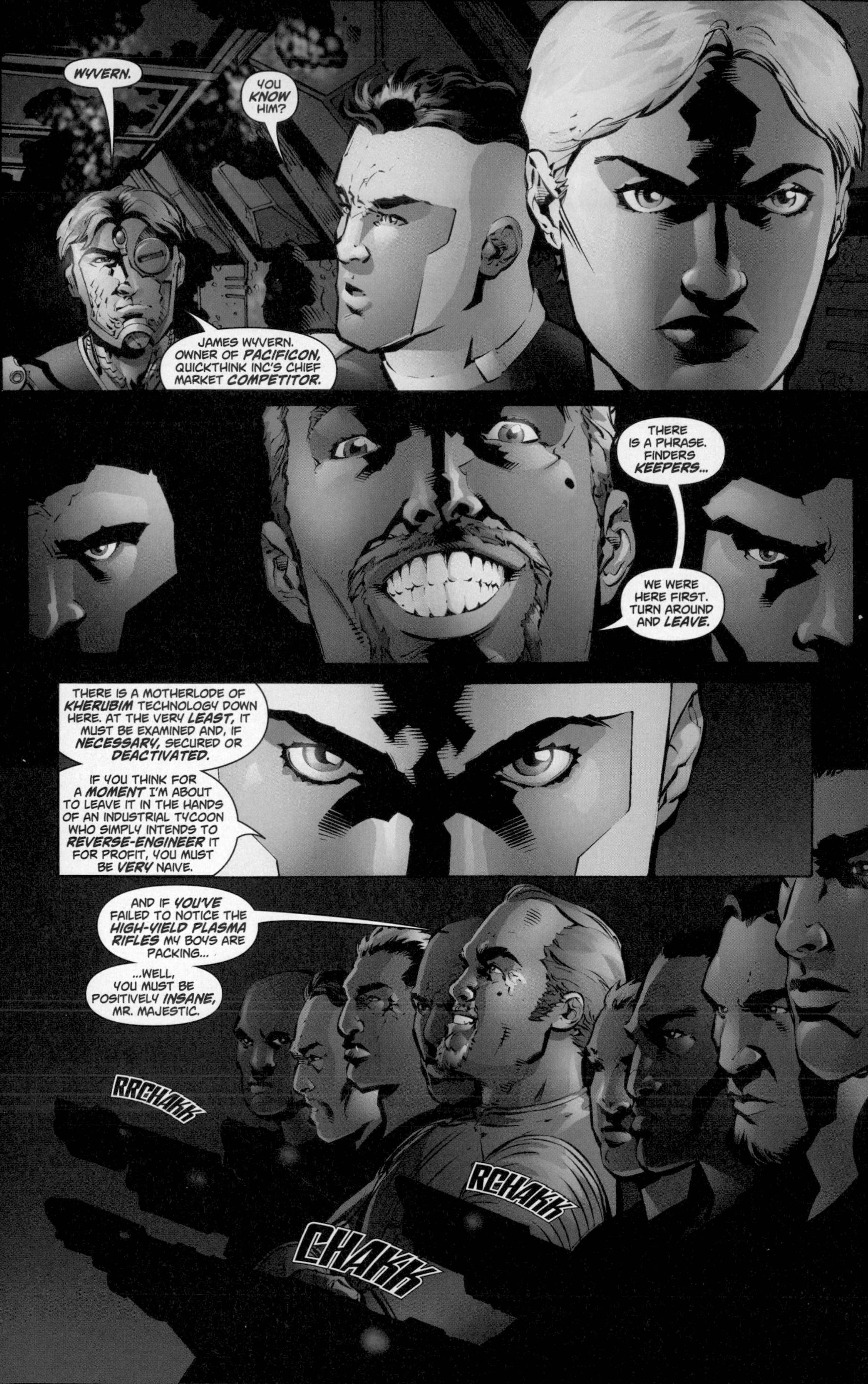
WYVERN.
YOU KNOW HIM?
JAMES WYVERN. OWNER OF PACIFICON, QUICKTHINK INC'S CHIEF MARKET COMPETITOR.
THERE IS A PHRASE. FINDERS KEEPERS...
WE WERE HERE FIRST. TURN AROUND AND LEAVE.
THERE IS A MOTHERLODE OF KHERUBIM TECHNOLOGY DOWN HERE. AT THE VERY LEAST, IT MUST BE EXAMINED AND, IF NECESSARY, SECURED OR DEACTIVATED.
IF YOU THINK FOR A MOMENT I'M ABOUT TO LEAVE IT IN THE HANDS OF AN INDUSTRIAL TYCOON WHO SIMPLY INTENDS TO REVERSE-ENGINEER IT FOR PROFIT, YOU MUST BE VERY NAIVE.
AND IF YOU'VE FAILED TO NOTICE THE HIGH-YIELD PLASMA RIFLES MY BOYS ARE PACKING...
...WELL, YOU MUST BE POSITIVELY INSANE, MR. MAJESTIC.
RRCHAKK
RCHAKK
CHAKK

Just Like Old Times

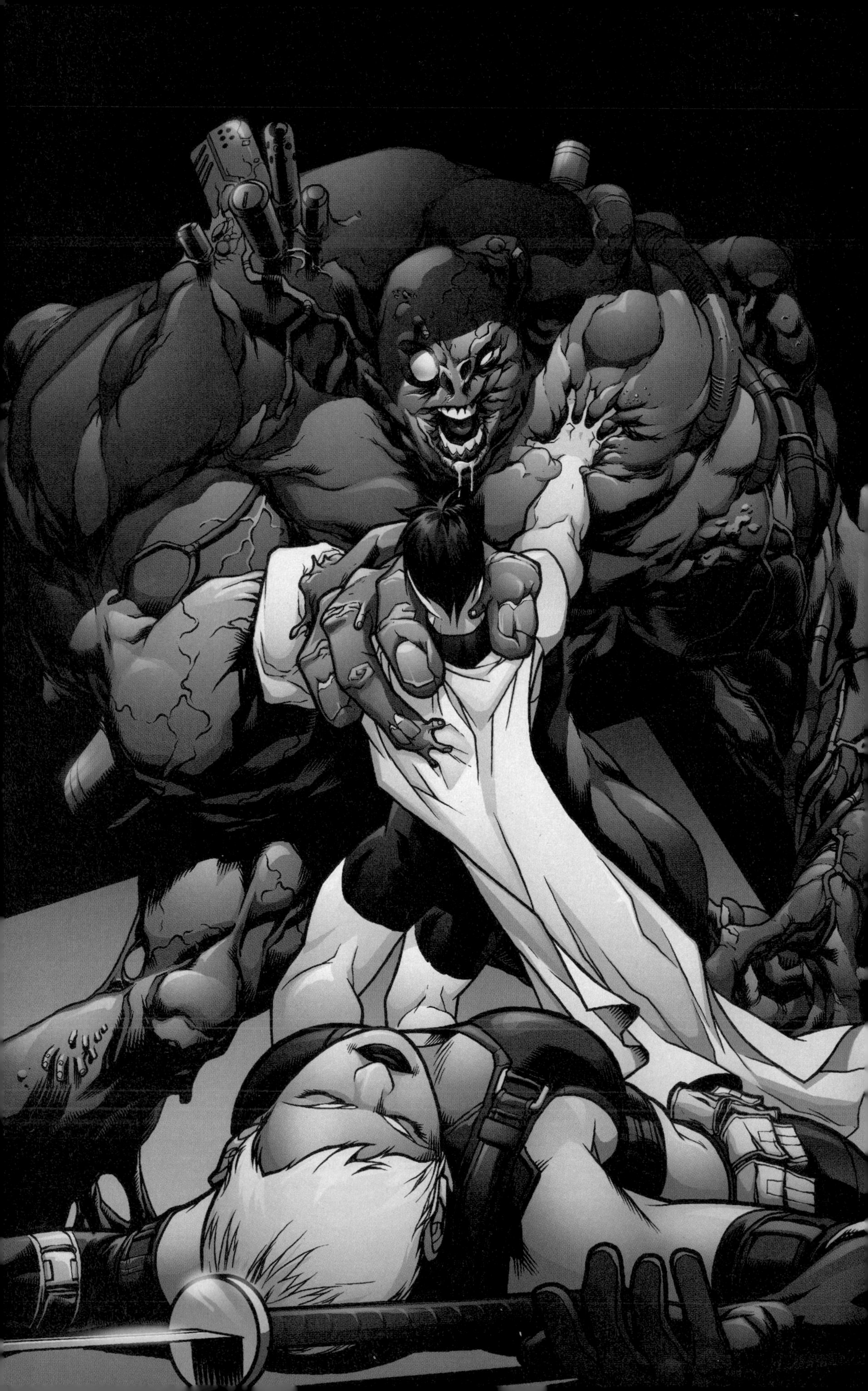

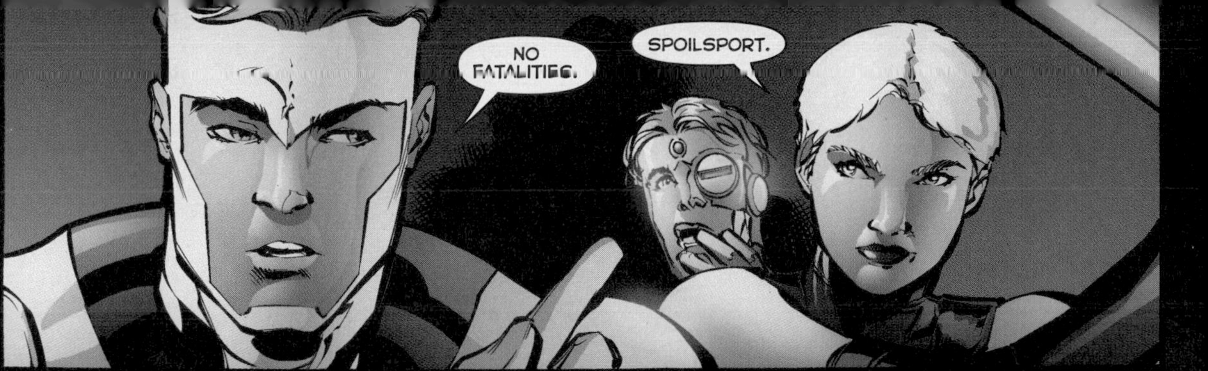
NO FATALITIES.
SPOILSPORT.

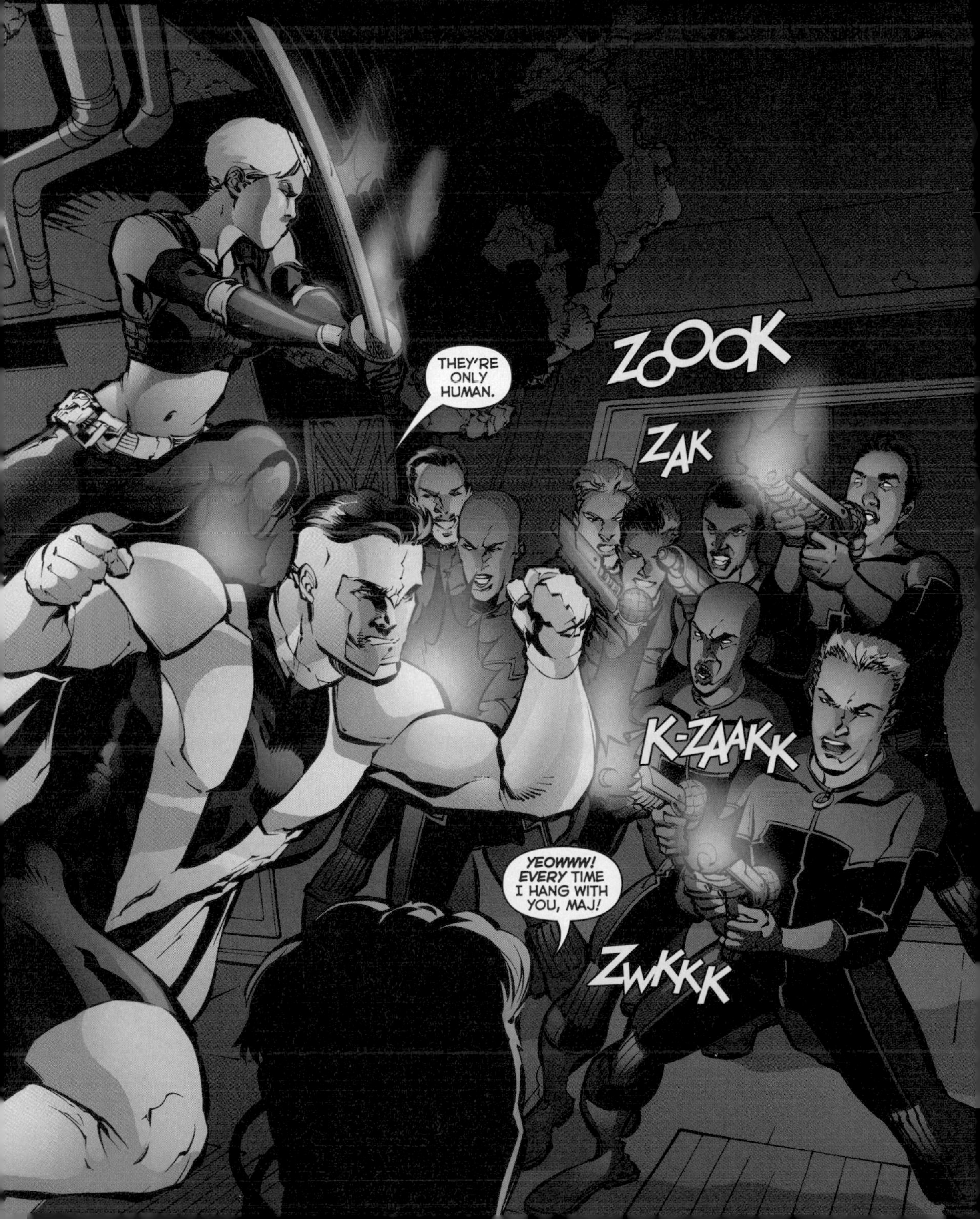
THEY'RE ONLY HUMAN.
ZOOOK
ZAK
K-ZAAKK
YEOWWW! EVERY TIME I HANG WITH YOU, MAJ!
ZWKKK

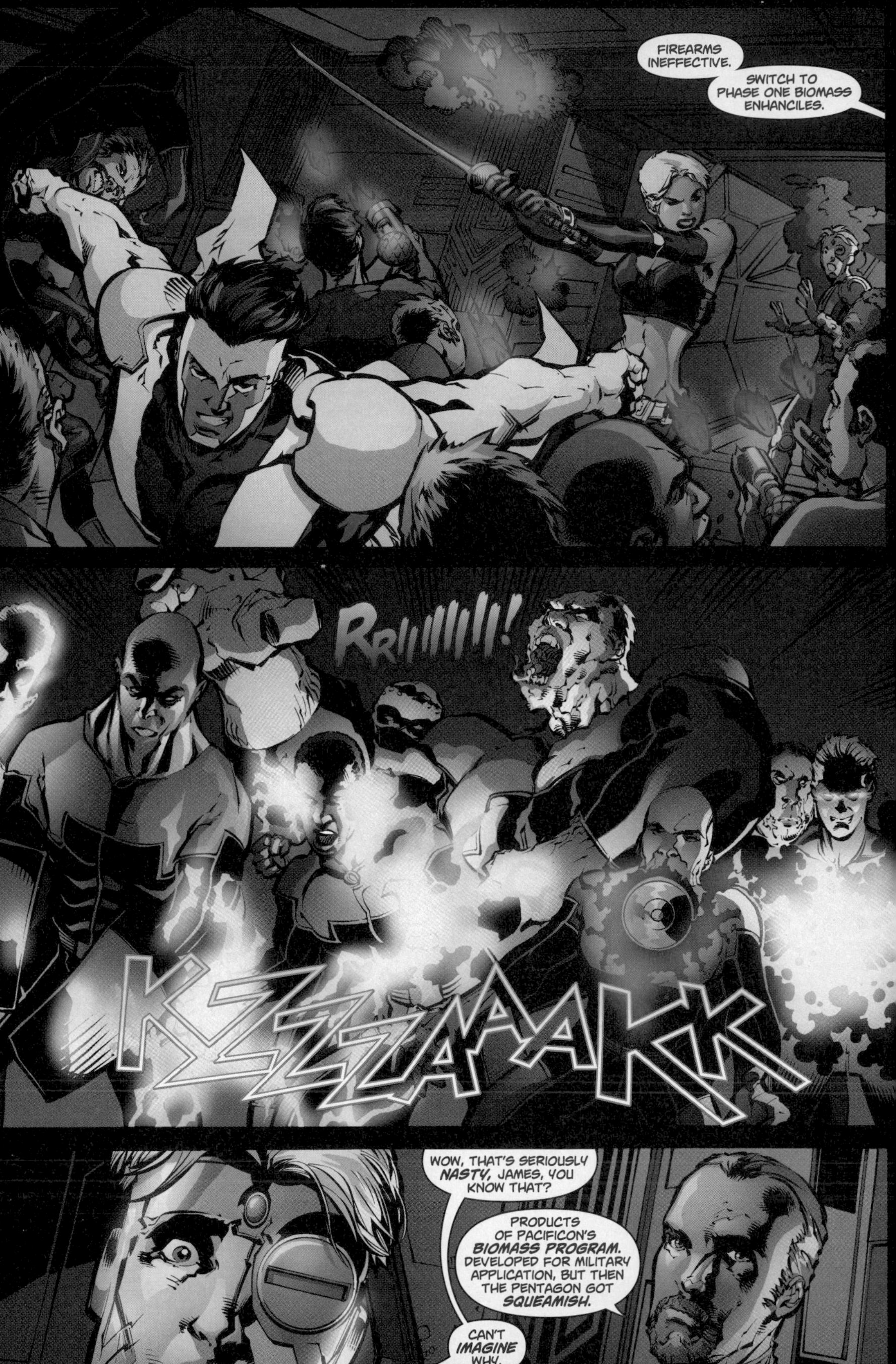
FIREARMS INEFFECTIVE.
SWITCH TO PHASE ONE BIOMASS ENHANCILES.
RRIIIIIIII!
KZZZAAAKK
WOW, THAT'S SERIOUSLY NASTY, JAMES, YOU KNOW THAT?
PRODUCTS OF PACIFICON'S BIOMASS PROGRAM. DEVELOPED FOR MILITARY APPLICATION, BUT THEN THE PENTAGON GOT SQUEAMISH.
CAN'T IMAGINE WHY.

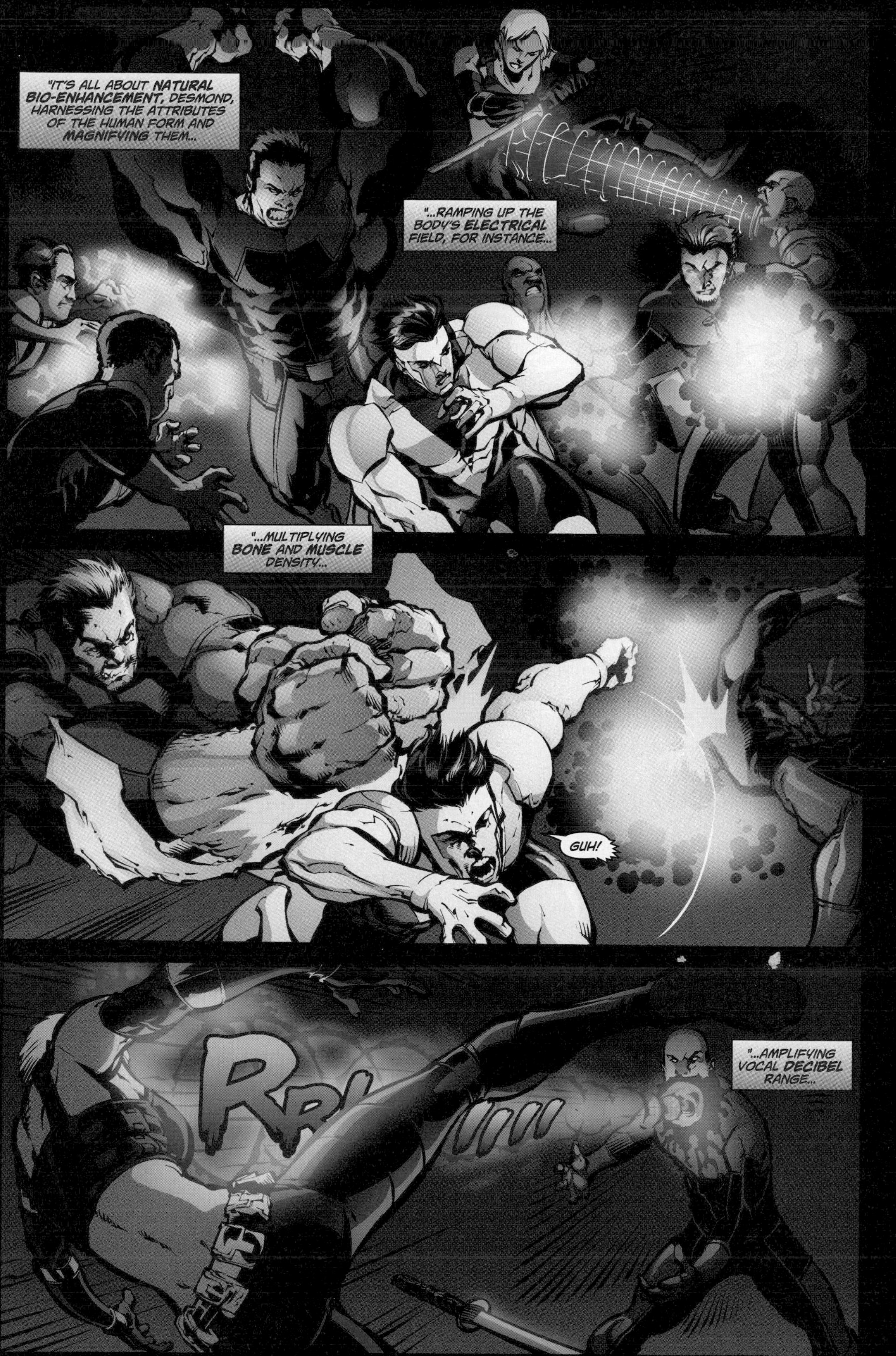
"IT'S ALL ABOUT NATURAL BIO-ENHANCEMENT, DESMOND, HARNESSING THE ATTRIBUTES OF THE HUMAN FORM AND MAGNIFYING THEM...
"...RAMPING UP THE BODY'S ELECTRICAL FIELD, FOR INSTANCE...
"...MULTIPLYING BONE AND MUSCLE DENSITY...
GUH!
"...AMPLIFYING VOCAL DECIBEL RANGE...
RRI

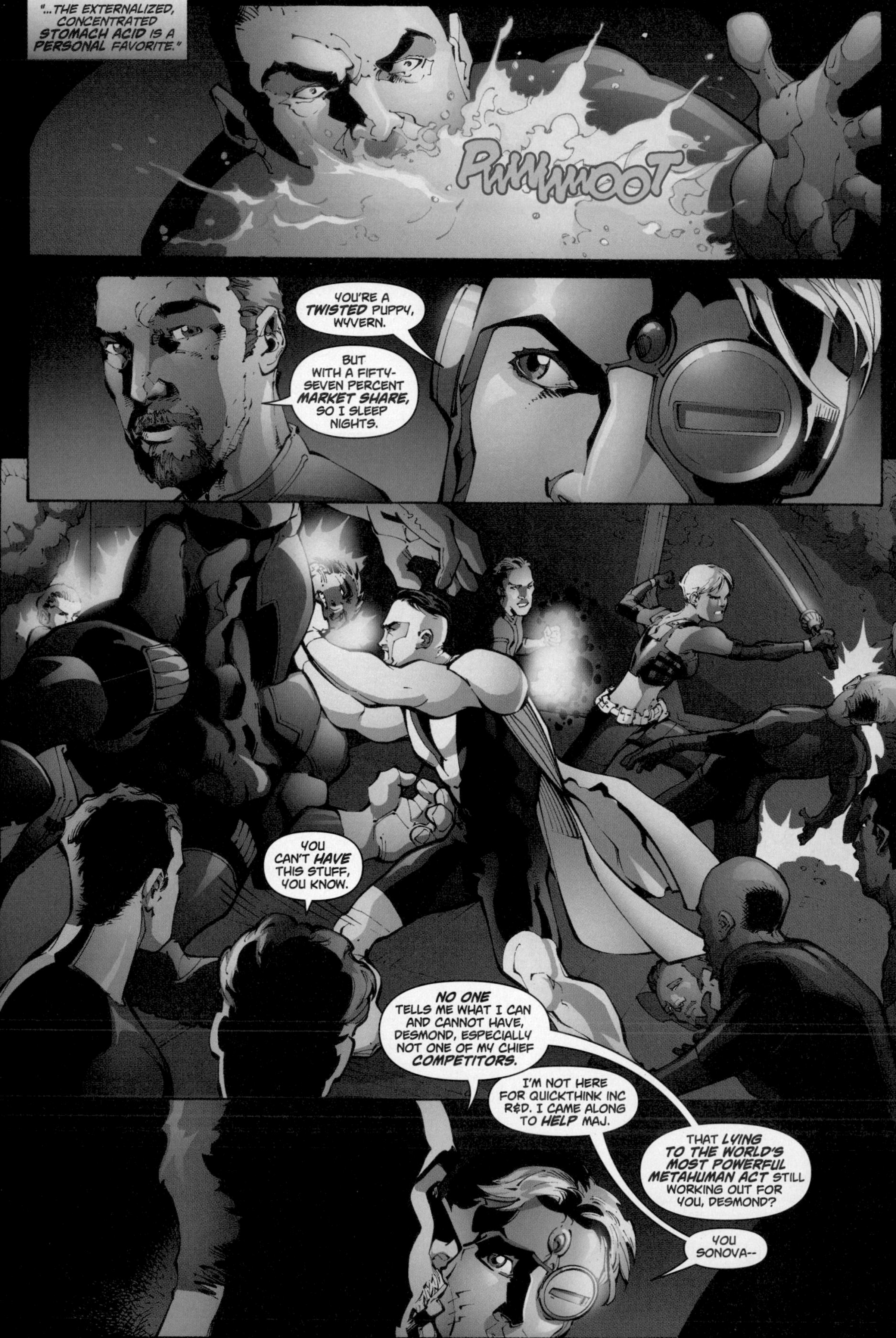
"...THE EXTERNALIZED, CONCENTRATED STOMACH ACID IS A PERSONAL FAVORITE."
PWWWMOOT
YOU'RE A TWISTED PUPPY, WYVERN.
BUT WITH A FIFTY-SEVEN PERCENT MARKET SHARE, SO I SLEEP NIGHTS.
YOU CAN'T HAVE THIS STUFF, YOU KNOW.
NO ONE TELLS ME WHAT I CAN AND CANNOT HAVE, DESMOND, ESPECIALLY NOT ONE OF MY CHIEF COMPETITORS.
I'M NOT HERE FOR QUICKTHINK INC R&D. I CAME ALONG TO HELP MAJ.
THAT LYING TO THE WORLD'S MOST POWERFUL METAHUMAN ACT STILL WORKING OUT FOR YOU, DESMOND?
YOU SONOVA--

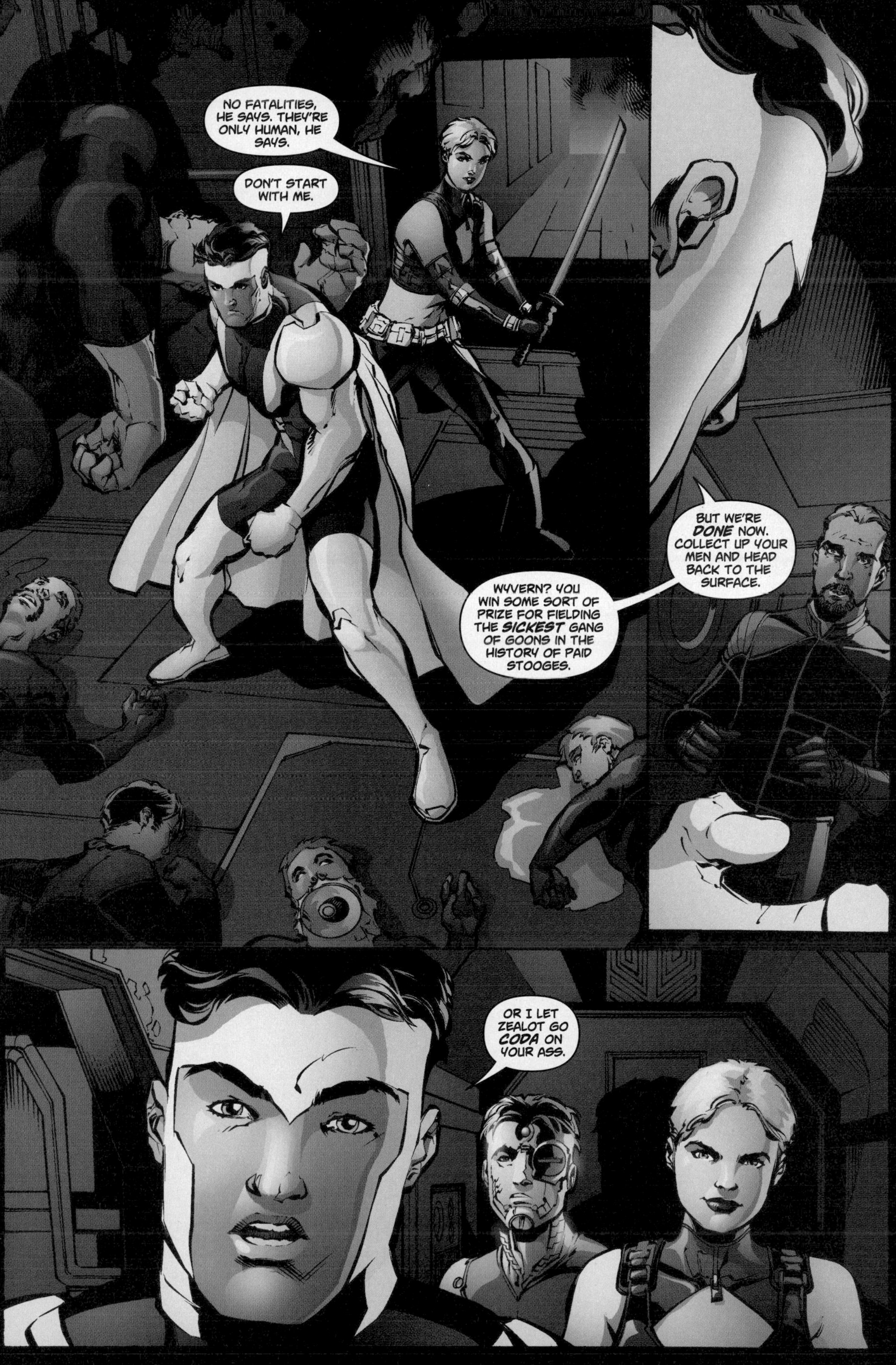
NO FATALITIES, HE SAYS. THEY'RE ONLY HUMAN, HE SAYS.
DON'T START WITH ME.
WYVERN? YOU WIN SOME SORT OF PRIZE FOR FIELDING THE SICKEST GANG OF GOONS IN THE HISTORY OF PAID STOOGES.
BUT WE'RE DONE NOW. COLLECT UP YOUR MEN AND HEAD BACK TO THE SURFACE.
OR I LET ZEALOT GO CODA ON YOUR ASS.

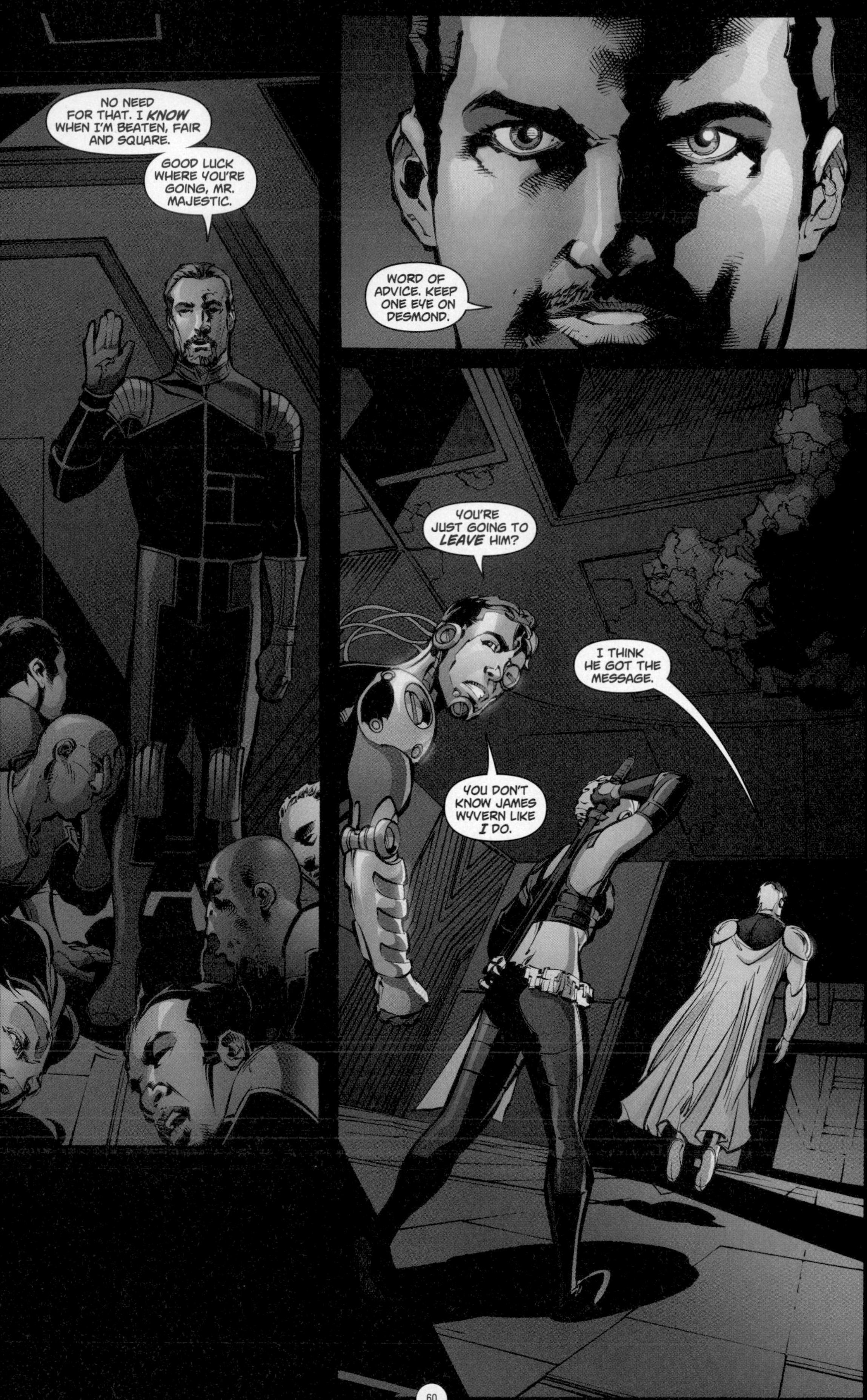
NO NEED FOR THAT. I *KNOW* WHEN I'M BEATEN, FAIR AND SQUARE.
GOOD LUCK WHERE YOU'RE GOING, MR. MAJESTIC.
WORD OF ADVICE. KEEP ONE EYE ON DESMOND.
YOU'RE JUST GOING TO *LEAVE* HIM?
YOU DON'T KNOW JAMES WYVERN LIKE *I* DO.
I THINK HE GOT THE MESSAGE.

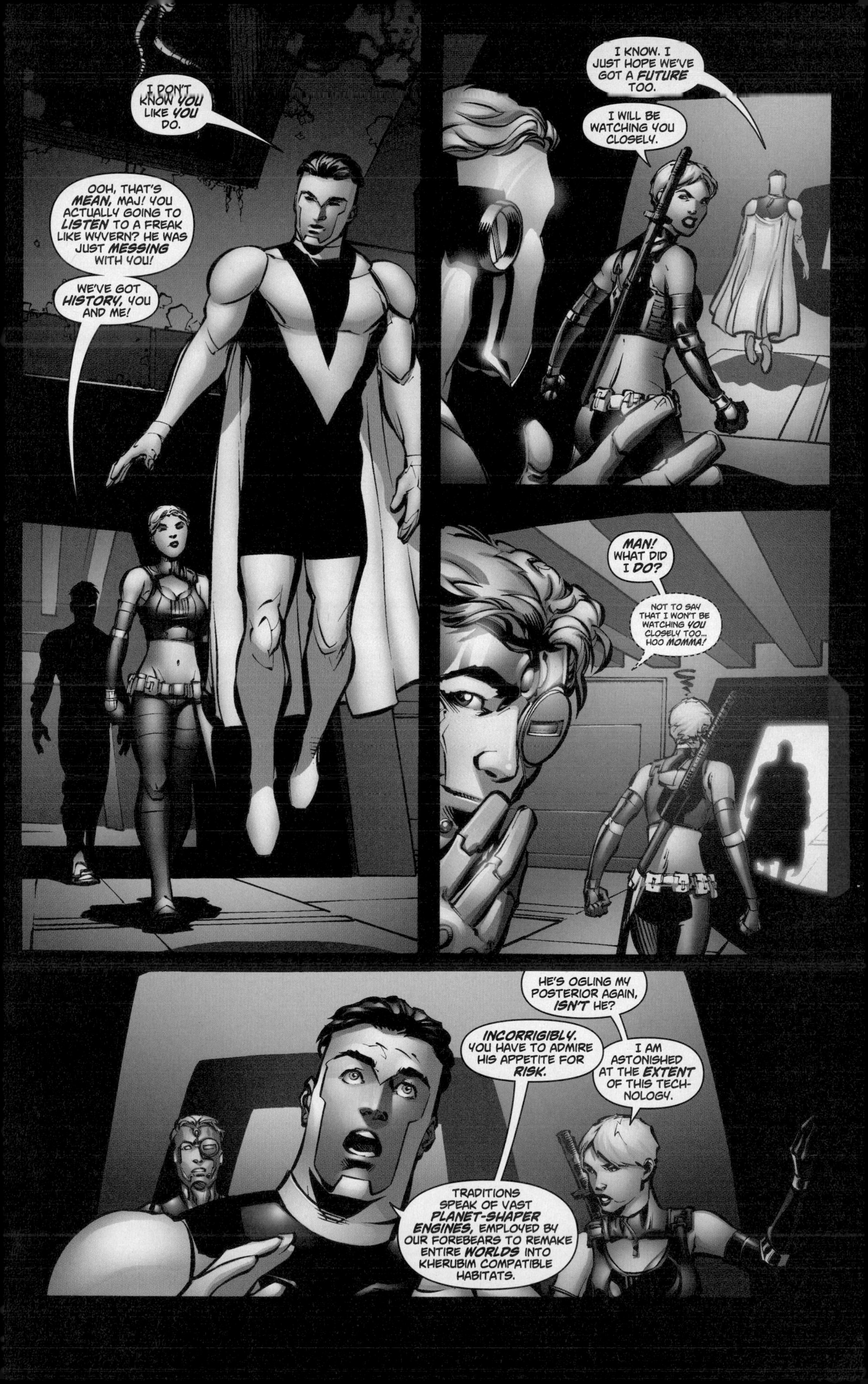
I DON'T KNOW YOU LIKE YOU DO.
OOH, THAT'S MEAN, MAJ! YOU ACTUALLY GOING TO LISTEN TO A FREAK LIKE WYVERN? HE WAS JUST MESSING WITH YOU!
WE'VE GOT HISTORY, YOU AND ME!
I KNOW. I JUST HOPE WE'VE GOT A FUTURE TOO.
I WILL BE WATCHING YOU CLOSELY.
MAN! WHAT DID I DO?
NOT TO SAY THAT I WON'T BE WATCHING YOU CLOSELY TOO... HOO MOMMA!
HE'S OGLING MY POSTERIOR AGAIN, ISN'T HE?
INCORRIGIBLY. YOU HAVE TO ADMIRE HIS APPETITE FOR RISK.
I AM ASTONISHED AT THE EXTENT OF THIS TECH-NOLOGY.
TRADITIONS SPEAK OF VAST PLANET-SHAPER ENGINES, EMPLOYED BY OUR FOREBEARS TO REMAKE ENTIRE WORLDS INTO KHERUBIM COMPATIBLE HABITATS.

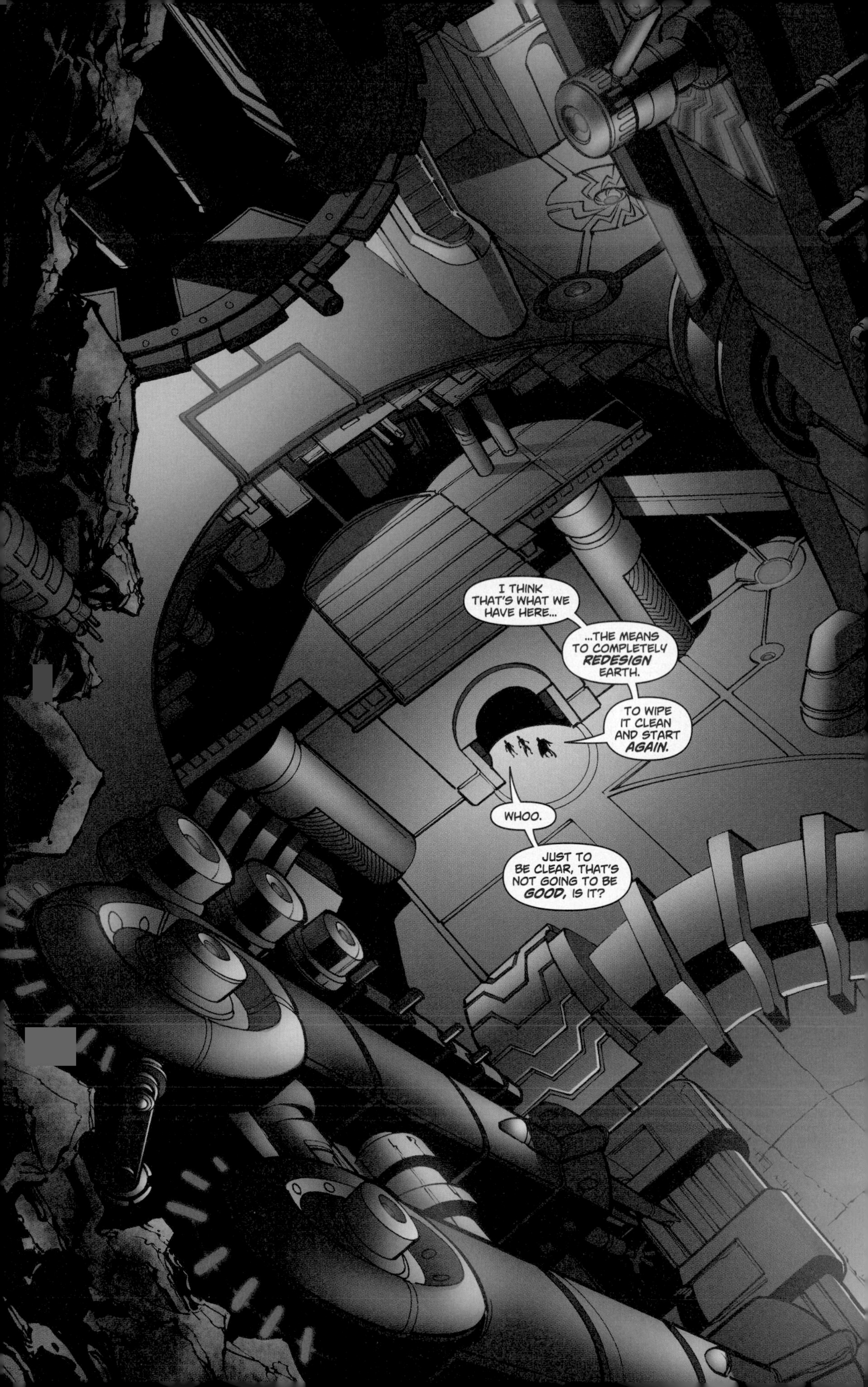
I THINK THAT'S WHAT WE HAVE HERE...
...THE MEANS TO COMPLETELY *REDESIGN* EARTH.
TO WIPE IT CLEAN AND START *AGAIN.*
WHOO.
JUST TO BE CLEAR, THAT'S NOT GOING TO BE *GOOD,* IS IT?

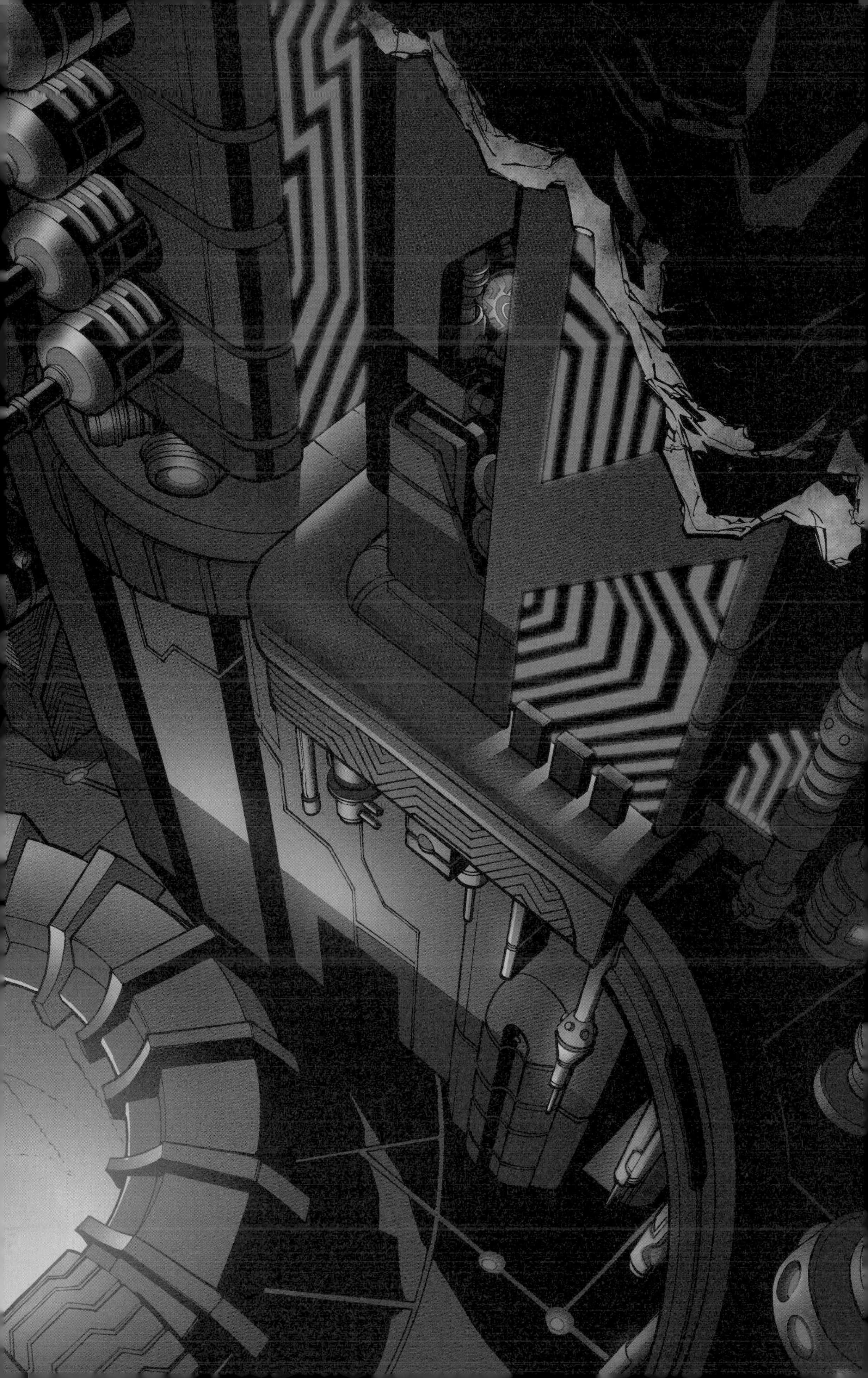

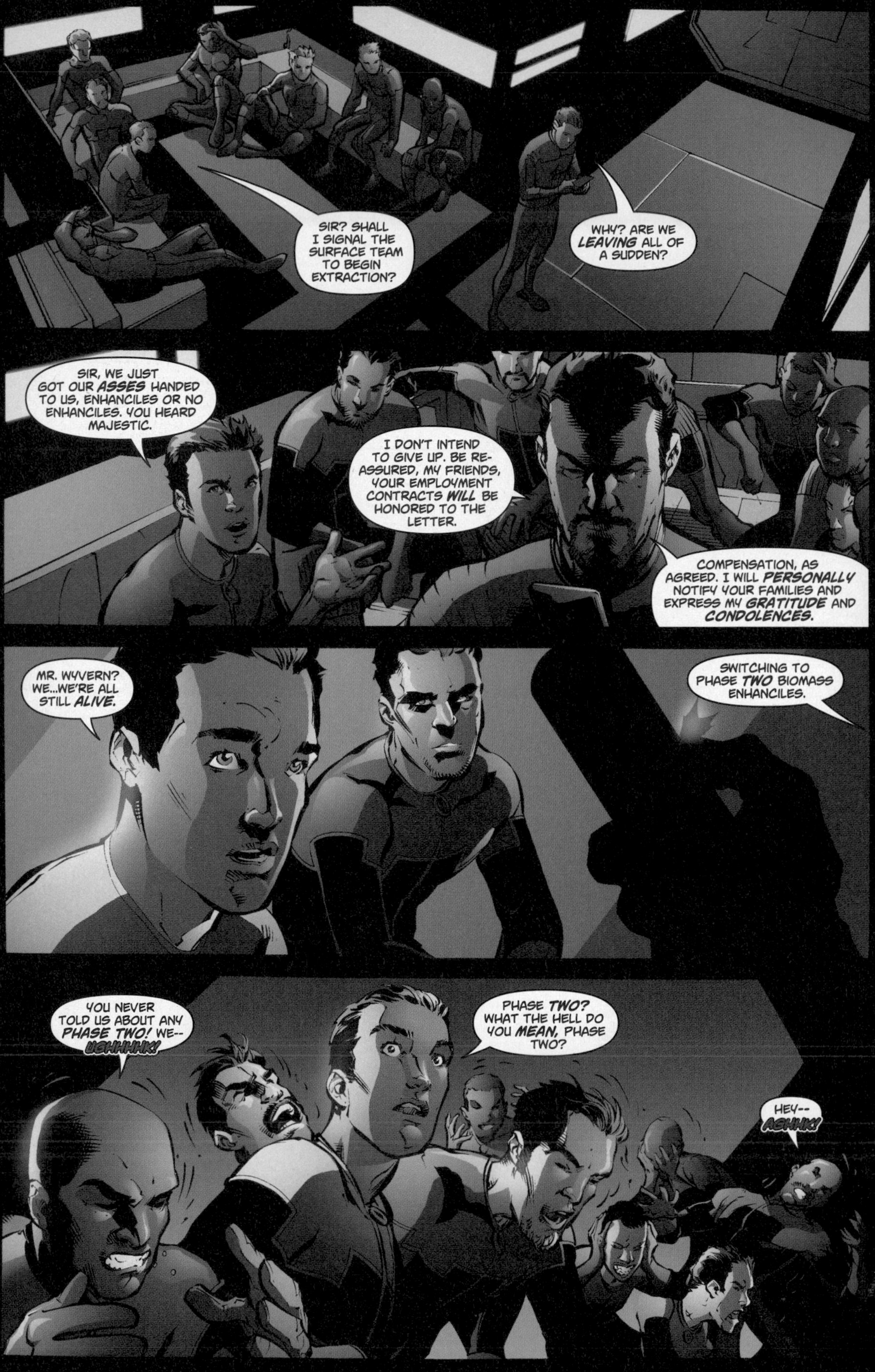
SIR? SHALL I SIGNAL THE SURFACE TEAM TO BEGIN EXTRACTION?
WHY? ARE WE LEAVING ALL OF A SUDDEN?
SIR, WE JUST GOT OUR ASSES HANDED TO US, ENHANCILES OR NO ENHANCILES. YOU HEARD MAJESTIC.
I DON'T INTEND TO GIVE UP. BE RE-ASSURED, MY FRIENDS, YOUR EMPLOYMENT CONTRACTS WILL BE HONORED TO THE LETTER.
COMPENSATION, AS AGREED. I WILL PERSONALLY NOTIFY YOUR FAMILIES AND EXPRESS MY GRATITUDE AND CONDOLENCES.
MR. WYVERN? WE...WE'RE ALL STILL ALIVE.
SWITCHING TO PHASE TWO BIOMASS ENHANCILES.
YOU NEVER TOLD US ABOUT ANY PHASE TWO! WE-- UGHHHHK!
PHASE TWO? WHAT THE HELL DO YOU MEAN, PHASE TWO?
HEY-- AGHHK!

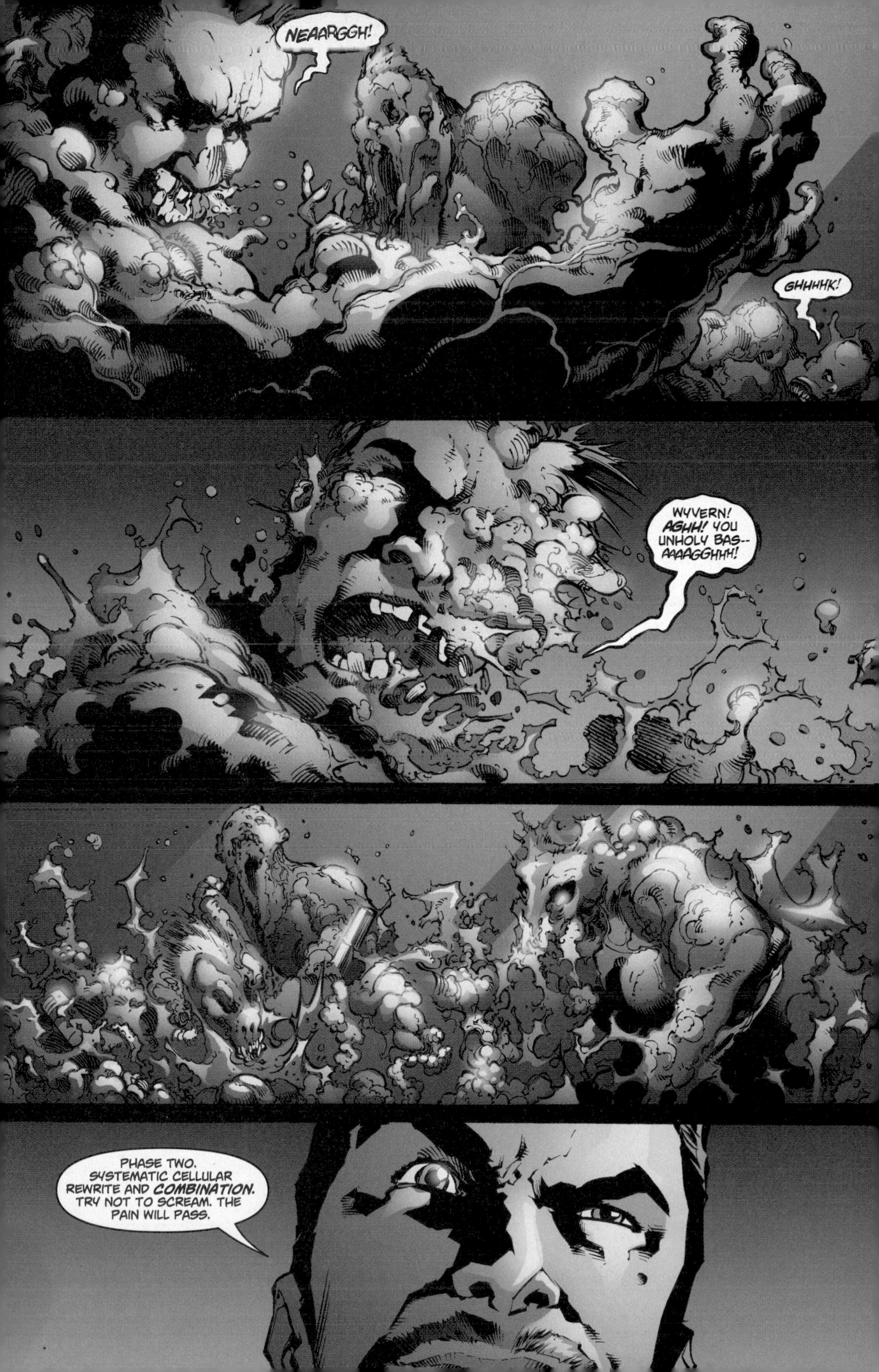
NEAARGGH!
GHHHHK!
WYVERN! AGHH! YOU UNHOLY BAS-- AAAAGGHHH!
PHASE TWO. SYSTEMATIC CELLULAR REWRITE AND COMBINATION. TRY NOT TO SCREAM. THE PAIN WILL PASS.

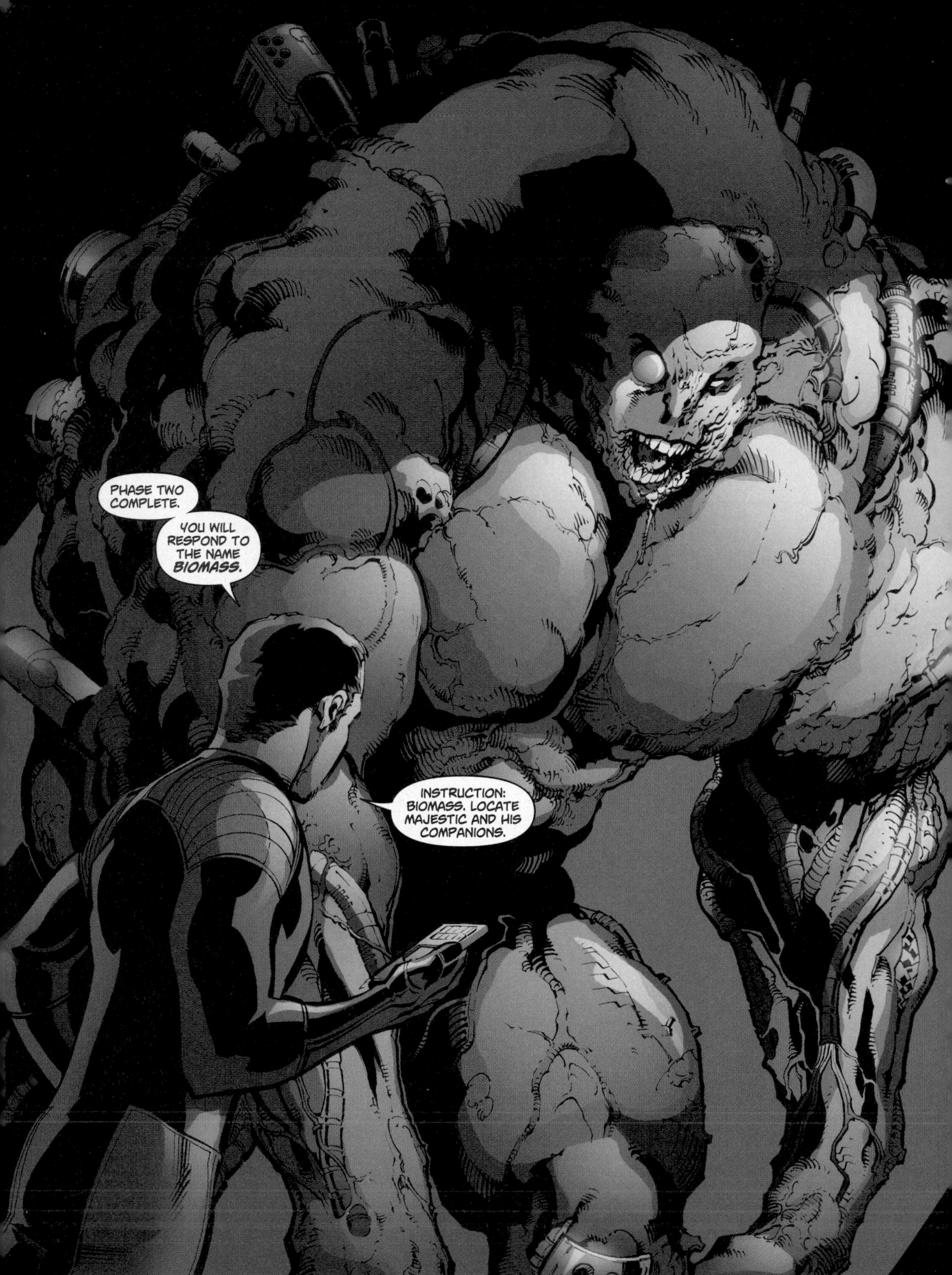
PHASE TWO COMPLETE.
YOU WILL RESPOND TO THE NAME BIOMASS.
INSTRUCTION: BIOMASS. LOCATE MAJESTIC AND HIS COMPANIONS.

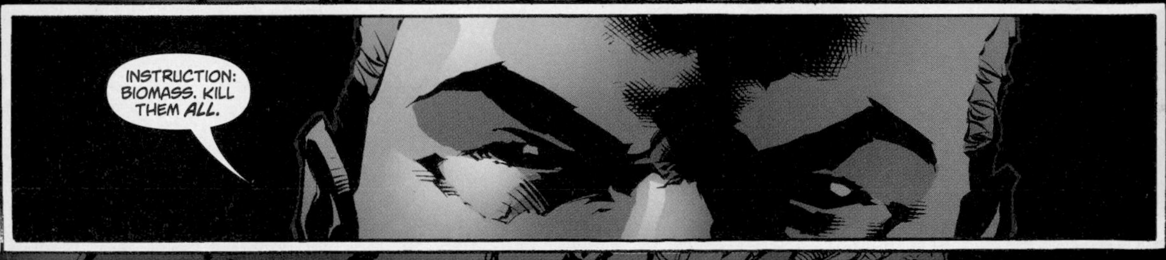
INSTRUCTION: BIOMASS. KILL THEM ALL.

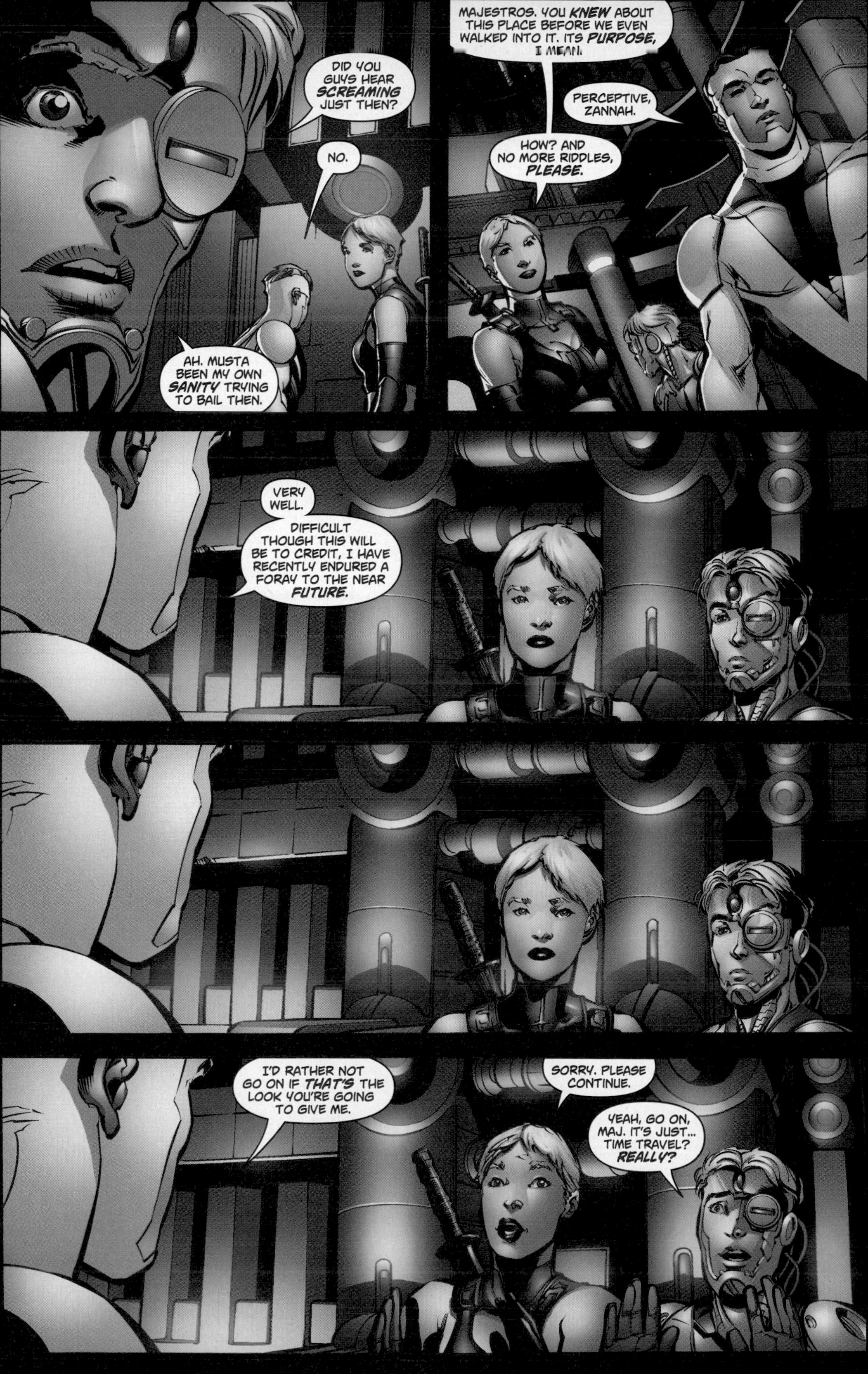
DID YOU GUYS HEAR SCREAMING JUST THEN?
NO.
AH. MUSTA BEEN MY OWN SANITY TRYING TO BAIL THEN.
MAJESTROS. YOU KNEW ABOUT THIS PLACE BEFORE WE EVEN WALKED INTO IT. ITS PURPOSE, I MEAN.
PERCEPTIVE, ZANNAH.
HOW? AND NO MORE RIDDLES, PLEASE.
VERY WELL.
DIFFICULT THOUGH THIS WILL BE TO CREDIT, I HAVE RECENTLY ENDURED A FORAY TO THE NEAR FUTURE.
I'D RATHER NOT GO ON IF THAT'S THE LOOK YOU'RE GOING TO GIVE ME.
SORRY. PLEASE CONTINUE.
YEAH, GO ON, MAJ. IT'S JUST... TIME TRAVEL? REALLY?

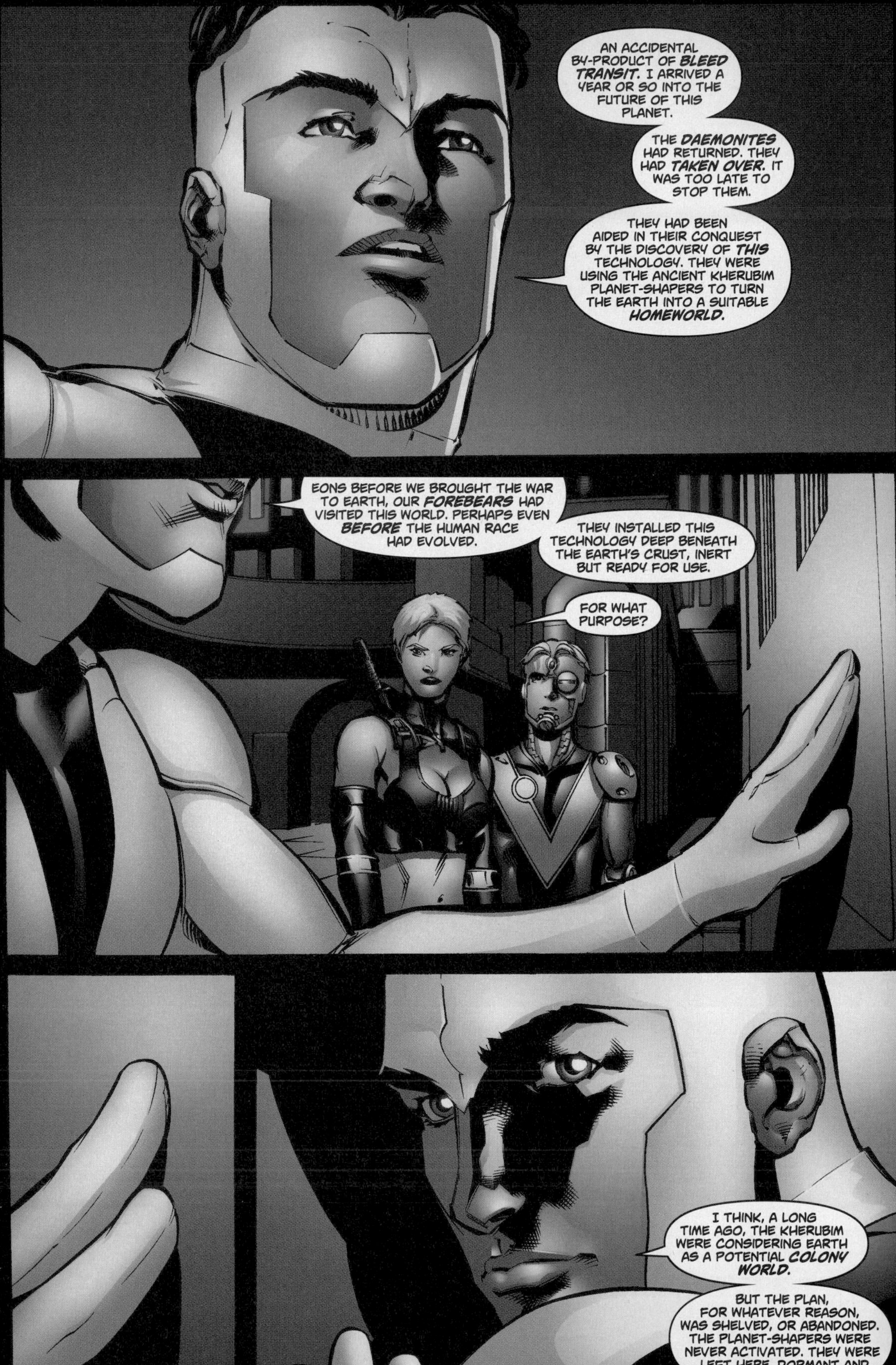
AN ACCIDENTAL BY-PRODUCT OF BLEED TRANSIT. I ARRIVED A YEAR OR SO INTO THE FUTURE OF THIS PLANET.
THE DAEMONITES HAD RETURNED. THEY HAD TAKEN OVER. IT WAS TOO LATE TO STOP THEM.
THEY HAD BEEN AIDED IN THEIR CONQUEST BY THE DISCOVERY OF THIS TECHNOLOGY. THEY WERE USING THE ANCIENT KHERUBIM PLANET-SHAPERS TO TURN THE EARTH INTO A SUITABLE HOMEWORLD.
EONS BEFORE WE BROUGHT THE WAR TO EARTH, OUR FOREBEARS HAD VISITED THIS WORLD. PERHAPS EVEN BEFORE THE HUMAN RACE HAD EVOLVED.
THEY INSTALLED THIS TECHNOLOGY DEEP BENEATH THE EARTH'S CRUST, INERT BUT READY FOR USE.
FOR WHAT PURPOSE?
I THINK, A LONG TIME AGO, THE KHERUBIM WERE CONSIDERING EARTH AS A POTENTIAL COLONY WORLD.
BUT THE PLAN, FOR WHATEVER REASON, WAS SHELVED, OR ABANDONED. THE PLANET-SHAPERS WERE NEVER ACTIVATED. THEY WERE LEFT HERE, DORMANT AND FORGOTTEN.

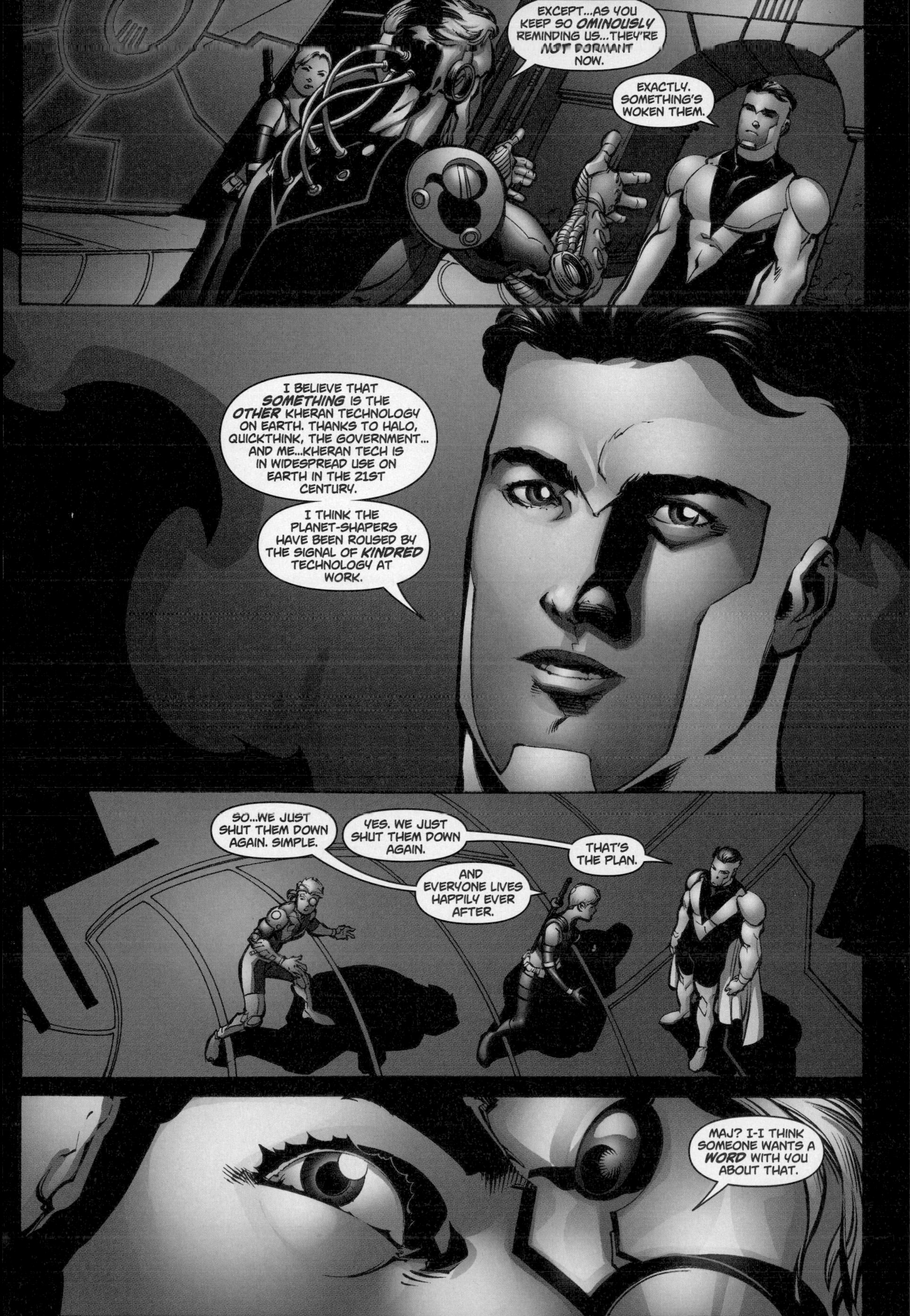

EXCEPT...AS YOU KEEP SO OMINOUSLY REMINDING US...THEY'RE NOT DORMANT NOW.
EXACTLY. SOMETHING'S WOKEN THEM.
I BELIEVE THAT SOMETHING IS THE OTHER KHERAN TECHNOLOGY ON EARTH. THANKS TO HALO, QUICKTHINK, THE GOVERNMENT... AND ME...KHERAN TECH IS IN WIDESPREAD USE ON EARTH IN THE 21ST CENTURY.
I THINK THE PLANET-SHAPERS HAVE BEEN ROUSED BY THE SIGNAL OF KINDRED TECHNOLOGY AT WORK.
SO...WE JUST SHUT THEM DOWN AGAIN. SIMPLE.
YES. WE JUST SHUT THEM DOWN AGAIN.
THAT'S THE PLAN.
AND EVERYONE LIVES HAPPILY EVER AFTER.
MAJ? I-I THINK SOMEONE WANTS A WORD WITH YOU ABOUT THAT.

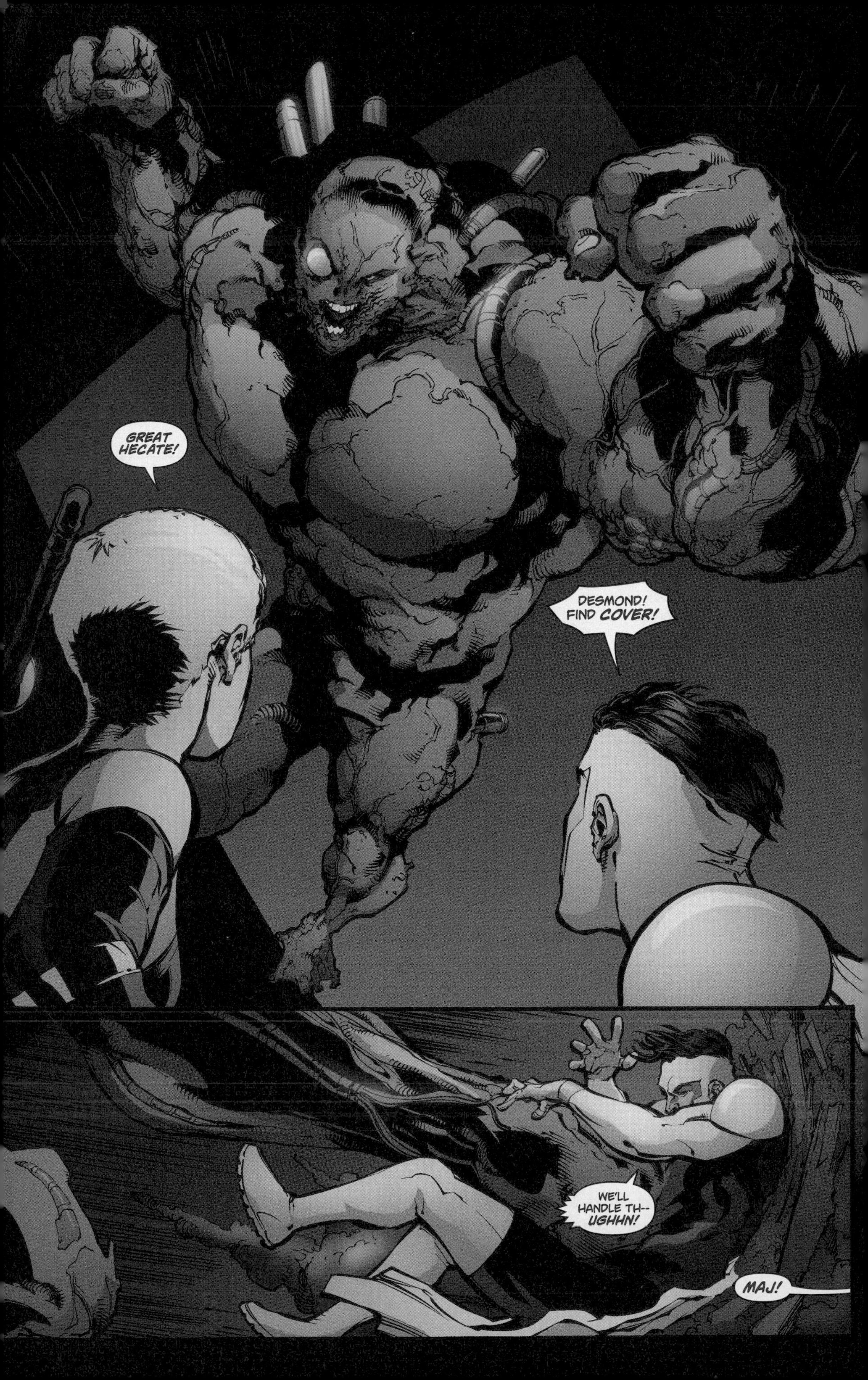
GREAT HECATE!
DESMOND! FIND COVER!
WE'LL HANDLE TH-- UGHHN!
MAJ!

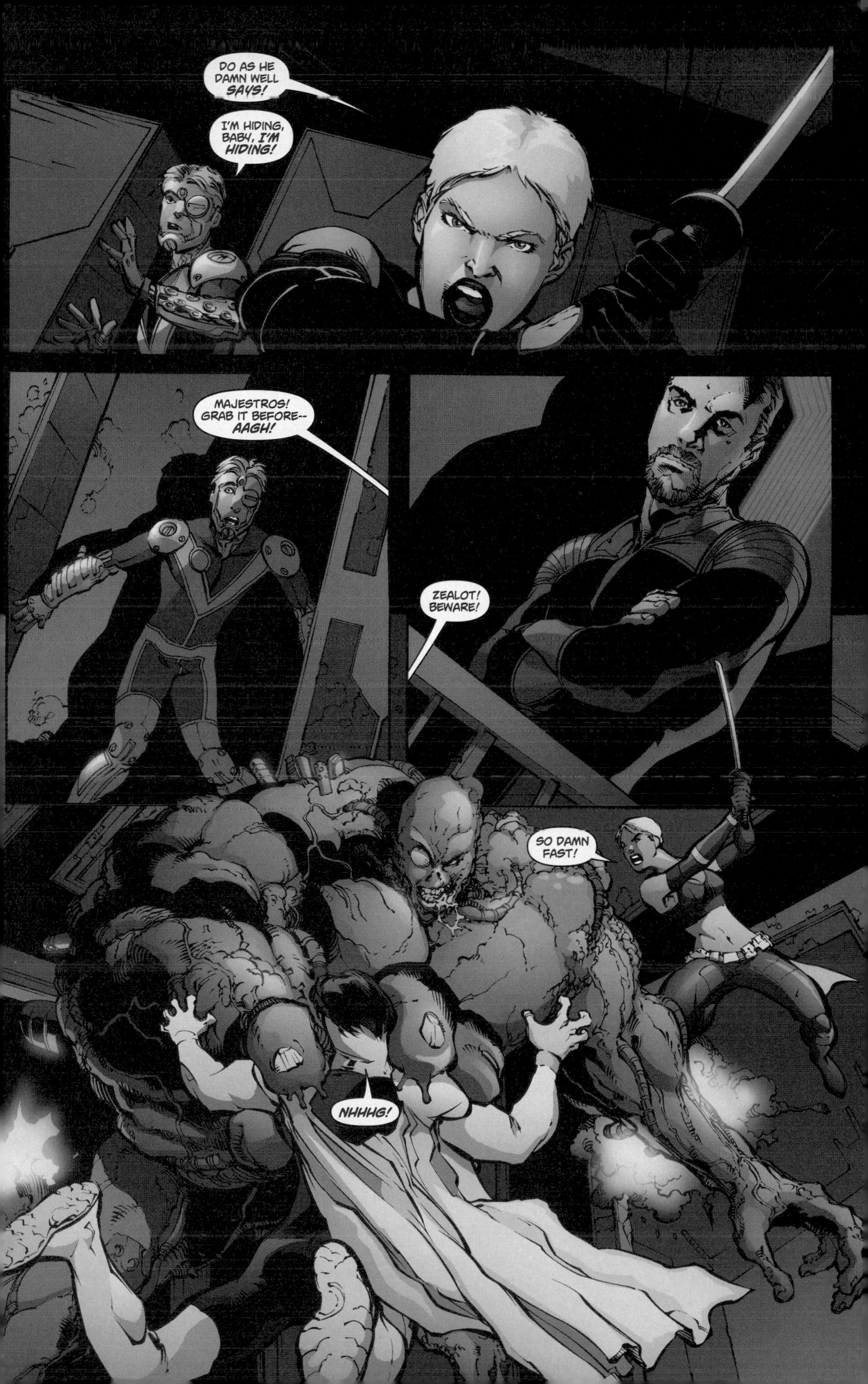
DO AS HE DAMN WELL SAYS!
I'M HIDING, BABY, I'M HIDING!
MAJESTROS! GRAB IT BEFORE-- AAGH!
ZEALOT! BEWARE!
SO DAMN FAST!
NHHHG!

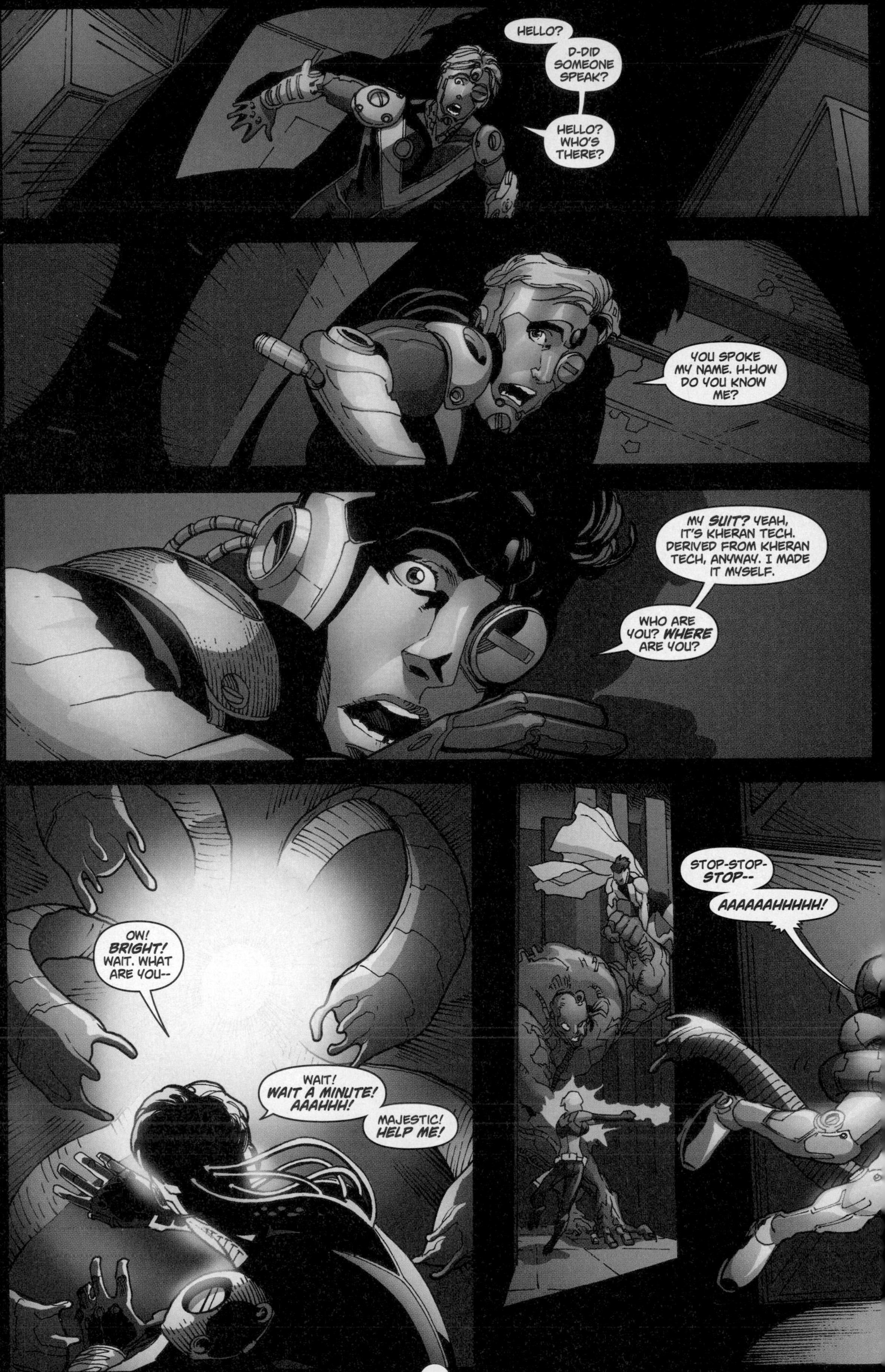
HELLO?
D-DID SOMEONE SPEAK?
HELLO? WHO'S THERE?
YOU SPOKE MY NAME. H-HOW DO YOU KNOW ME?
MY SUIT? YEAH, IT'S KHERAN TECH. DERIVED FROM KHERAN TECH, ANYWAY. I MADE IT MYSELF.
WHO ARE YOU? WHERE ARE YOU?
OW! BRIGHT! WAIT. WHAT ARE YOU--
WAIT! WAIT A MINUTE! AAAHHH!
MAJESTIC! HELP ME!
STOP-STOP-STOP--
AAAAAAHHHHH!

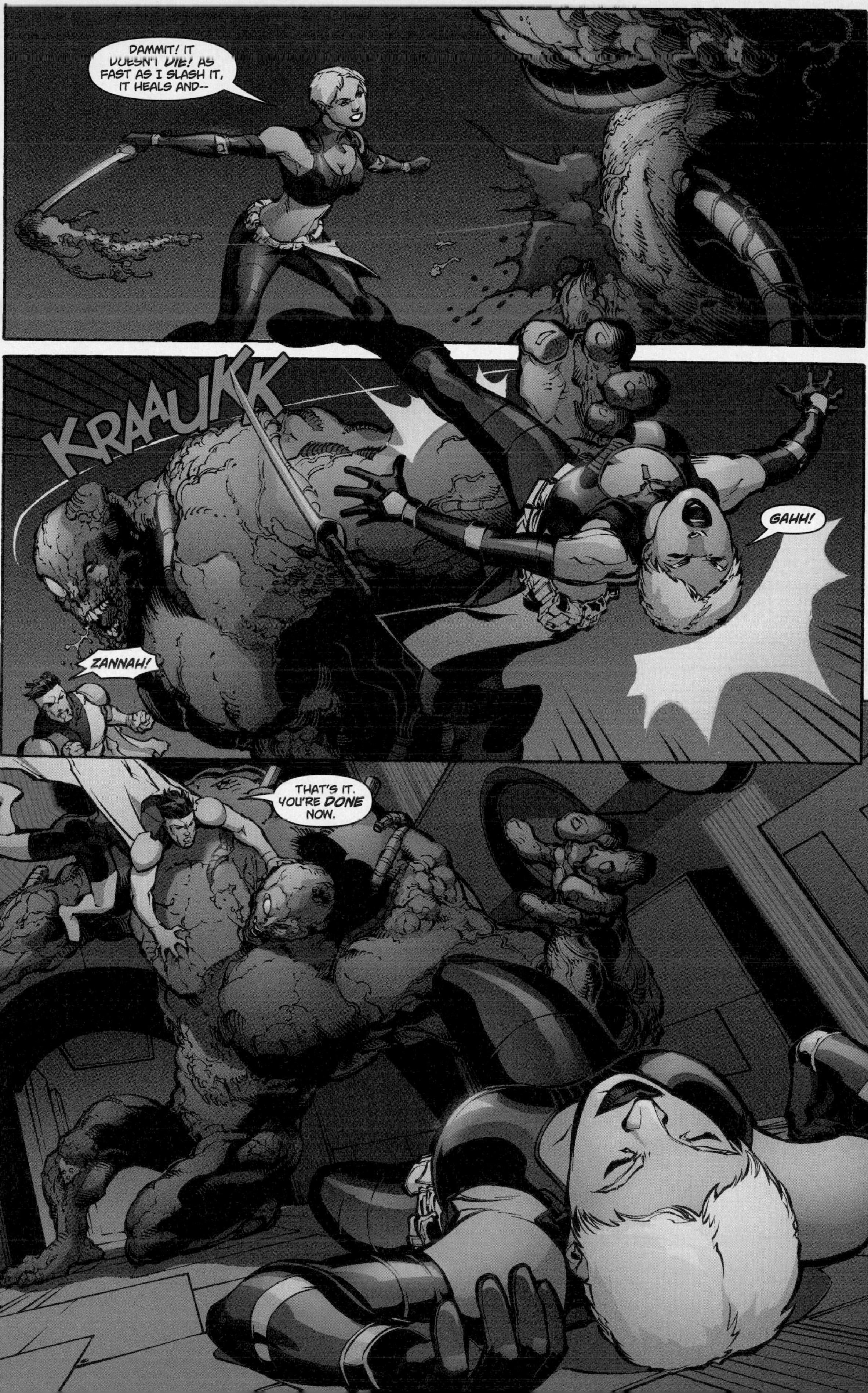
DAMMIT! IT DOESN'T DIE! AS FAST AS I SLASH IT, IT HEALS AND--
KRAAUKK
GAHH!
ZANNAH!
THAT'S IT. YOU'RE DONE NOW.

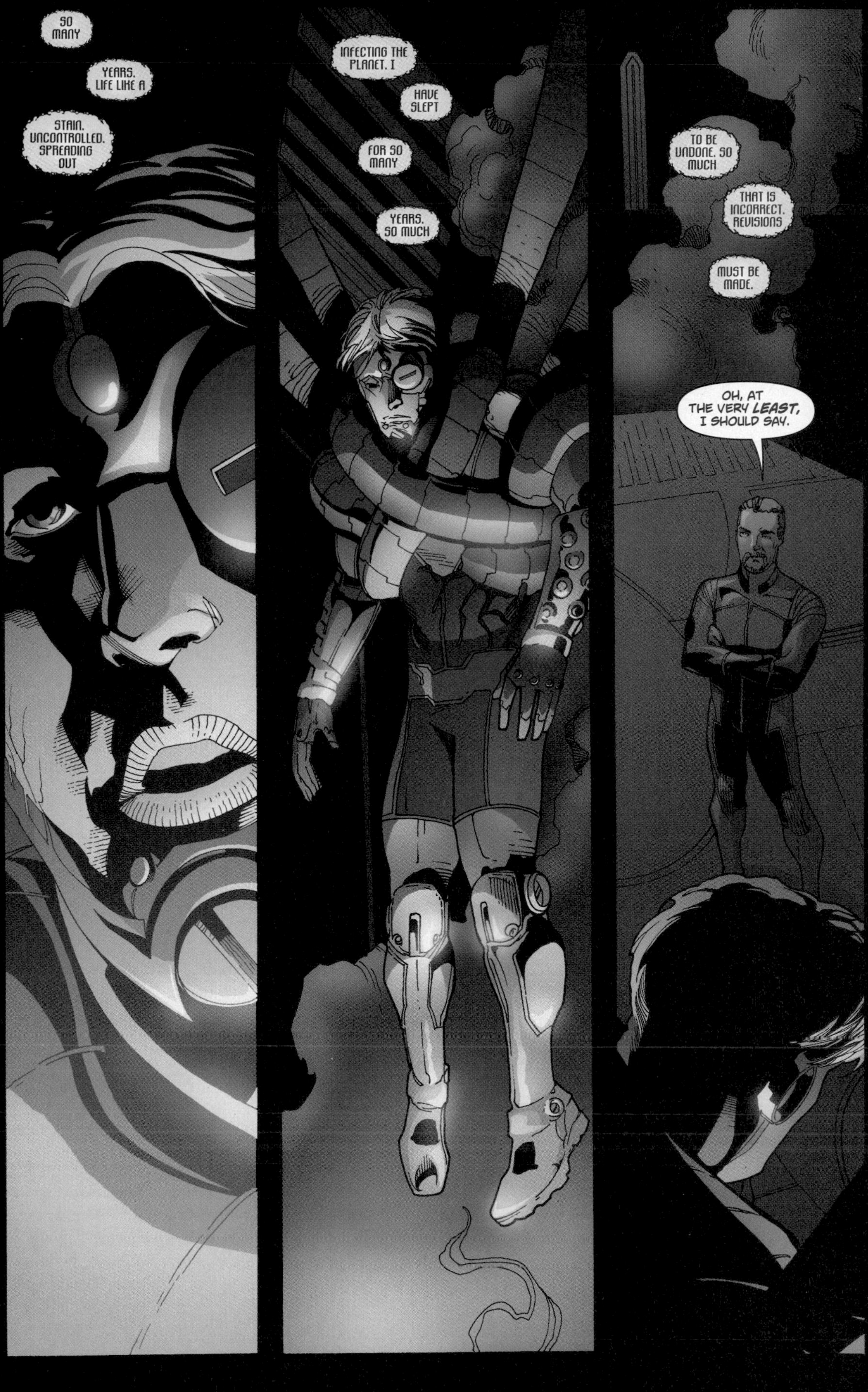
SO MANY
YEARS. LIFE LIKE A
STAIN. UNCONTROLLED. SPREADING OUT
INFECTING THE PLANET. I
HAVE SLEPT
FOR SO MANY
YEARS. SO MUCH
TO BE UNDONE. SO MUCH
THAT IS INCORRECT. REVISIONS
MUST BE MADE.
OH, AT THE VERY LEAST, I SHOULD SAY.

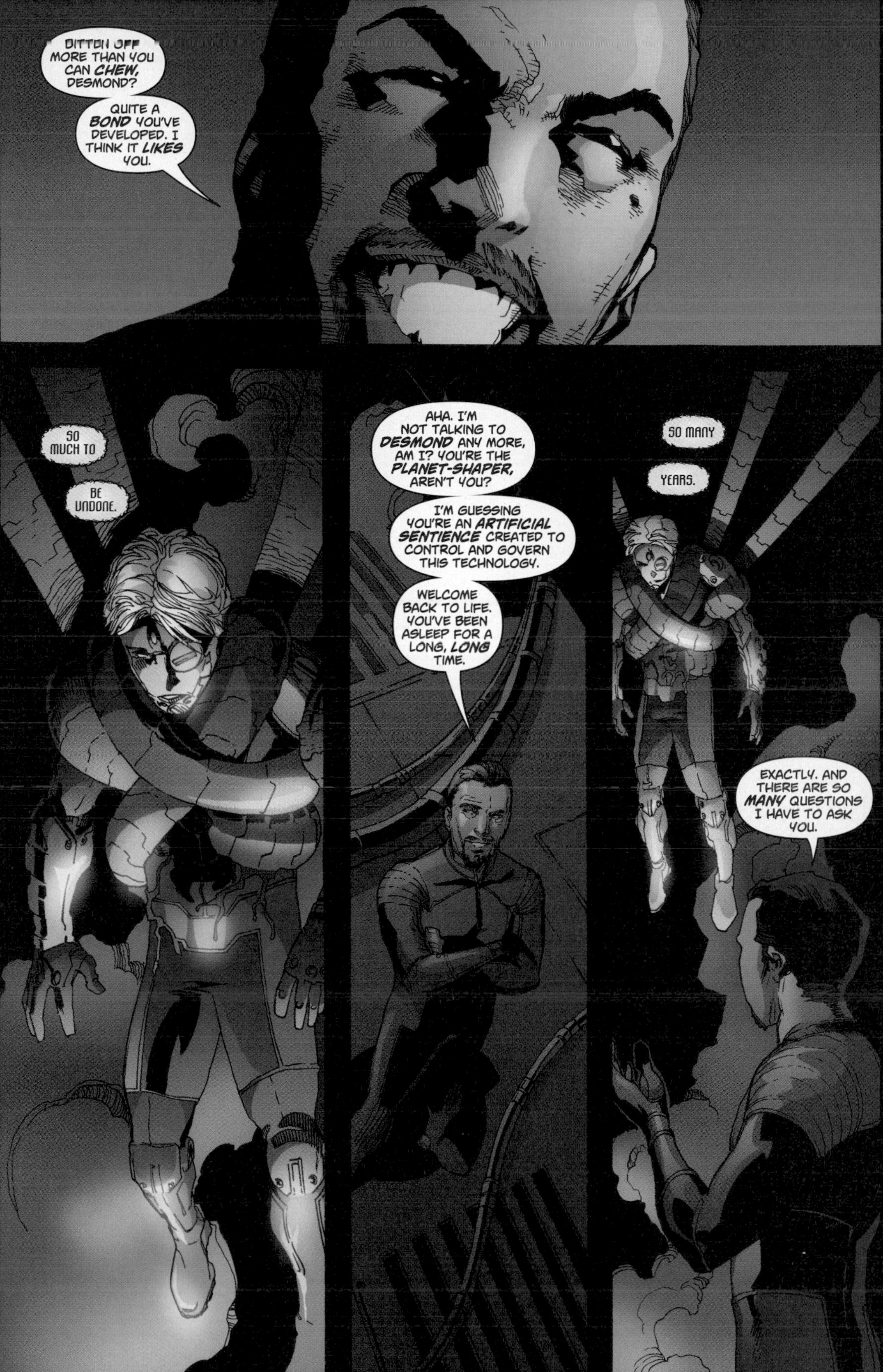
BITTEN OFF MORE THAN YOU CAN **CHEW,** DESMOND?
QUITE A **BOND** YOU'VE DEVELOPED. I THINK IT **LIKES** YOU.
SO MUCH TO
BE UNDONE.
AHA. I'M NOT TALKING TO **DESMOND** ANY MORE, AM I? YOU'RE THE **PLANET-SHAPER,** AREN'T YOU?
I'M GUESSING YOU'RE AN **ARTIFICIAL SENTIENCE** CREATED TO CONTROL AND GOVERN THIS TECHNOLOGY.
WELCOME BACK TO LIFE. YOU'VE BEEN ASLEEP FOR A LONG, **LONG** TIME.
SO MANY
YEARS.
EXACTLY. AND THERE ARE SO **MANY** QUESTIONS I HAVE TO ASK YOU.

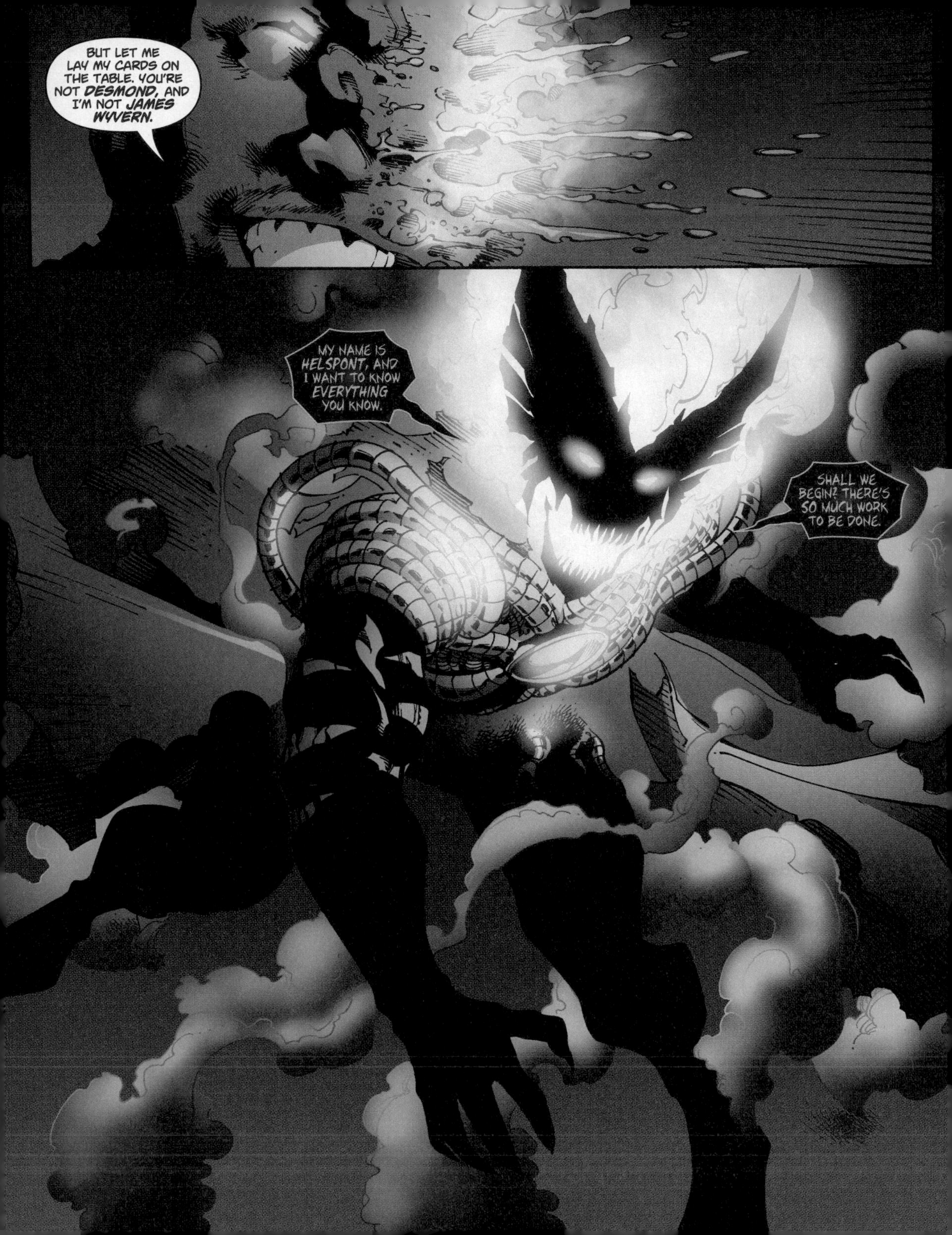
BUT LET ME LAY MY CARDS ON THE TABLE. YOU'RE NOT DESMOND, AND I'M NOT JAMES WYVERN.
MY NAME IS HELSPONT, AND I WANT TO KNOW EVERYTHING YOU KNOW.
SHALL WE BEGIN? THERE'S SO MUCH WORK TO BE DONE.

Shapers Of Destiny

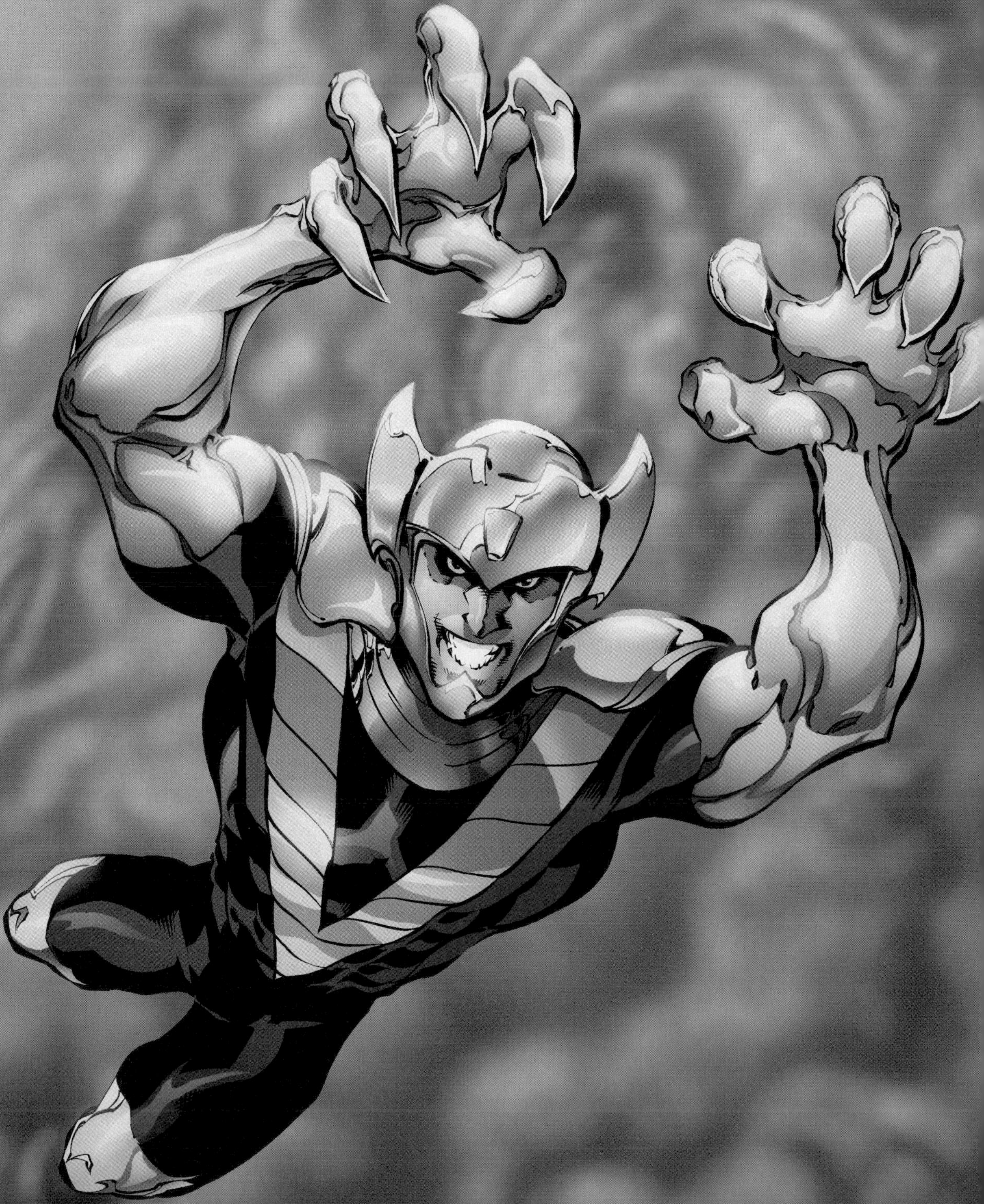

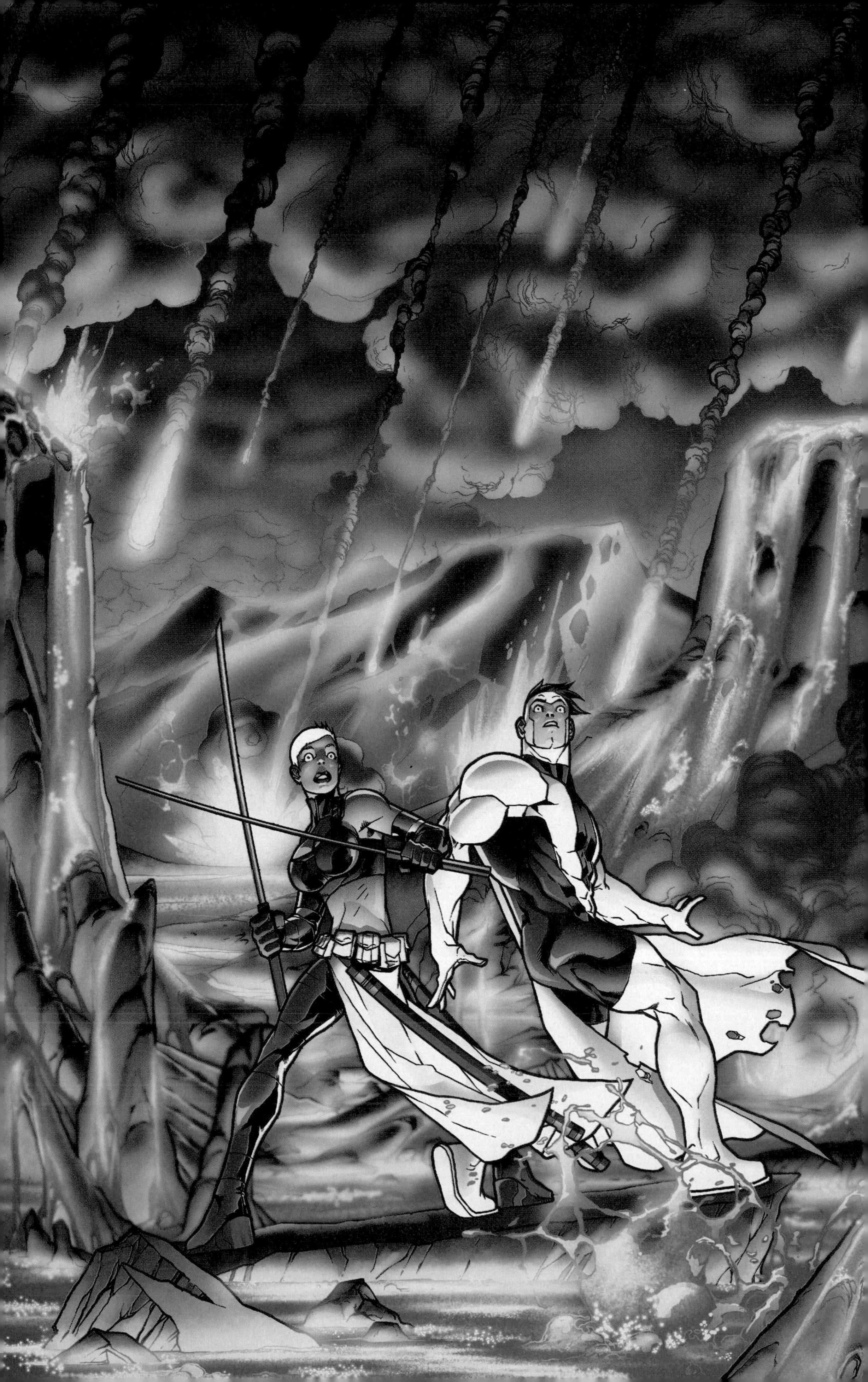

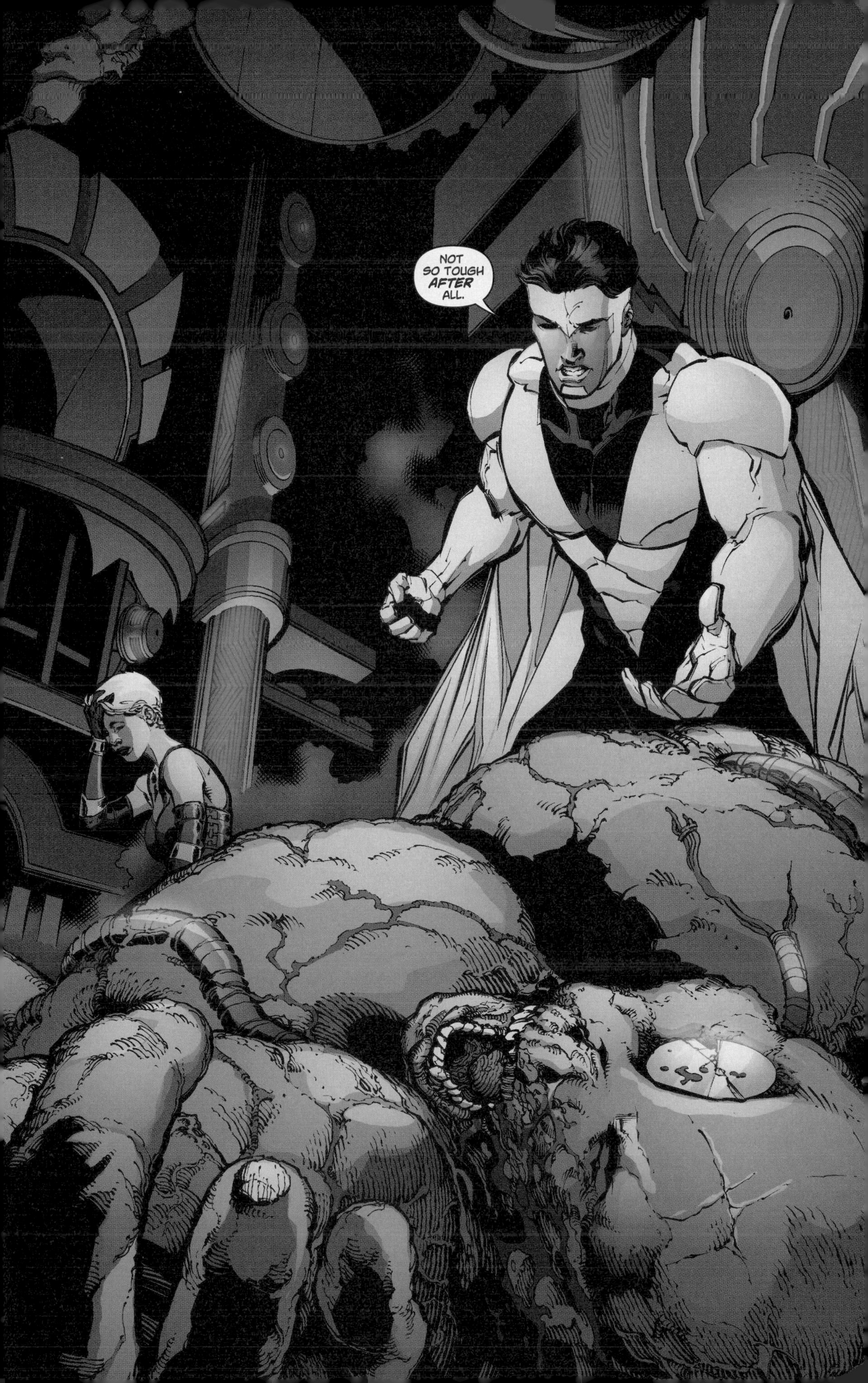
NOT SO TOUGH AFTER ALL.

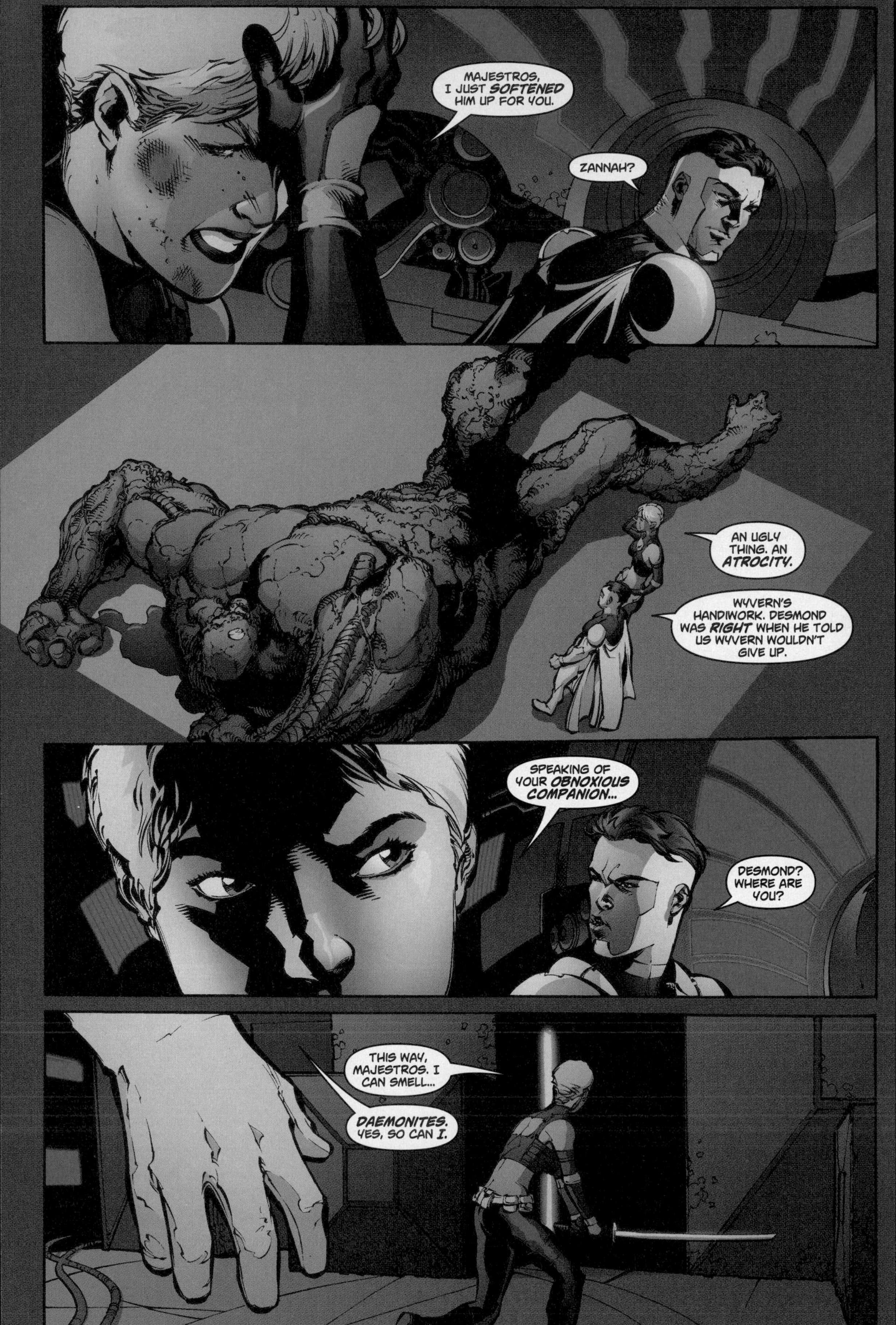
MAJESTROS, I JUST SOFTENED HIM UP FOR YOU.
ZANNAH?
AN UGLY THING. AN ATROCITY.
WYVERN'S HANDIWORK. DESMOND WAS RIGHT WHEN HE TOLD US WYVERN WOULDN'T GIVE UP.
SPEAKING OF YOUR OBNOXIOUS COMPANION...
DESMOND? WHERE ARE YOU?
THIS WAY, MAJESTROS. I CAN SMELL...
DAEMONITES. YES, SO CAN I.

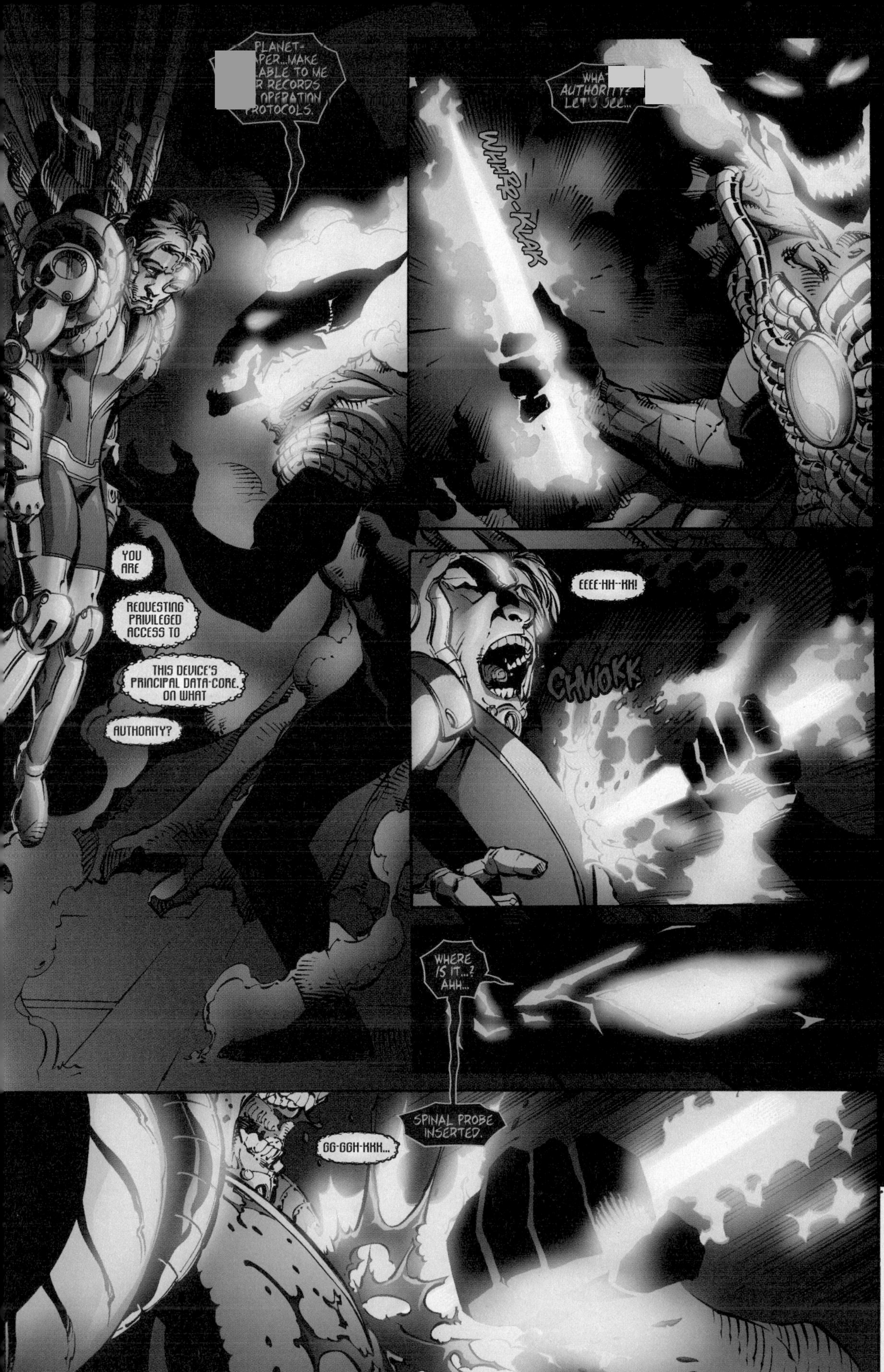
PLANET- ...APER...MAKE ...LABLE TO ME ...R RECORDS ...OPERATION PROTOCOLS.
YOU ARE
REQUESTING PRIVILEGED ACCESS TO
THIS DEVICE'S PRINCIPAL DATA-CORE. ON WHAT
AUTHORITY?
WHAT AUTHORITY? LET'S SEE...
WHIRR-KLAK
EEEE-HH--KK!
CHWOKK
WHERE IS IT...? AHH...
SPINAL PROBE INSERTED.
GG-GGH-HKK...

ESTABLISHING PROBE LINK. OVERRIDES ENABLED.

HOW'S *THAT?*

GGK--

AUTHORITY RECOGNIZED.

WELCOME, USER NAME "HELSPONT."

YOU HAVE REQUESTED

ACCESS TO THE PRINCIPAL DATA-CORE.

SPIIK

I WANT TO KNOW YOUR *HISTORY,* PLANET SHAPER. YOUR *PURPOSE.* YOUR *MEANS OF OPERATION.*

WAIT. ACCESSING DATA.

DO YOU REQUIRE TEXT DISPLAY

AUDIO COMMENTARY OR

FULL IMMERSION?

OH, FULL IMMERSION, I THINK.

WAIT. IMMERSION PACKAGE UPLOADING...

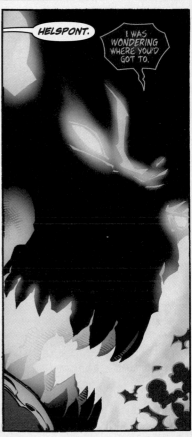

HELSPONT.

I WAS WONDERING WHERE YOU'D GOT TO.

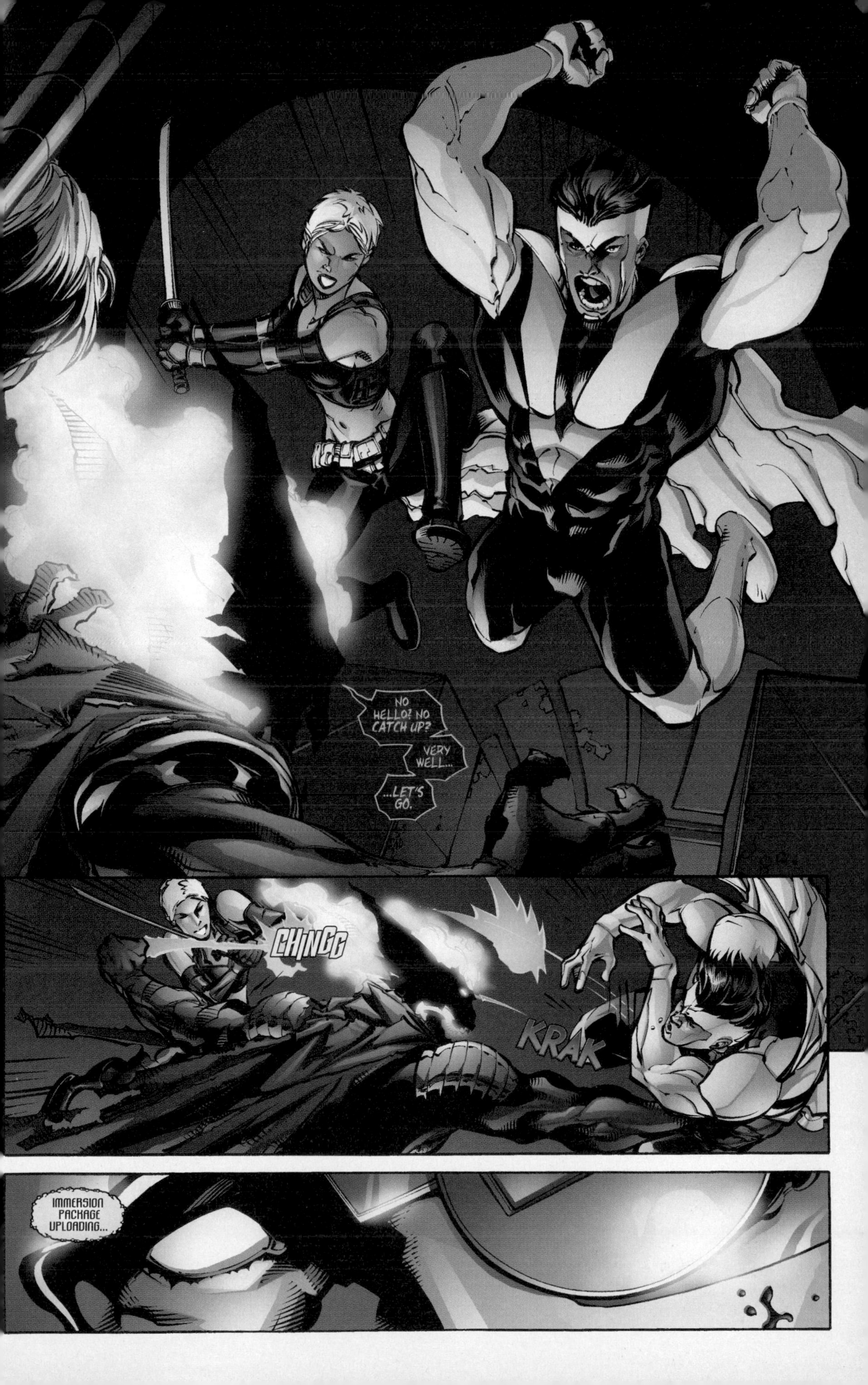
NO HELLO? NO CATCH UP?
VERY WELL...
...LET'S GO.
CHINGG
KRAK
IMMERSION PACKAGE UPLOADING...

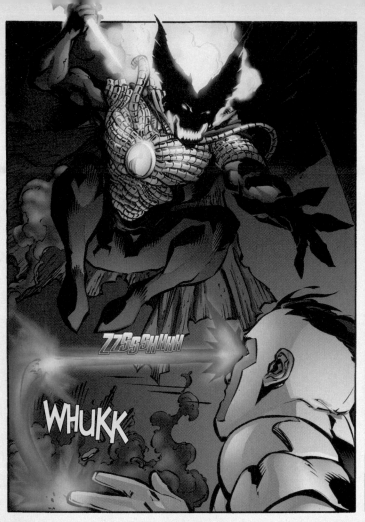

ZZSsSSHHHH

WHUKK

NHF.

HI, REMEMBER ME?

IMMERSION PACKAGE UPLOADING...

BRAKKATCH

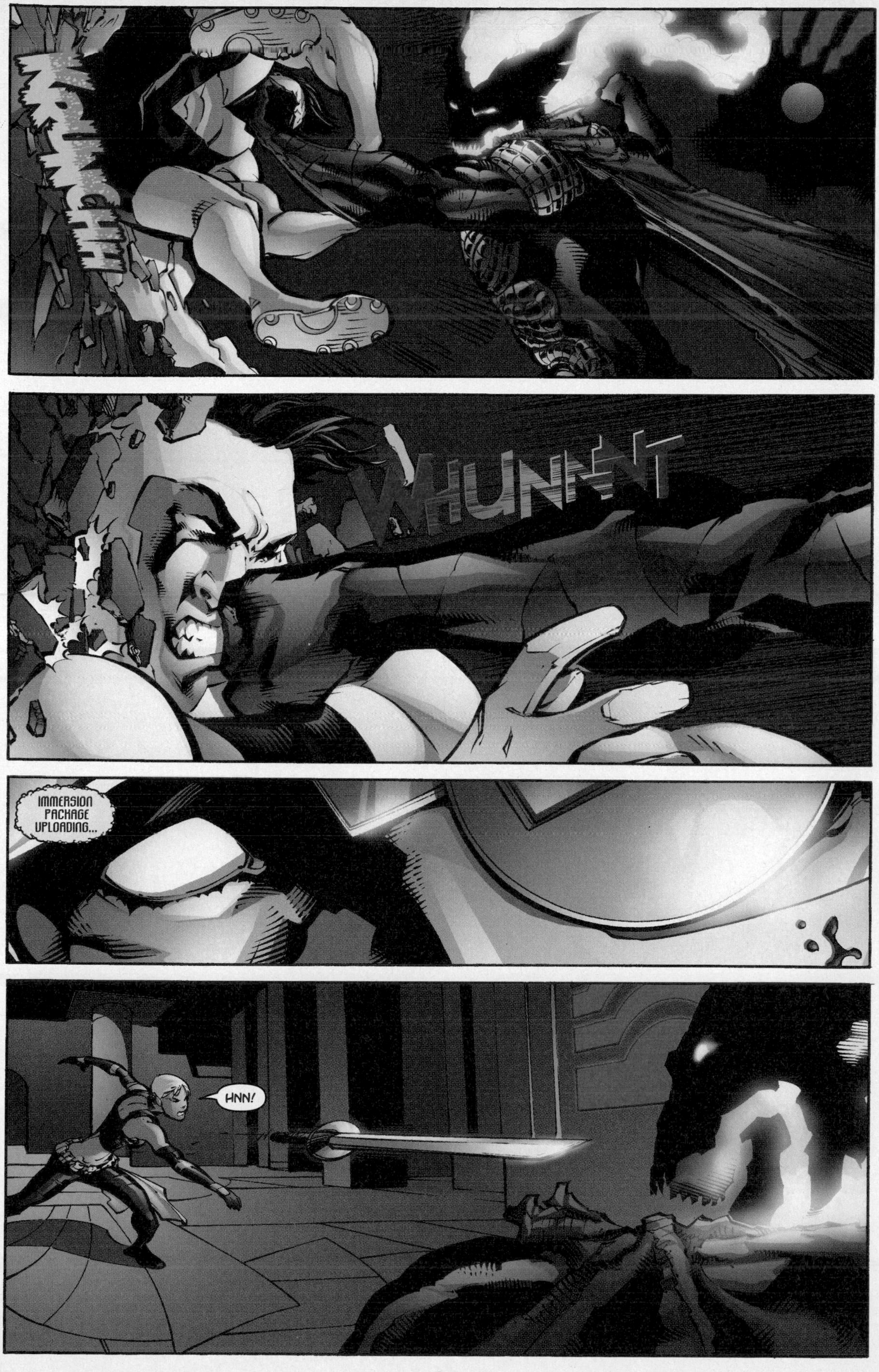
WHUNNNT
IMMERSION PACKAGE UPLOADING...
HNN!

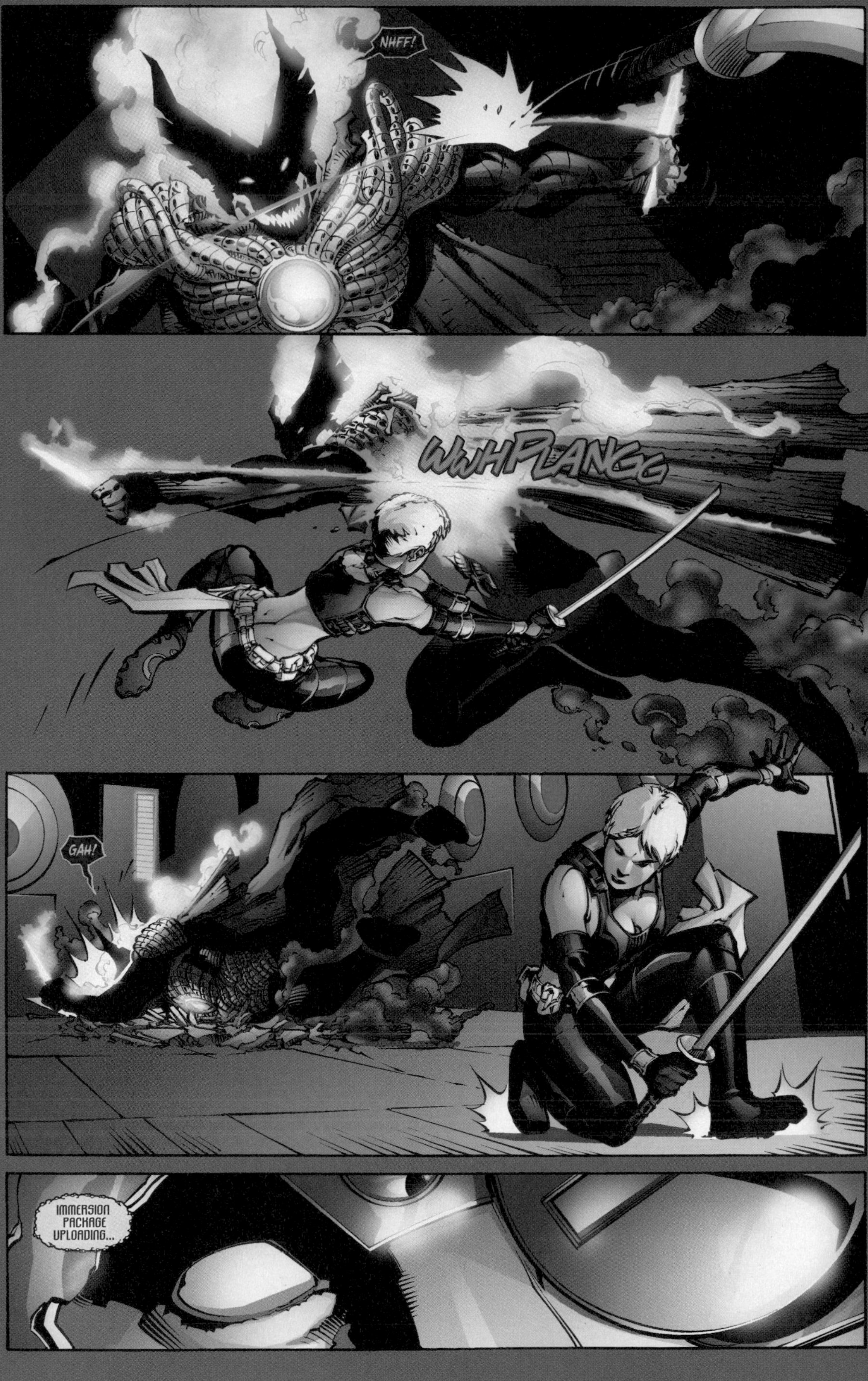
NHFF!
WWHPLANGG
GAH!
IMMERSION PACKAGE UPLOADING...

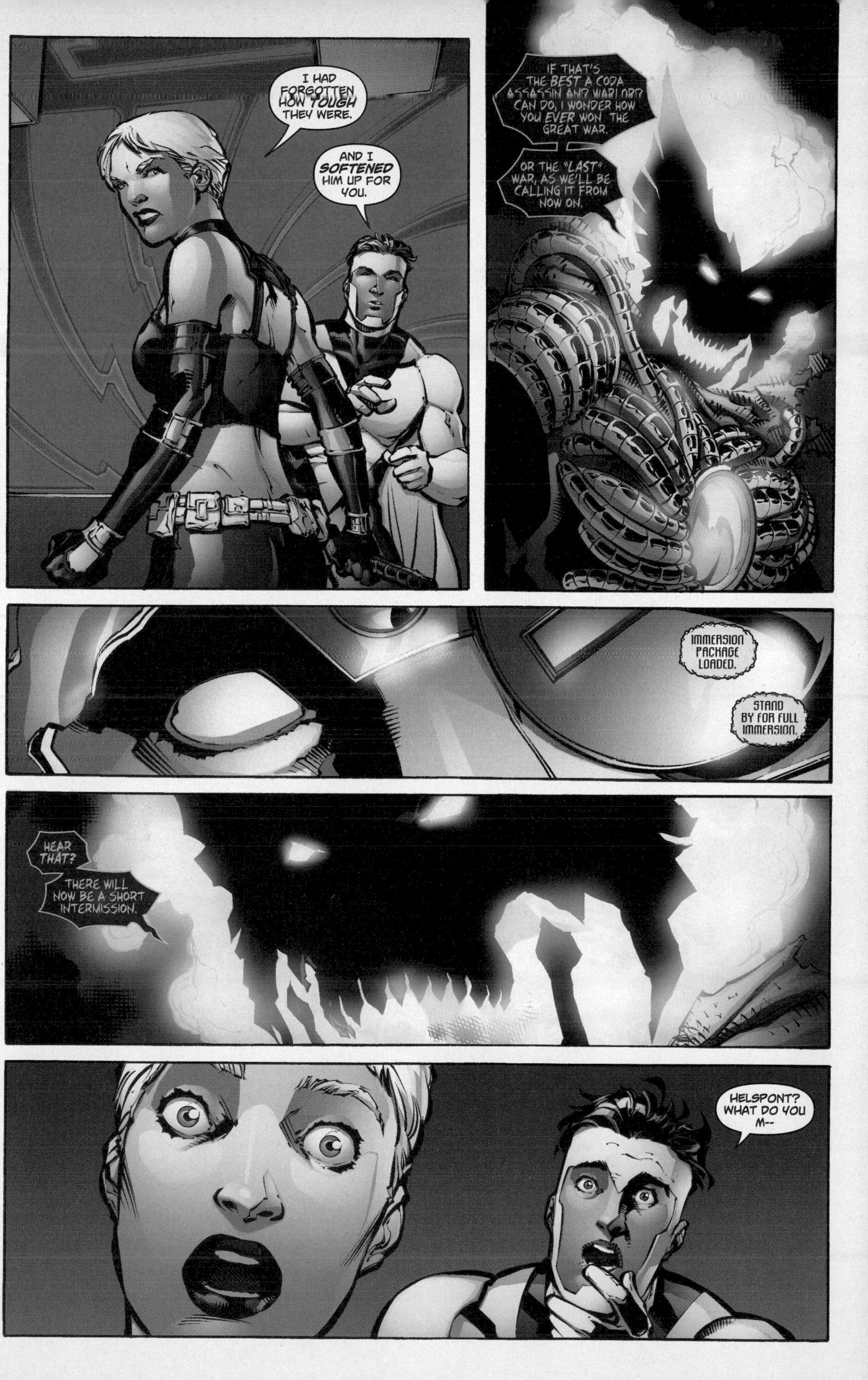
I HAD FORGOTTEN HOW TOUGH THEY WERE.
AND I SOFTENED HIM UP FOR YOU.
IF THAT'S THE BEST A CODA ASSASSIN AND WARLORD CAN DO, I WONDER HOW YOU EVER WON THE GREAT WAR.
OR THE "LAST" WAR, AS WE'LL BE CALLING IT FROM NOW ON.
IMMERSION PACKAGE LOADED.
STAND BY FOR FULL IMMERSION.
HEAR THAT?
THERE WILL NOW BE A SHORT INTERMISSION.
HELSPONT? WHAT DO YOU M--

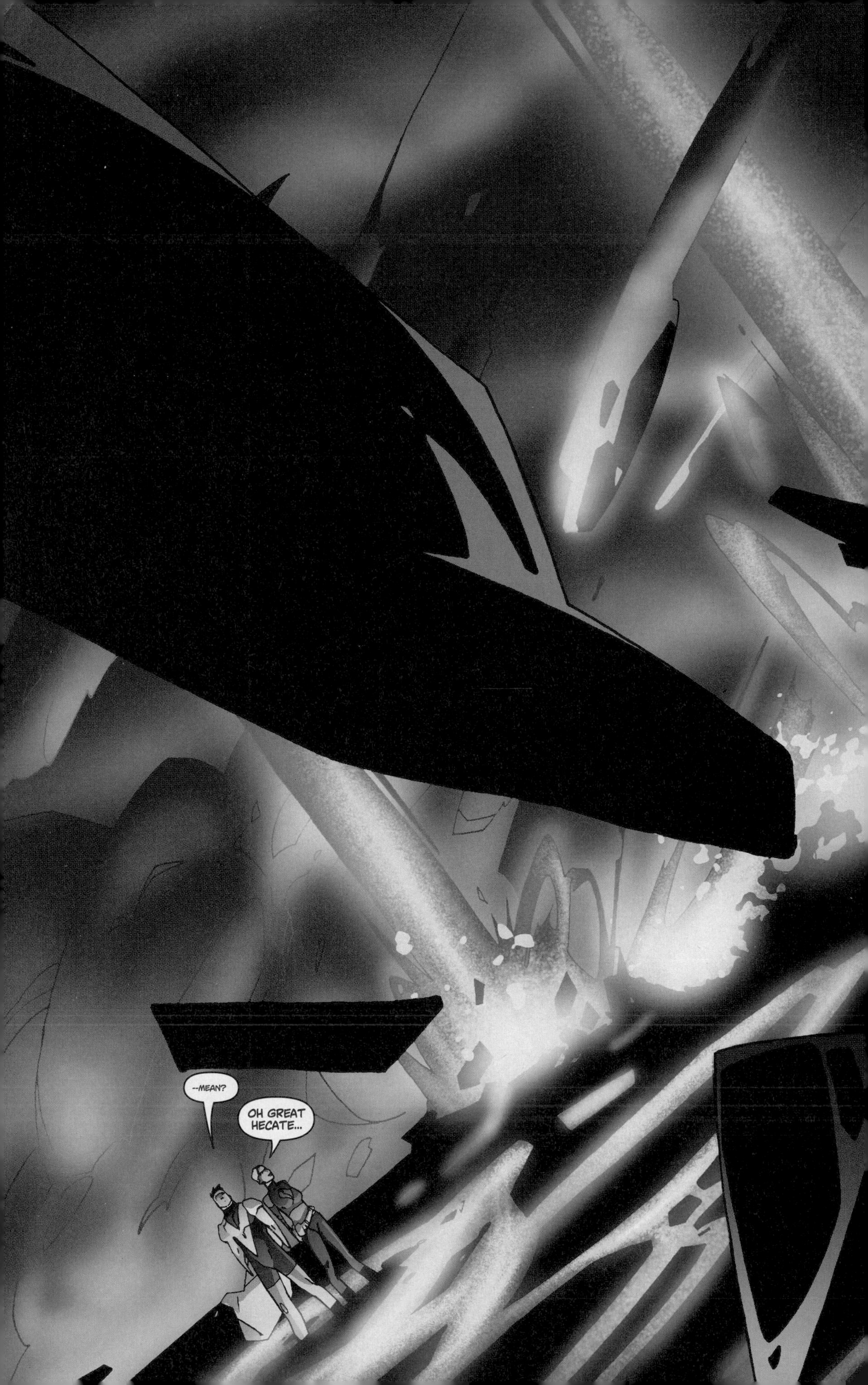
--MEAN?
OH GREAT HECATE...

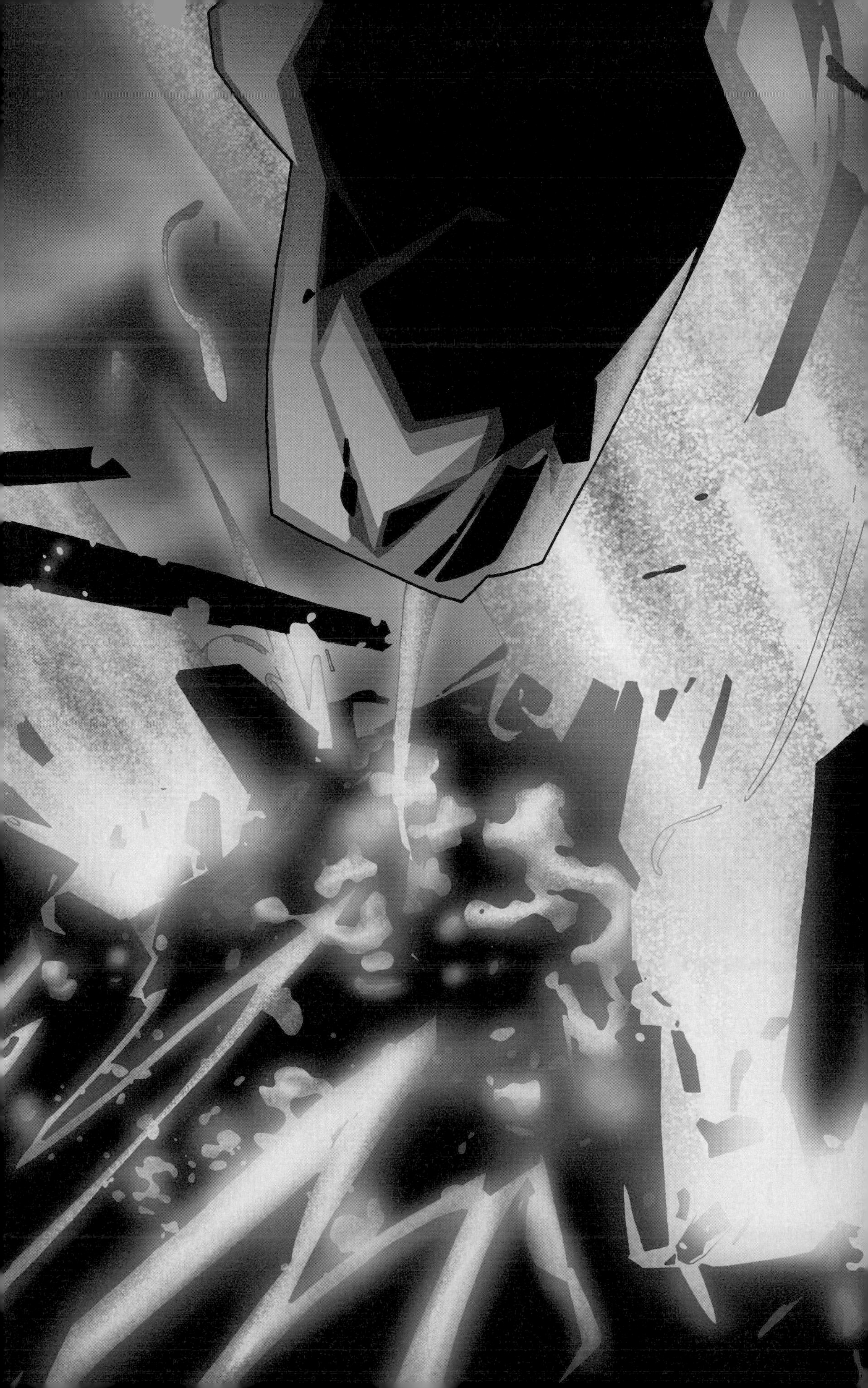

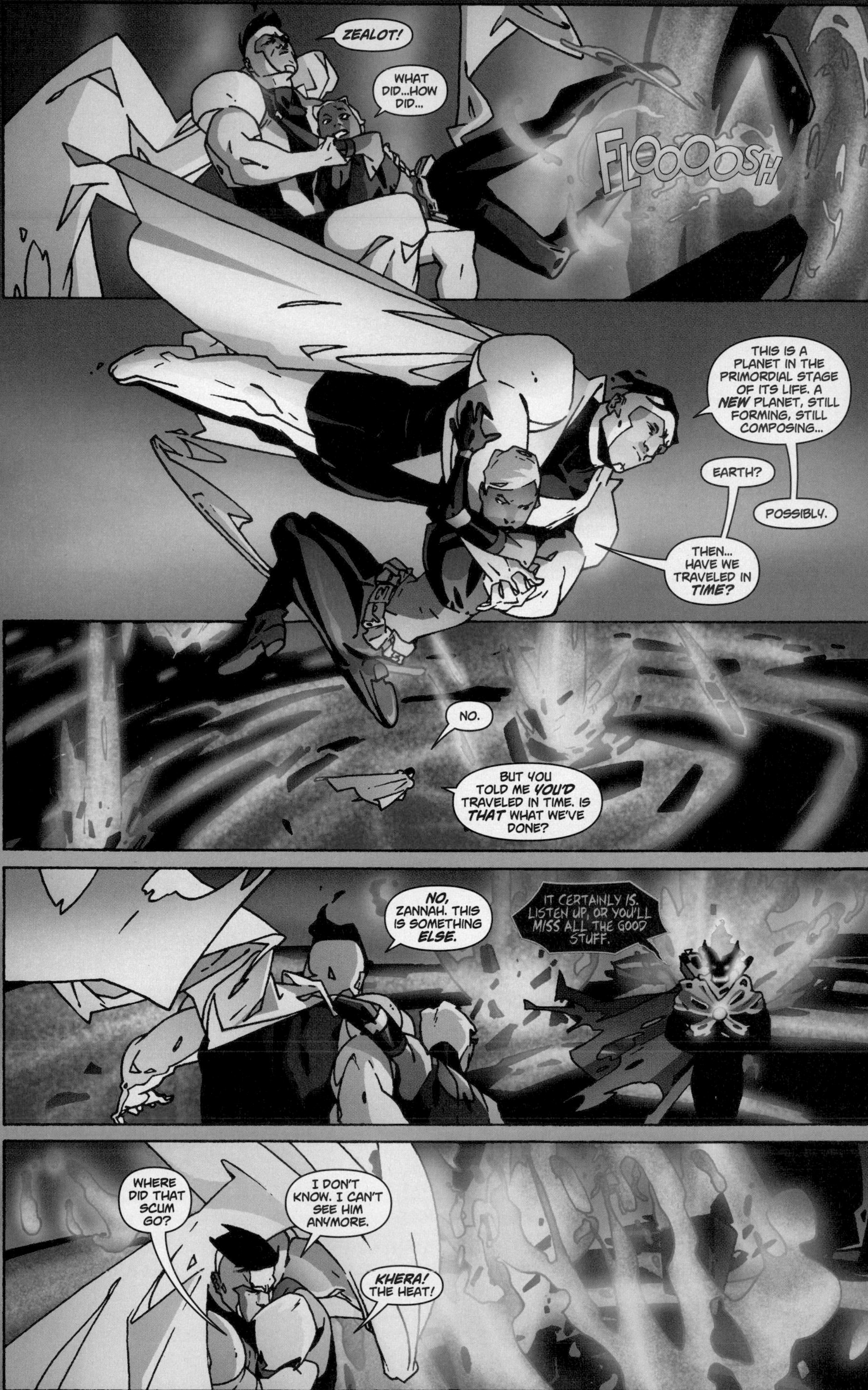
ZEALOT!
WHAT DID...HOW DID...
FLOOOOSH
THIS IS A PLANET IN THE PRIMORDIAL STAGE OF ITS LIFE. A NEW PLANET, STILL FORMING, STILL COMPOSING...
EARTH?
POSSIBLY.
THEN... HAVE WE TRAVELED IN TIME?
NO.
BUT YOU TOLD ME YOU'D TRAVELED IN TIME. IS THAT WHAT WE'VE DONE?
NO, ZANNAH. THIS IS SOMETHING ELSE.
IT CERTAINLY IS. LISTEN UP, OR YOU'LL MISS ALL THE GOOD STUFF.
WHERE DID THAT SCUM GO?
I DON'T KNOW. I CAN'T SEE HIM ANYMORE.
KHERA! THE HEAT!

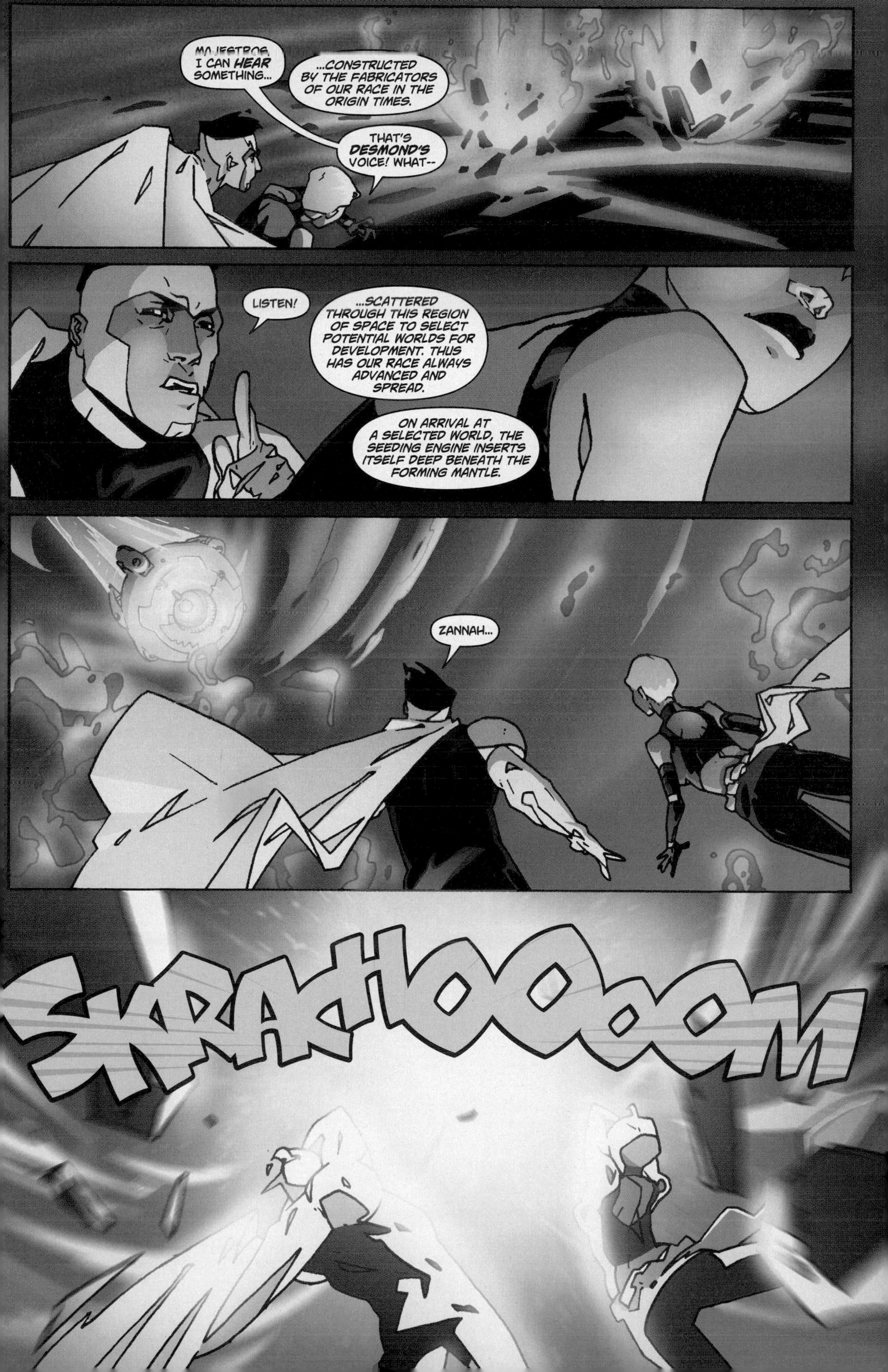
MAJESTROS, I CAN HEAR SOMETHING...
...CONSTRUCTED BY THE FABRICATORS OF OUR RACE IN THE ORIGIN TIMES.
THAT'S DESMOND'S VOICE! WHAT--
LISTEN!
...SCATTERED THROUGH THIS REGION OF SPACE TO SELECT POTENTIAL WORLDS FOR DEVELOPMENT. THUS HAS OUR RACE ALWAYS ADVANCED AND SPREAD.
ON ARRIVAL AT A SELECTED WORLD, THE SEEDING ENGINE INSERTS ITSELF DEEP BENEATH THE FORMING MANTLE.
ZANNAH...
SKRATHOOOOOM

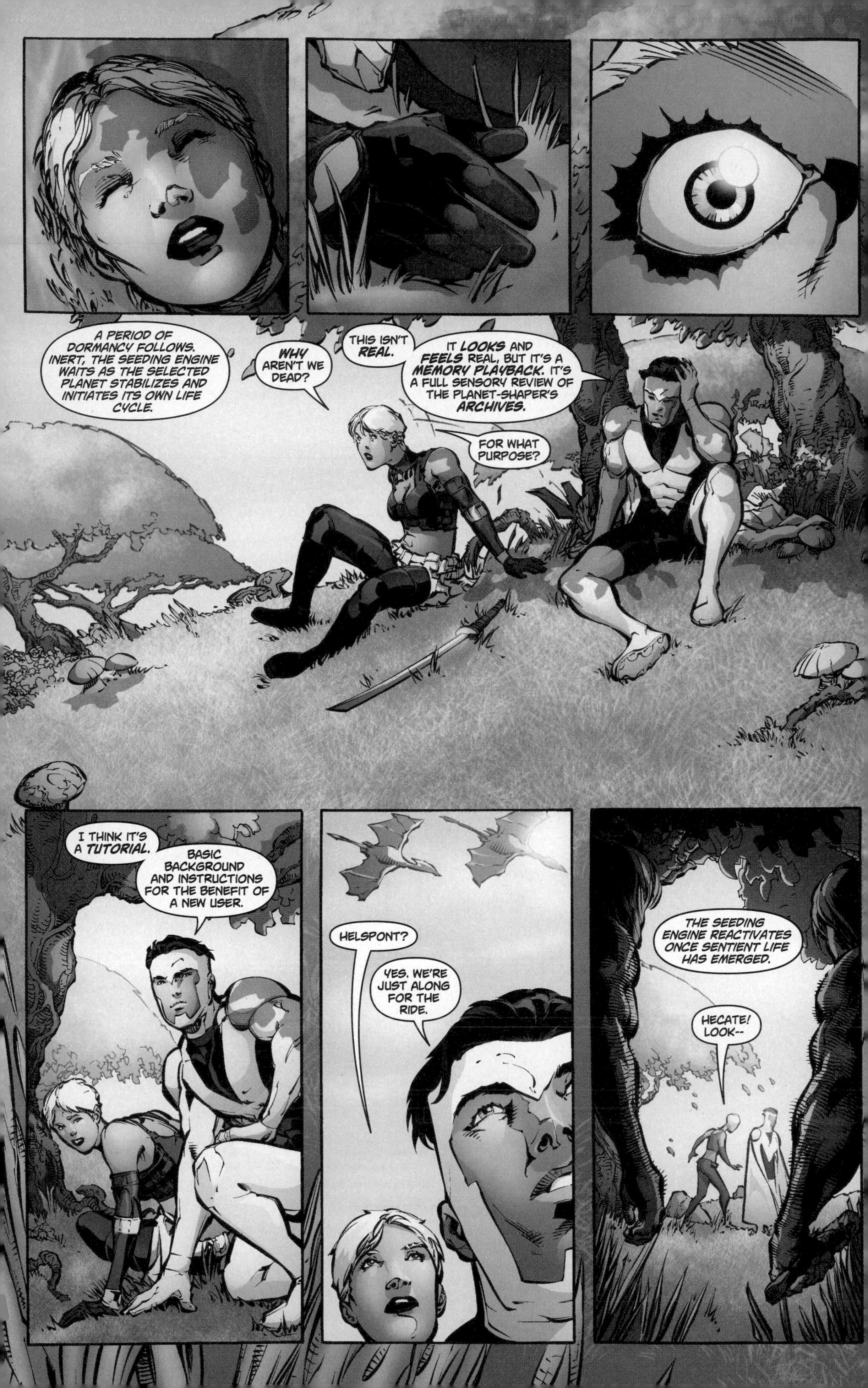
A PERIOD OF DORMANCY FOLLOWS. INERT, THE SEEDING ENGINE WAITS AS THE SELECTED PLANET STABILIZES AND INITIATES ITS OWN LIFE CYCLE.
WHY AREN'T WE DEAD?
THIS ISN'T REAL.
IT LOOKS AND FEELS REAL, BUT IT'S A MEMORY PLAYBACK. IT'S A FULL SENSORY REVIEW OF THE PLANET-SHAPER'S ARCHIVES.
FOR WHAT PURPOSE?
I THINK IT'S A TUTORIAL.
BASIC BACKGROUND AND INSTRUCTIONS FOR THE BENEFIT OF A NEW USER.
HELSPONT?
YES. WE'RE JUST ALONG FOR THE RIDE.
THE SEEDING ENGINE REACTIVATES ONCE SENTIENT LIFE HAS EMERGED.
HECATE! LOOK--

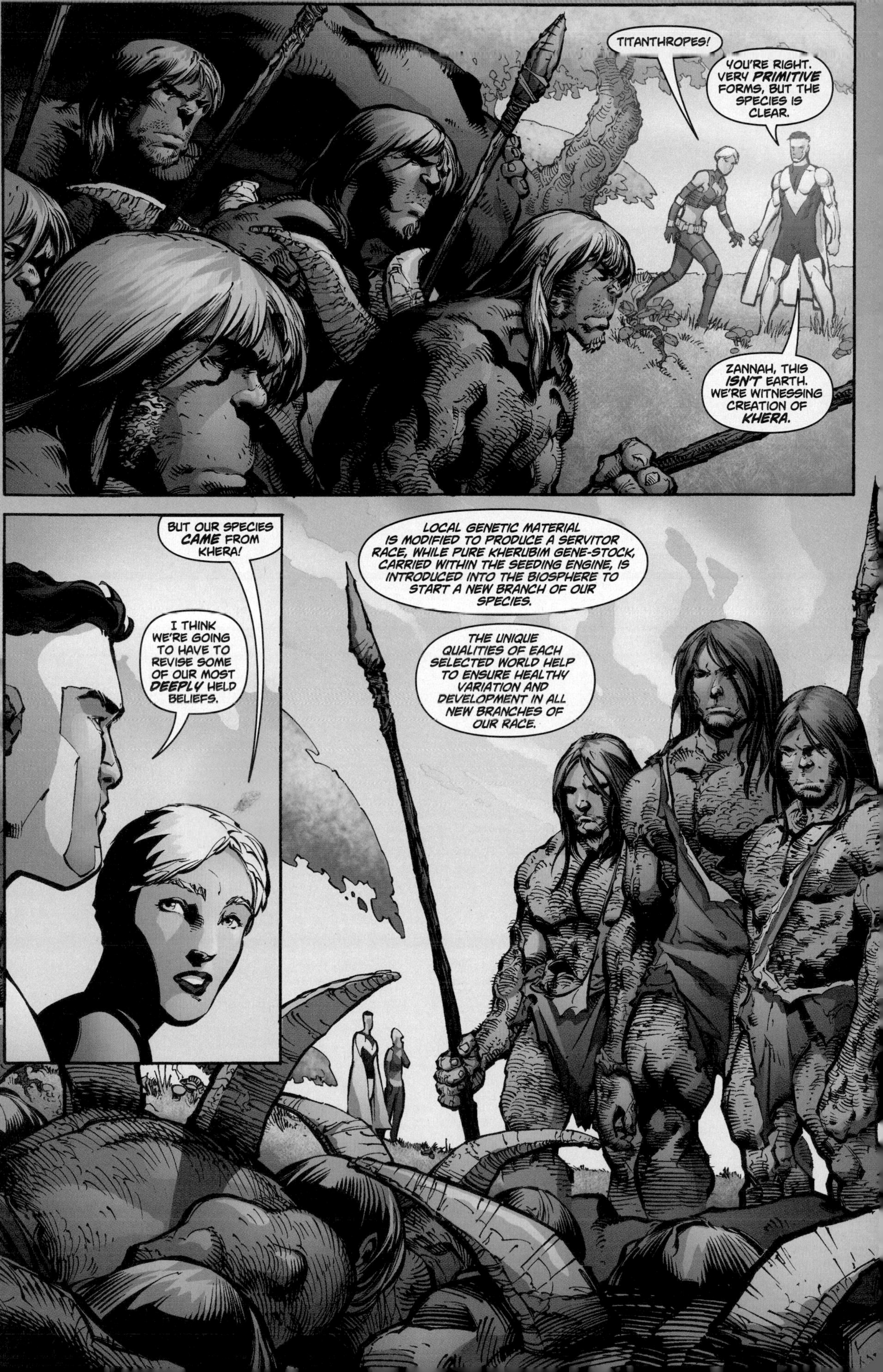
TITANTHROPES!
YOU'RE RIGHT. VERY PRIMITIVE FORMS, BUT THE SPECIES IS CLEAR.
ZANNAH, THIS ISN'T EARTH. WE'RE WITNESSING CREATION OF KHERA.
BUT OUR SPECIES CAME FROM KHERA!
I THINK WE'RE GOING TO HAVE TO REVISE SOME OF OUR MOST DEEPLY HELD BELIEFS.
LOCAL GENETIC MATERIAL IS MODIFIED TO PRODUCE A SERVITOR RACE, WHILE PURE KHERUBIM GENE-STOCK, CARRIED WITHIN THE SEEDING ENGINE, IS INTRODUCED INTO THE BIOSPHERE TO START A NEW BRANCH OF OUR SPECIES.
THE UNIQUE QUALITIES OF EACH SELECTED WORLD HELP TO ENSURE HEALTHY VARIATION AND DEVELOPMENT IN ALL NEW BRANCHES OF OUR RACE.

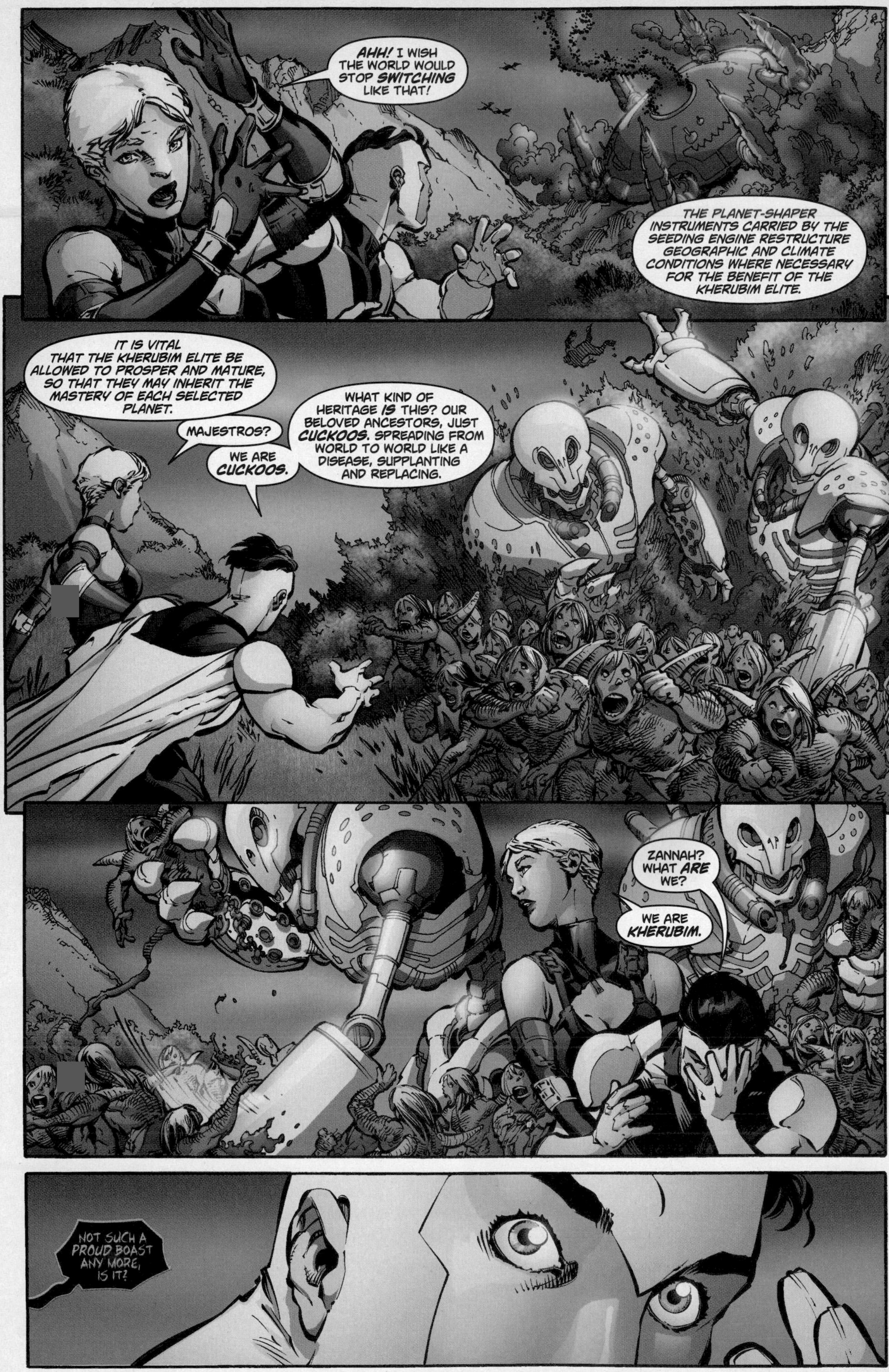
AHH! I WISH THE WORLD WOULD STOP SWITCHING LIKE THAT!
THE PLANET-SHAPER INSTRUMENTS CARRIED BY THE SEEDING ENGINE RESTRUCTURE GEOGRAPHIC AND CLIMATE CONDITIONS WHERE NECESSARY FOR THE BENEFIT OF THE KHERUBIM ELITE.
IT IS VITAL THAT THE KHERUBIM ELITE BE ALLOWED TO PROSPER AND MATURE, SO THAT THEY MAY INHERIT THE MASTERY OF EACH SELECTED PLANET.
MAJESTROS?
WE ARE CUCKOOS.
WHAT KIND OF HERITAGE IS THIS? OUR BELOVED ANCESTORS, JUST CUCKOOS. SPREADING FROM WORLD TO WORLD LIKE A DISEASE, SUPPLANTING AND REPLACING.
ZANNAH? WHAT ARE WE?
WE ARE KHERUBIM.
NOT SUCH A PROUD BOAST ANY MORE, IS IT?

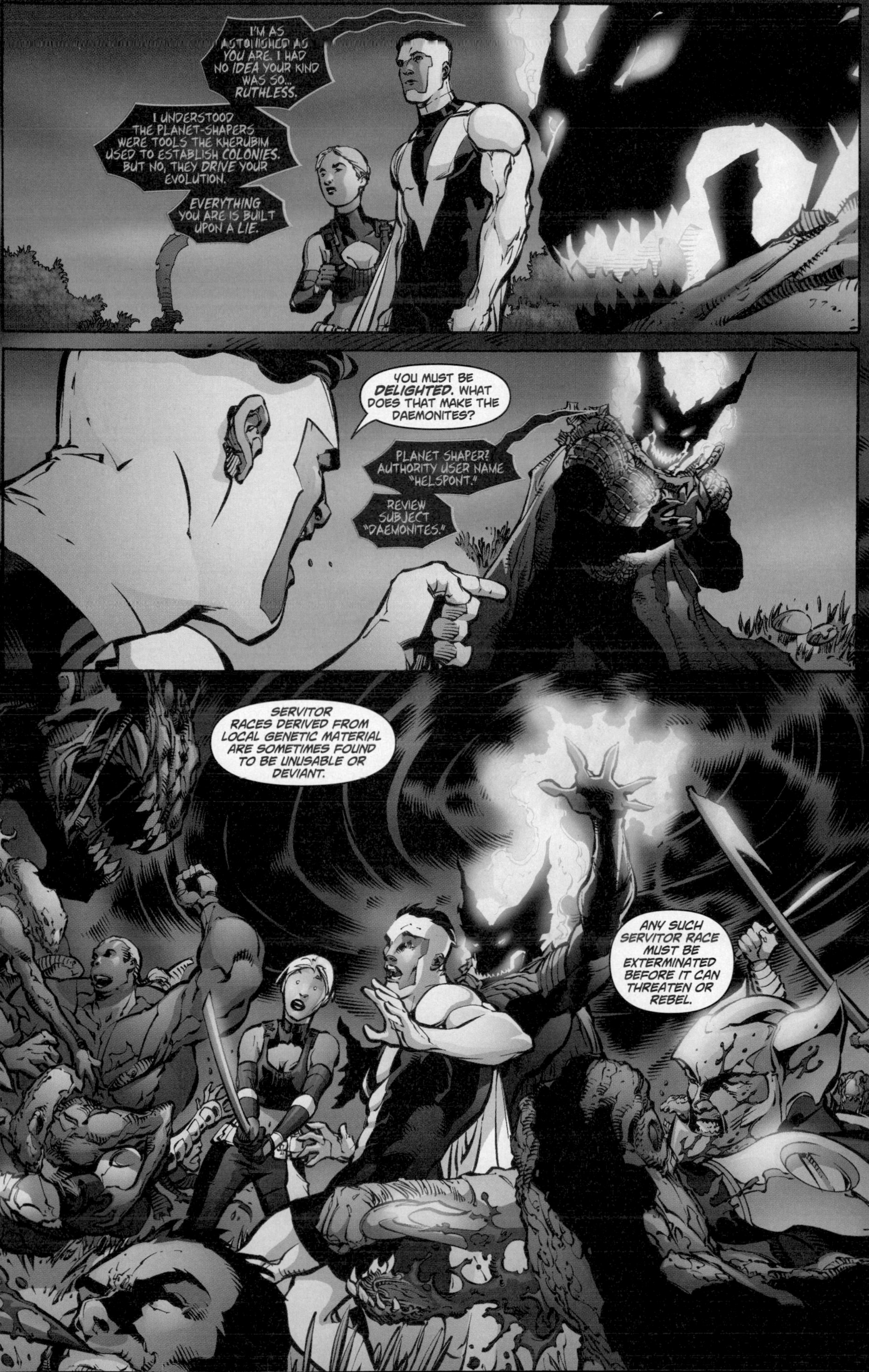
I'M AS ASTONISHED AS YOU ARE. I HAD NO IDEA YOUR KIND WAS SO... RUTHLESS.
I UNDERSTOOD THE PLANET-SHAPERS WERE TOOLS THE KHERUBIM USED TO ESTABLISH COLONIES. BUT NO, THEY DRIVE YOUR EVOLUTION.
EVERYTHING YOU ARE IS BUILT UPON A LIE.
YOU MUST BE DELIGHTED. WHAT DOES THAT MAKE THE DAEMONITES?
PLANET SHAPER? AUTHORITY USER NAME "HELSPONT."
REVIEW SUBJECT "DAEMONITES."
SERVITOR RACES DERIVED FROM LOCAL GENETIC MATERIAL ARE SOMETIMES FOUND TO BE UNUSABLE OR DEVIANT.
ANY SUCH SERVITOR RACE MUST BE EXTERMINATED BEFORE IT CAN THREATEN OR REBEL.

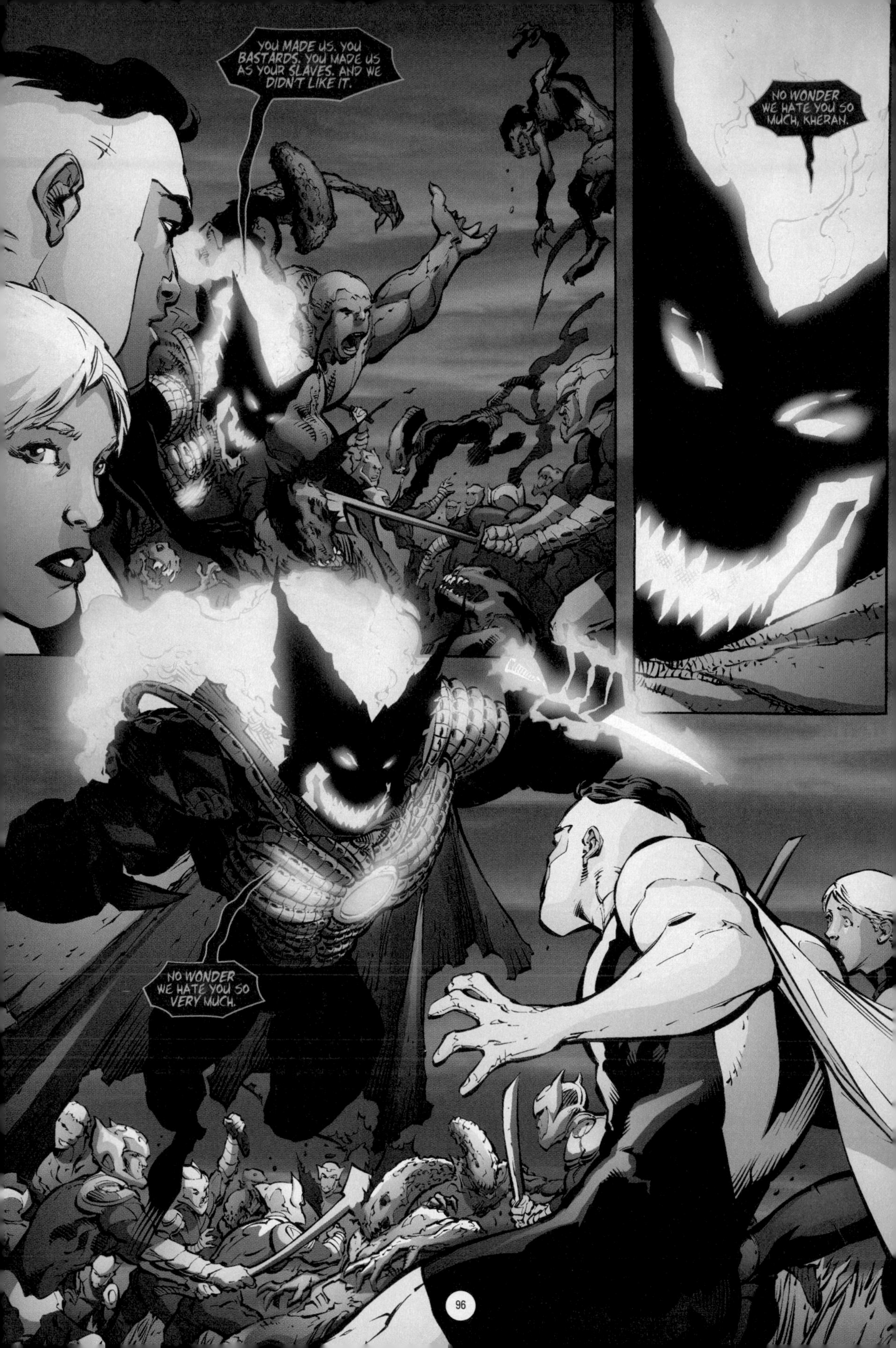
YOU MADE US. YOU BASTARDS. YOU MADE US AS YOUR SLAVES. AND WE DIDN'T LIKE IT.
NO WONDER WE HATE YOU SO MUCH, KHERAN.
NO WONDER WE HATE YOU SO VERY MUCH.

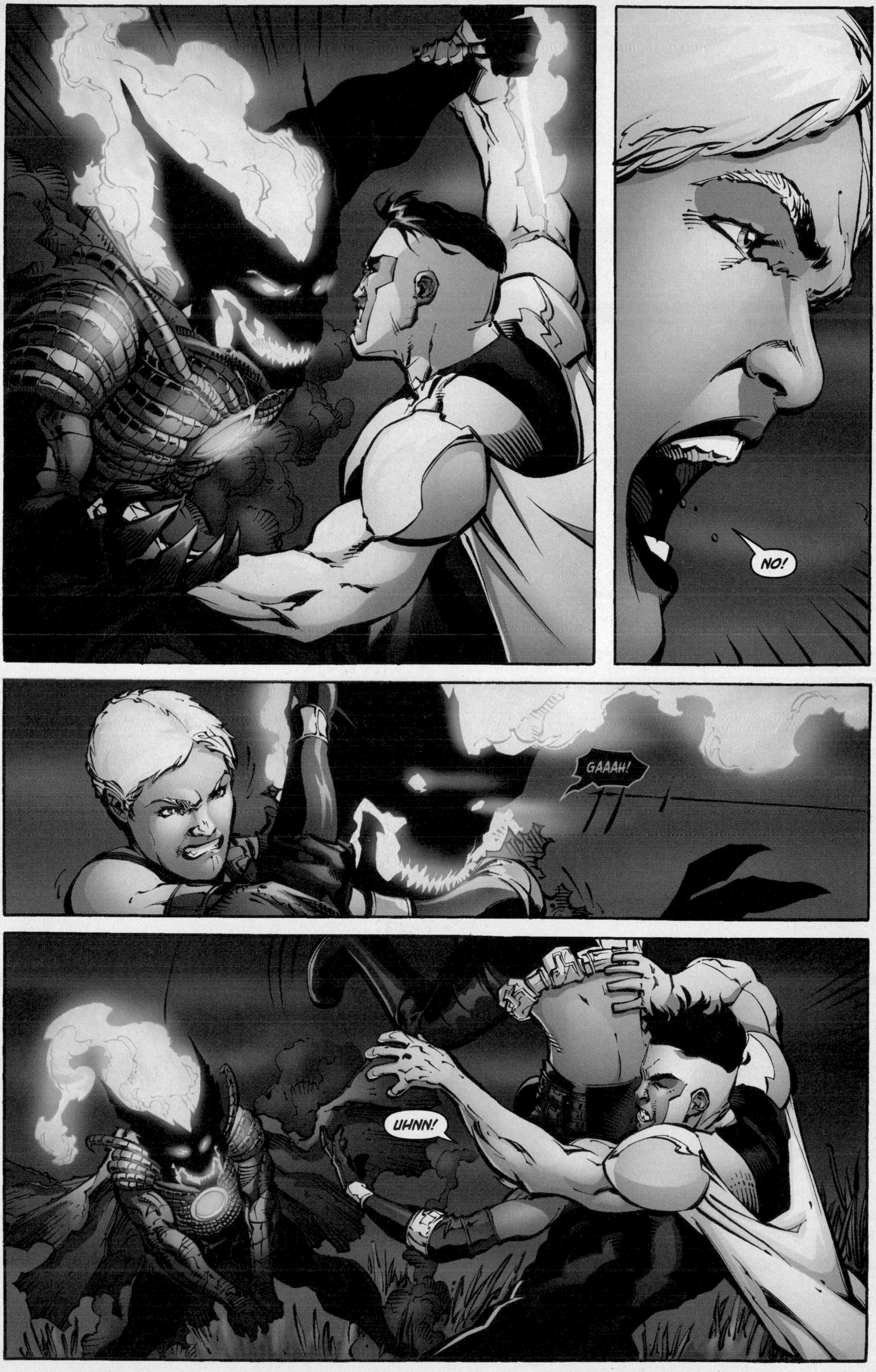
NO!
GAAAH!
UHNN!

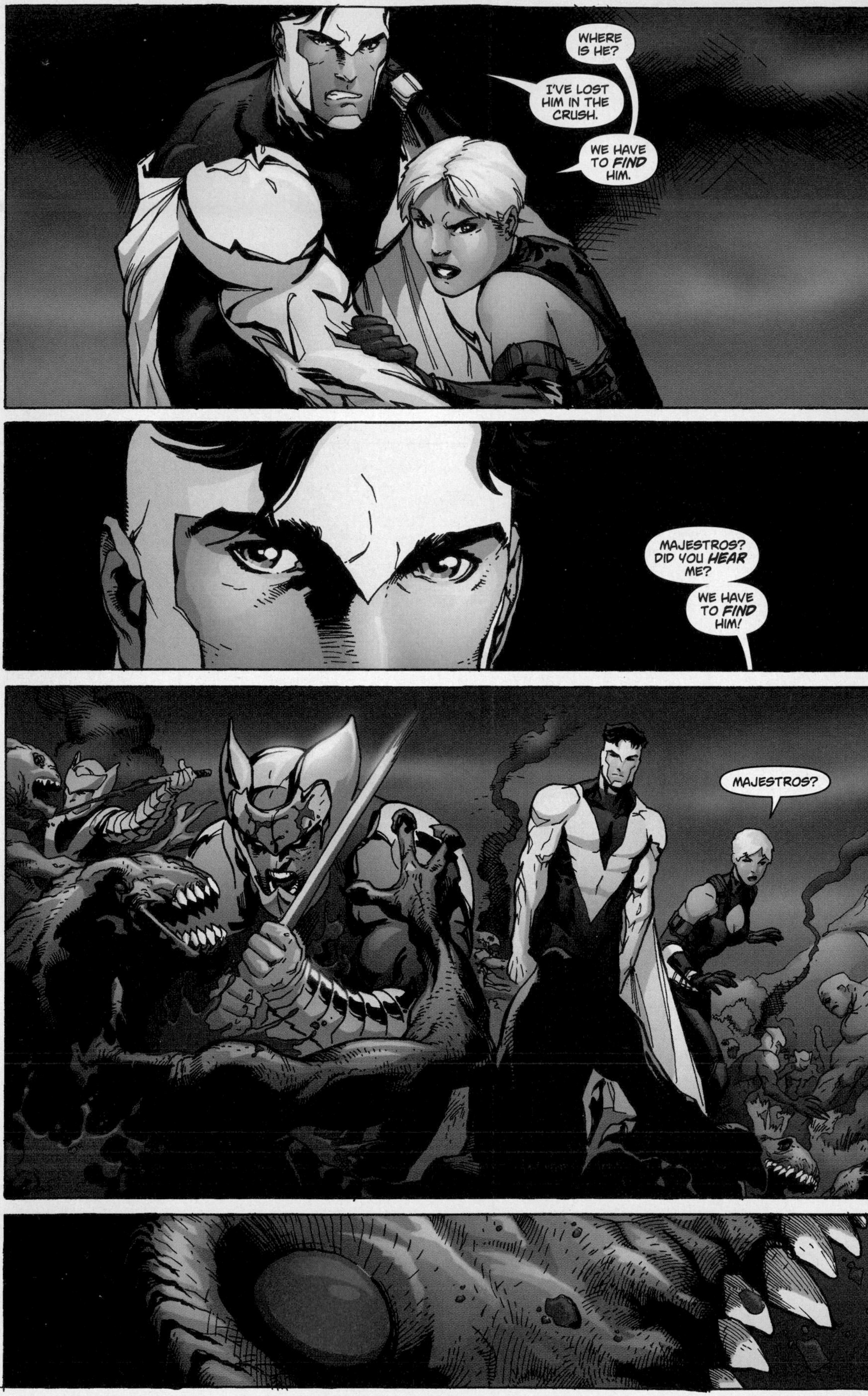
WHERE IS HE?
I'VE LOST HIM IN THE CRUSH.
WE HAVE TO FIND HIM.
MAJESTROS? DID YOU HEAR ME?
WE HAVE TO FIND HIM!
MAJESTROS?

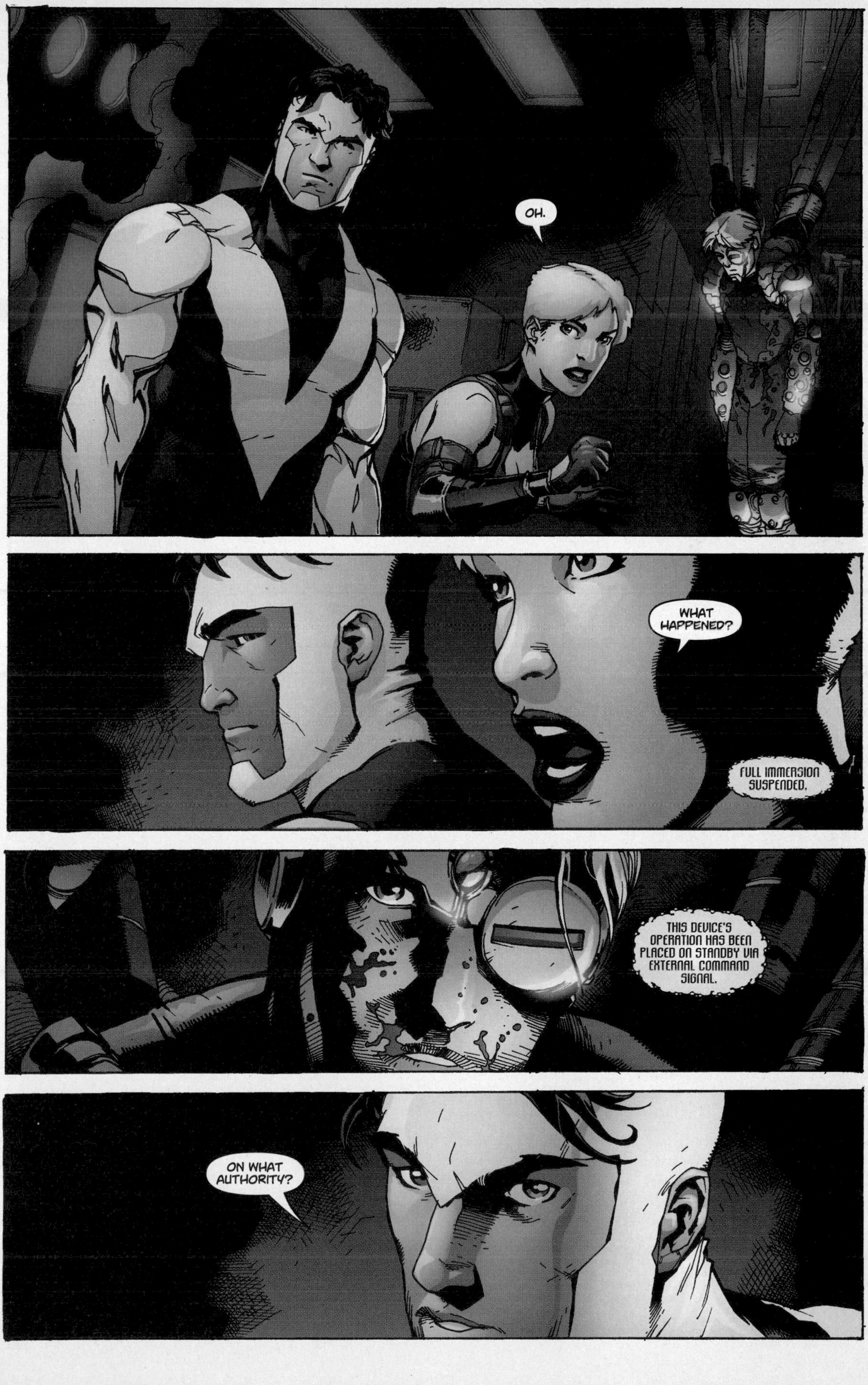
OH.
WHAT HAPPENED?
FULL IMMERSION SUSPENDED.
THIS DEVICE'S OPERATION HAS BEEN PLACED ON STANDBY VIA EXTERNAL COMMAND SIGNAL.
ON WHAT AUTHORITY?

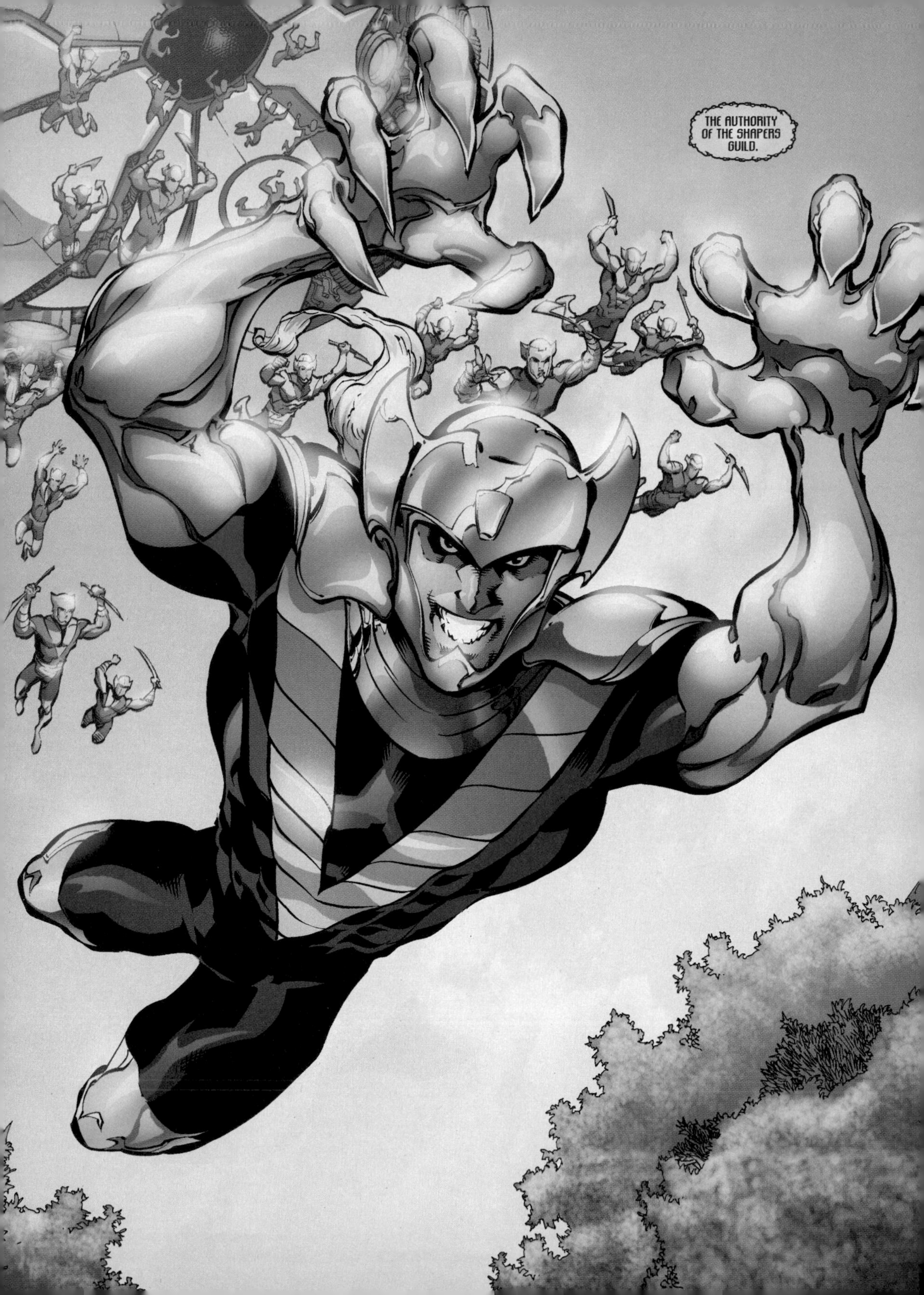
THE AUTHORITY OF THE SHAPERS GUILD.

Noble Blood

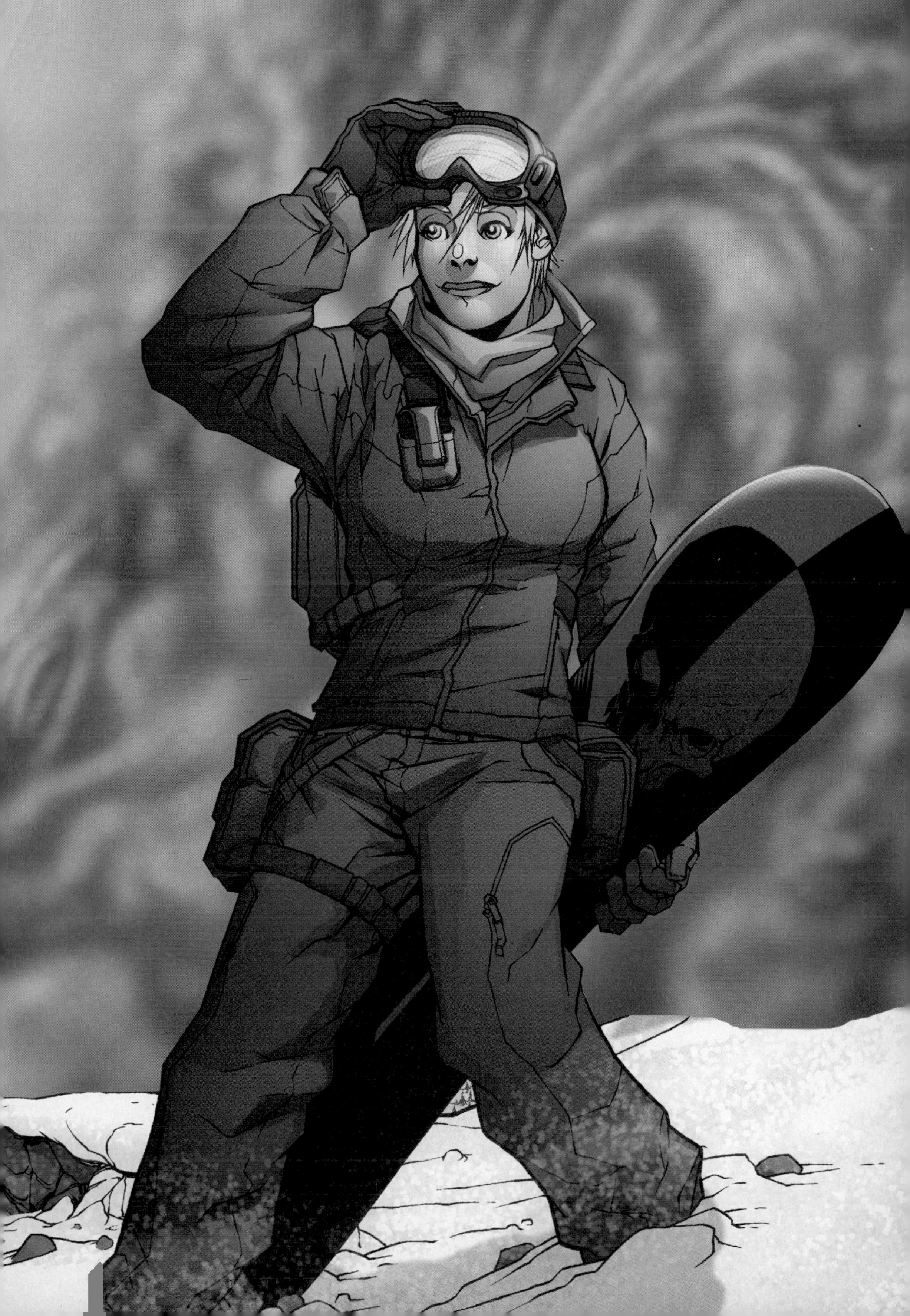

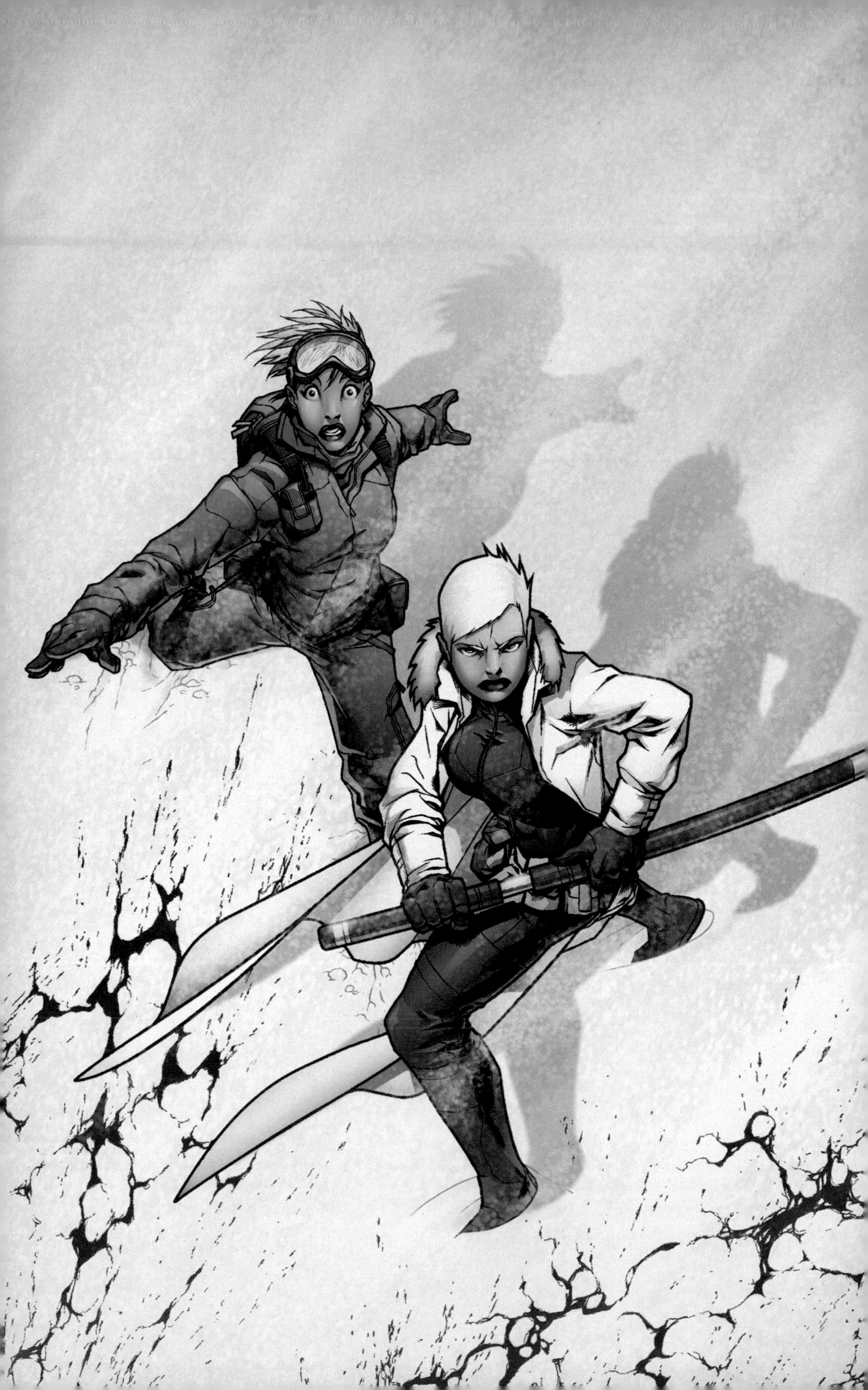

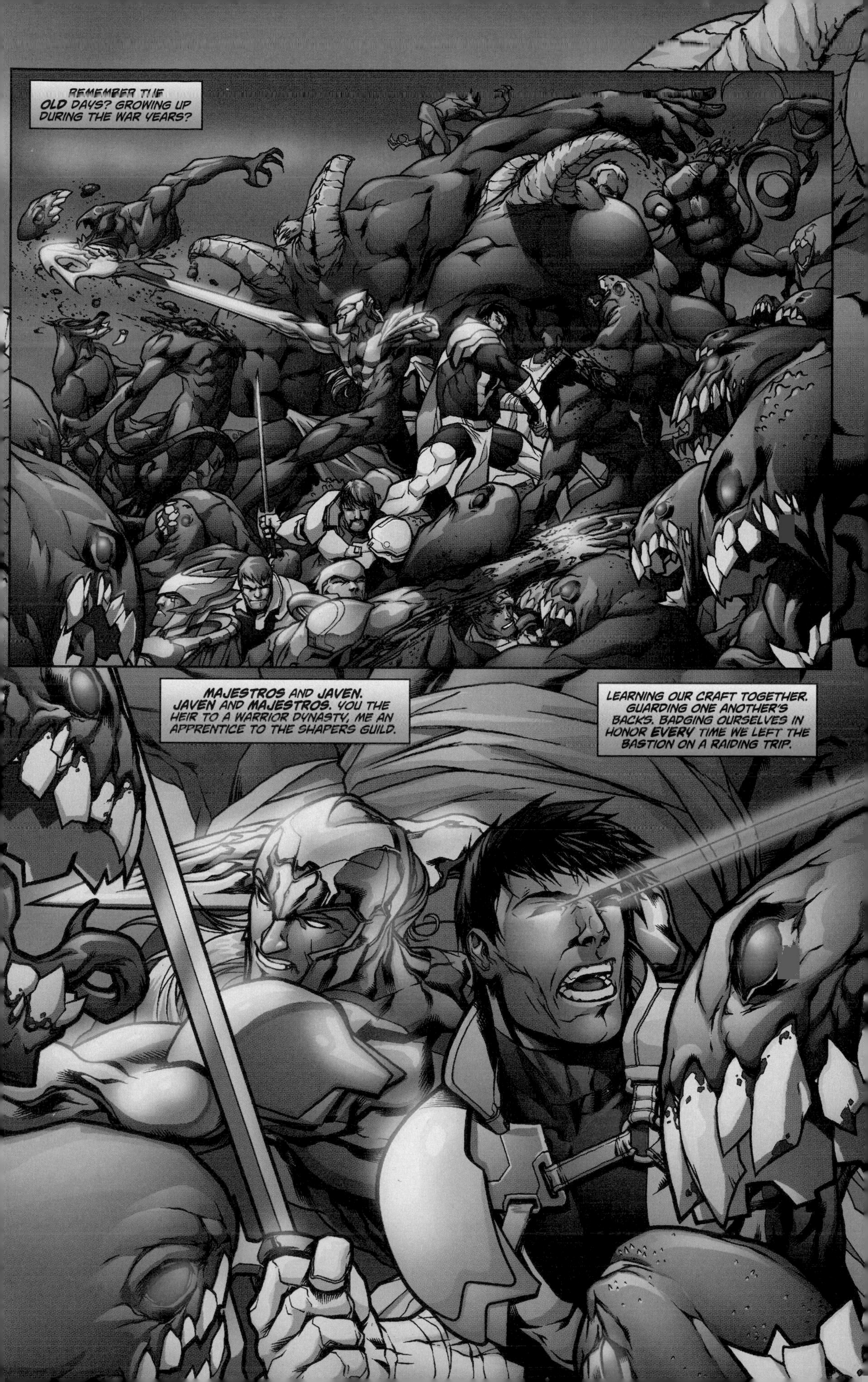

REMEMBER THE OLD DAYS? GROWING UP DURING THE WAR YEARS?
MAJESTROS AND JAVEN. JAVEN AND MAJESTROS. YOU THE HEIR TO A WARRIOR DYNASTY, ME AN APPRENTICE TO THE SHAPERS GUILD.
LEARNING OUR CRAFT TOGETHER. GUARDING ONE ANOTHER'S BACKS. BADGING OURSELVES IN HONOR EVERY TIME WE LEFT THE BASTION ON A RAIDING TRIP.

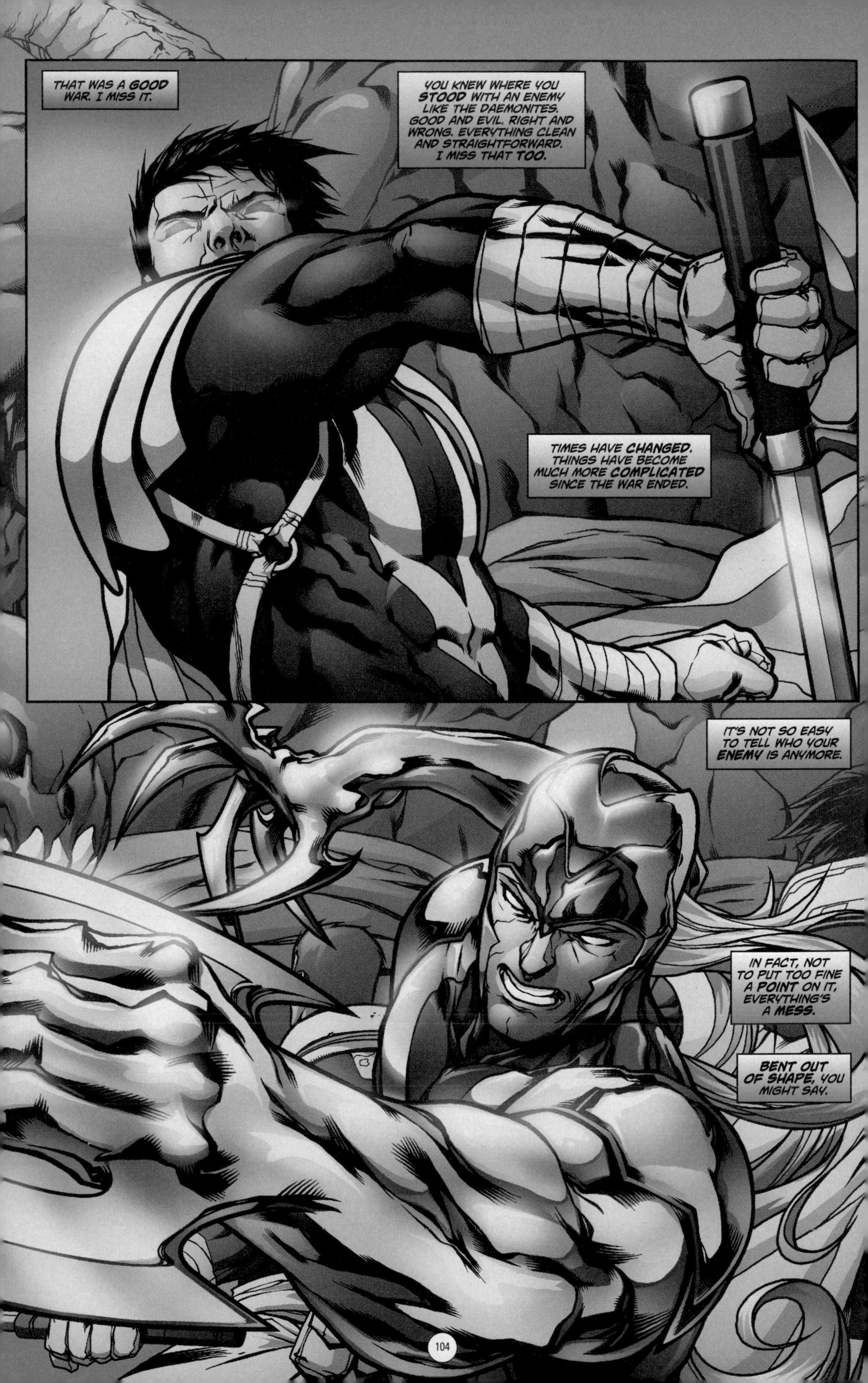
THAT WAS A GOOD WAR. I MISS IT.
YOU KNEW WHERE YOU STOOD WITH AN ENEMY LIKE THE DAEMONITES. GOOD AND EVIL. RIGHT AND WRONG. EVERYTHING CLEAN AND STRAIGHTFORWARD. I MISS THAT TOO.
TIMES HAVE CHANGED. THINGS HAVE BECOME MUCH MORE COMPLICATED SINCE THE WAR ENDED.
IT'S NOT SO EASY TO TELL WHO YOUR ENEMY IS ANYMORE.
IN FACT, NOT TO PUT TOO FINE A POINT ON IT, EVERYTHING'S A MESS.
BENT OUT OF SHAPE, YOU MIGHT SAY.

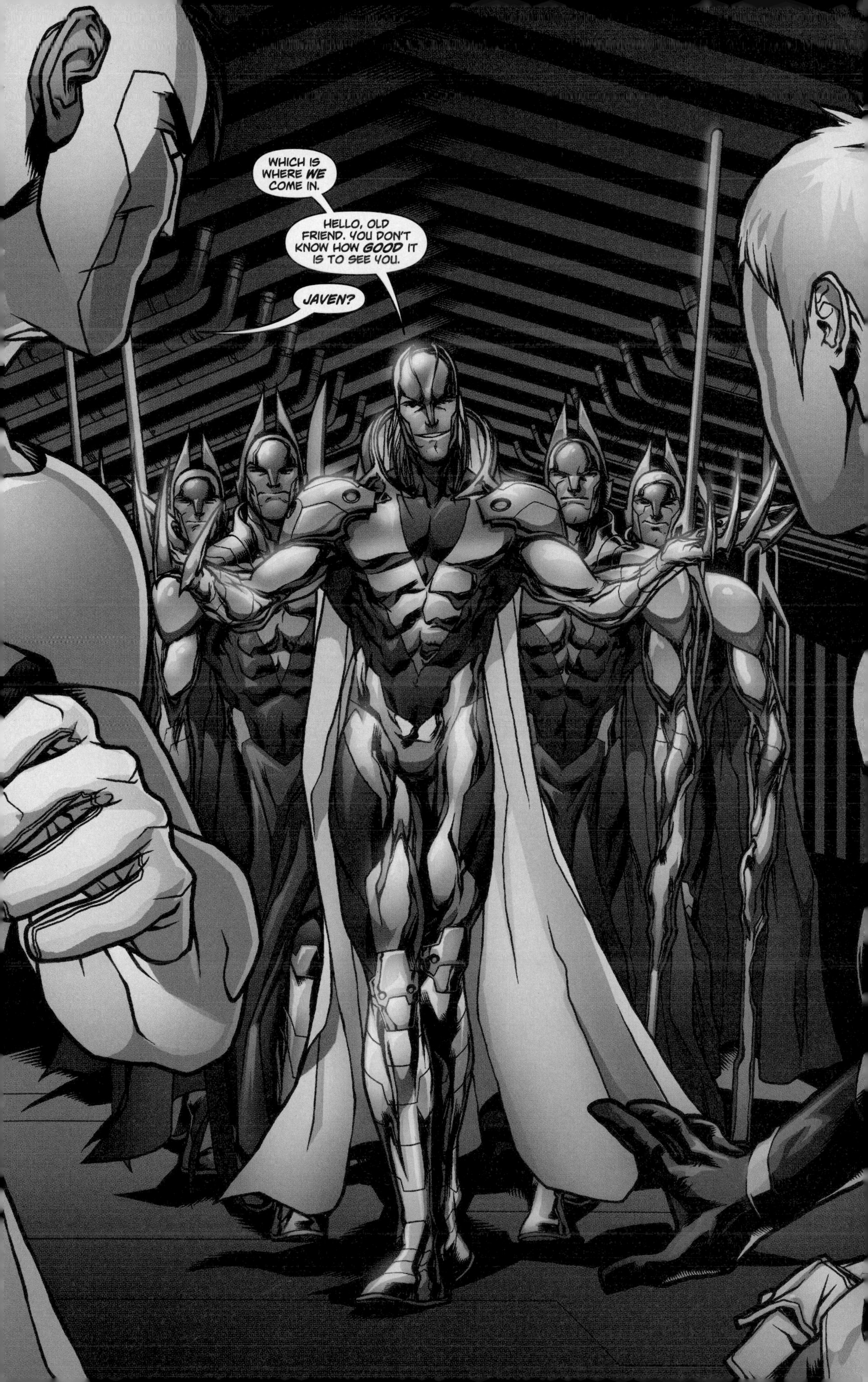
WHICH IS WHERE WE COME IN.
HELLO, OLD FRIEND. YOU DON'T KNOW HOW GOOD IT IS TO SEE YOU.
JAVEN?

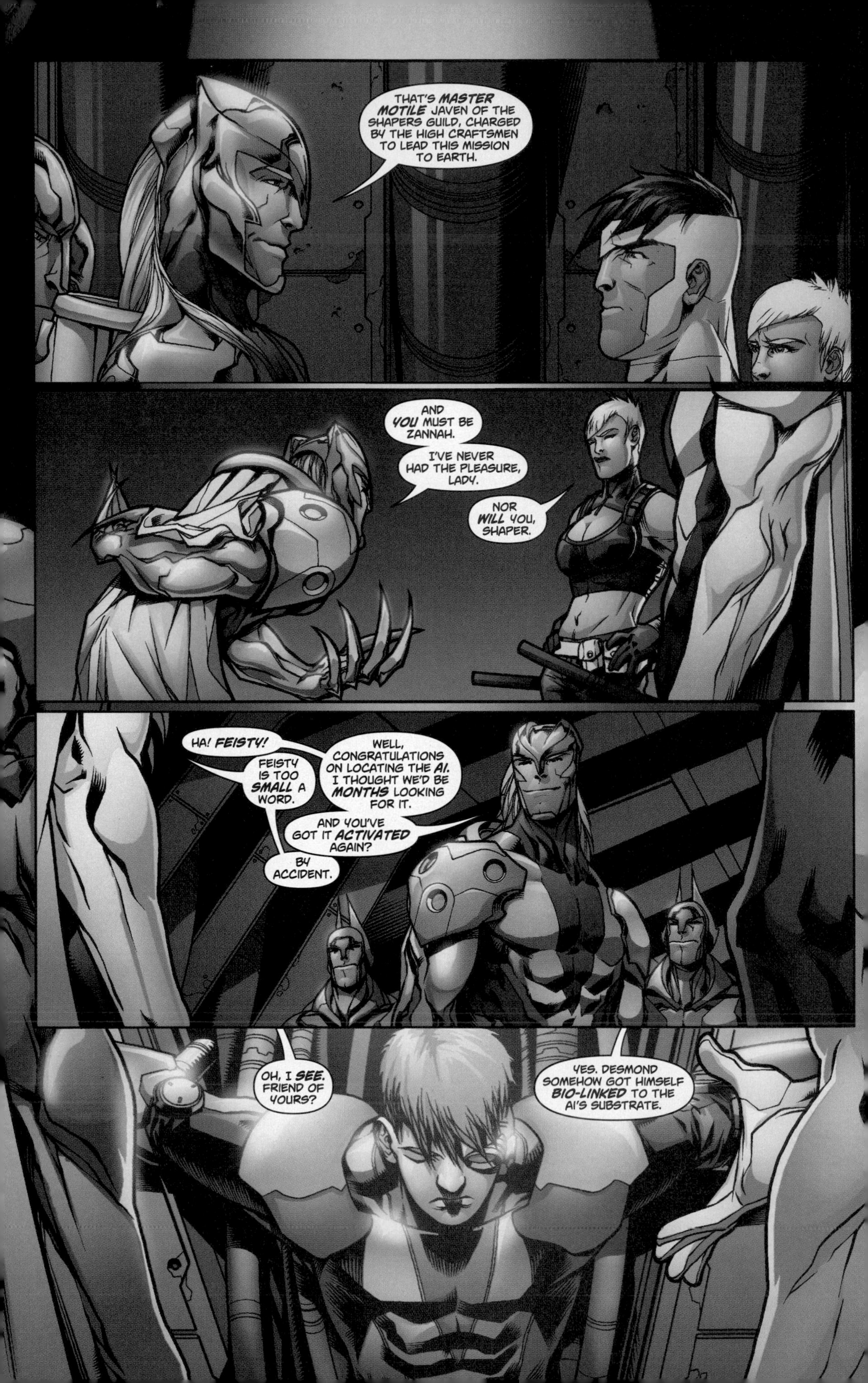
THAT'S MASTER MOTILE JAVEN OF THE SHAPERS GUILD, CHARGED BY THE HIGH CRAFTSMEN TO LEAD THIS MISSION TO EARTH.
AND YOU MUST BE ZANNAH.
I'VE NEVER HAD THE PLEASURE, LADY.
NOR WILL YOU, SHAPER.
HA! FEISTY!
FEISTY IS TOO SMALL A WORD.
WELL, CONGRATULATIONS ON LOCATING THE AI. I THOUGHT WE'D BE MONTHS LOOKING FOR IT.
AND YOU'VE GOT IT ACTIVATED AGAIN?
BY ACCIDENT.
OH, I SEE. FRIEND OF YOURS?
YES. DESMOND SOMEHOW GOT HIMSELF BIO-LINKED TO THE AI'S SUBSTRATE.

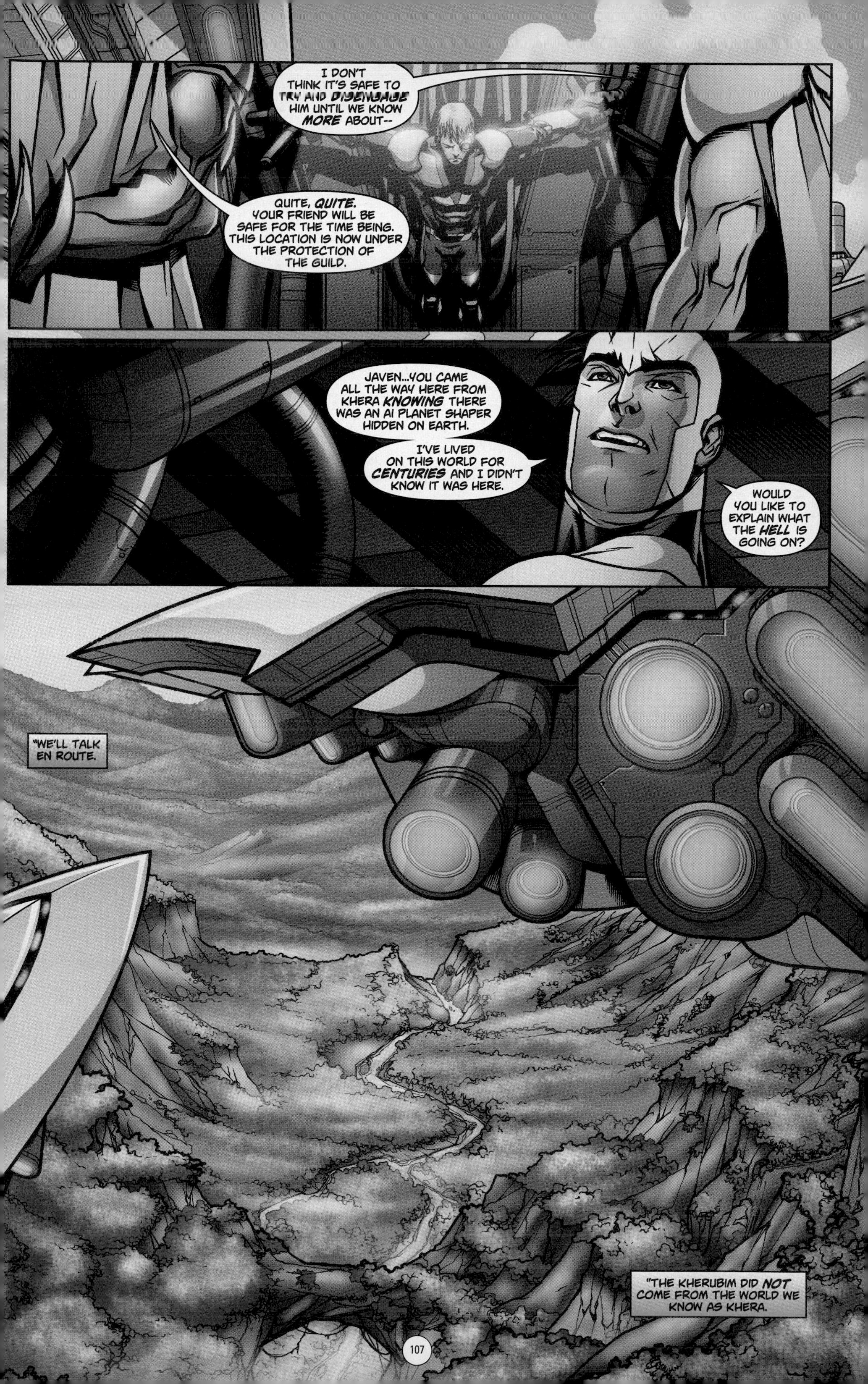
I DON'T THINK IT'S SAFE TO TRY AND DISENGAGE HIM UNTIL WE KNOW MORE ABOUT--
QUITE, QUITE. YOUR FRIEND WILL BE SAFE FOR THE TIME BEING. THIS LOCATION IS NOW UNDER THE PROTECTION OF THE GUILD.
JAVEN...YOU CAME ALL THE WAY HERE FROM KHERA KNOWING THERE WAS AN AI PLANET SHAPER HIDDEN ON EARTH.
I'VE LIVED ON THIS WORLD FOR CENTURIES AND I DIDN'T KNOW IT WAS HERE.
WOULD YOU LIKE TO EXPLAIN WHAT THE HELL IS GOING ON?
"WE'LL TALK EN ROUTE.
"THE KHERUBIM DID NOT COME FROM THE WORLD WE KNOW AS KHERA.

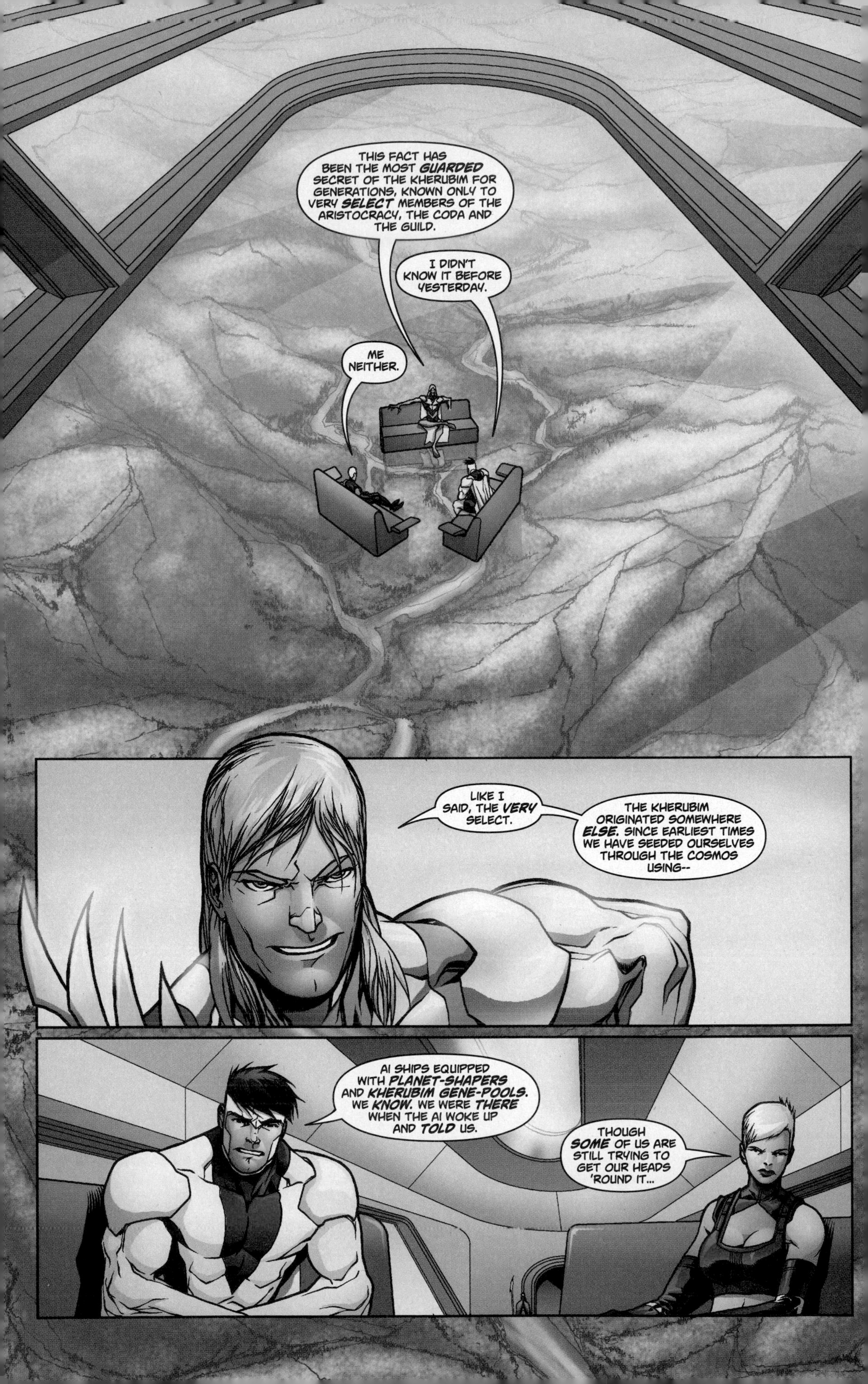
THIS FACT HAS BEEN THE MOST GUARDED SECRET OF THE KHERUBIM FOR GENERATIONS, KNOWN ONLY TO VERY SELECT MEMBERS OF THE ARISTOCRACY, THE CODA AND THE GUILD.
I DIDN'T KNOW IT BEFORE YESTERDAY.
ME NEITHER.
LIKE I SAID, THE VERY SELECT.
THE KHERUBIM ORIGINATED SOMEWHERE ELSE. SINCE EARLIEST TIMES WE HAVE SEEDED OURSELVES THROUGH THE COSMOS USING--
AI SHIPS EQUIPPED WITH PLANET-SHAPERS AND KHERUBIM GENE-POOLS. WE KNOW. WE WERE THERE WHEN THE AI WOKE UP AND TOLD US.
THOUGH SOME OF US ARE STILL TRYING TO GET OUR HEADS 'ROUND IT...

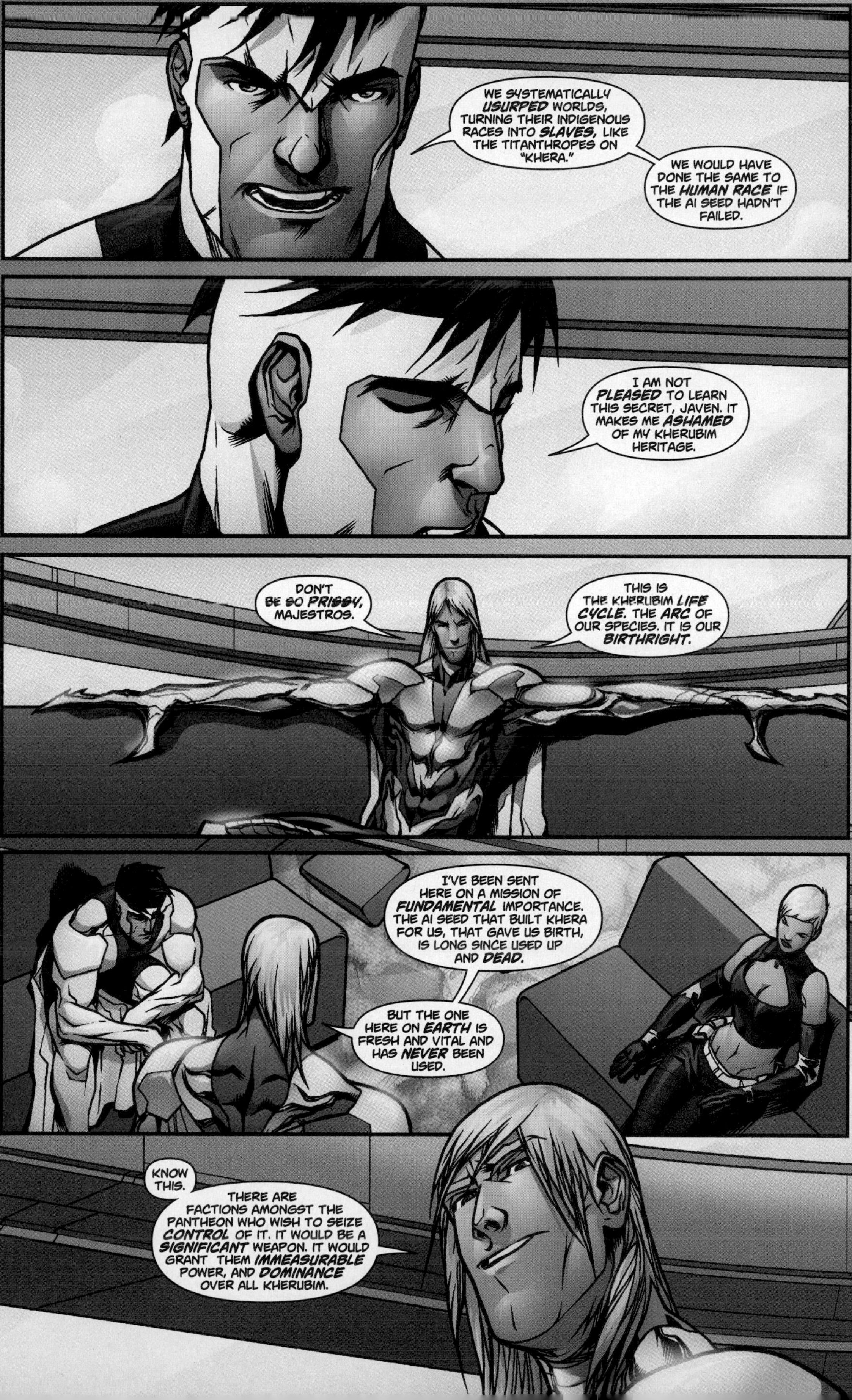
WE SYSTEMATICALLY USURPED WORLDS, TURNING THEIR INDIGENOUS RACES INTO SLAVES, LIKE THE TITANTHROPES ON "KHERA."
WE WOULD HAVE DONE THE SAME TO THE HUMAN RACE IF THE AI SEED HADN'T FAILED.
I AM NOT PLEASED TO LEARN THIS SECRET, JAVEN. IT MAKES ME ASHAMED OF MY KHERUBIM HERITAGE.
DON'T BE SO PRISSY, MAJESTROS.
THIS IS THE KHERUBIM LIFE CYCLE. THE ARC OF OUR SPECIES. IT IS OUR BIRTHRIGHT.
I'VE BEEN SENT HERE ON A MISSION OF FUNDAMENTAL IMPORTANCE. THE AI SEED THAT BUILT KHERA FOR US, THAT GAVE US BIRTH, IS LONG SINCE USED UP AND DEAD.
BUT THE ONE HERE ON EARTH IS FRESH AND VITAL AND HAS NEVER BEEN USED.
KNOW THIS.
THERE ARE FACTIONS AMONGST THE PANTHEON WHO WISH TO SEIZE CONTROL OF IT. IT WOULD BE A SIGNIFICANT WEAPON. IT WOULD GRANT THEM IMMEASURABLE POWER, AND DOMINANCE OVER ALL KHERUBIM.

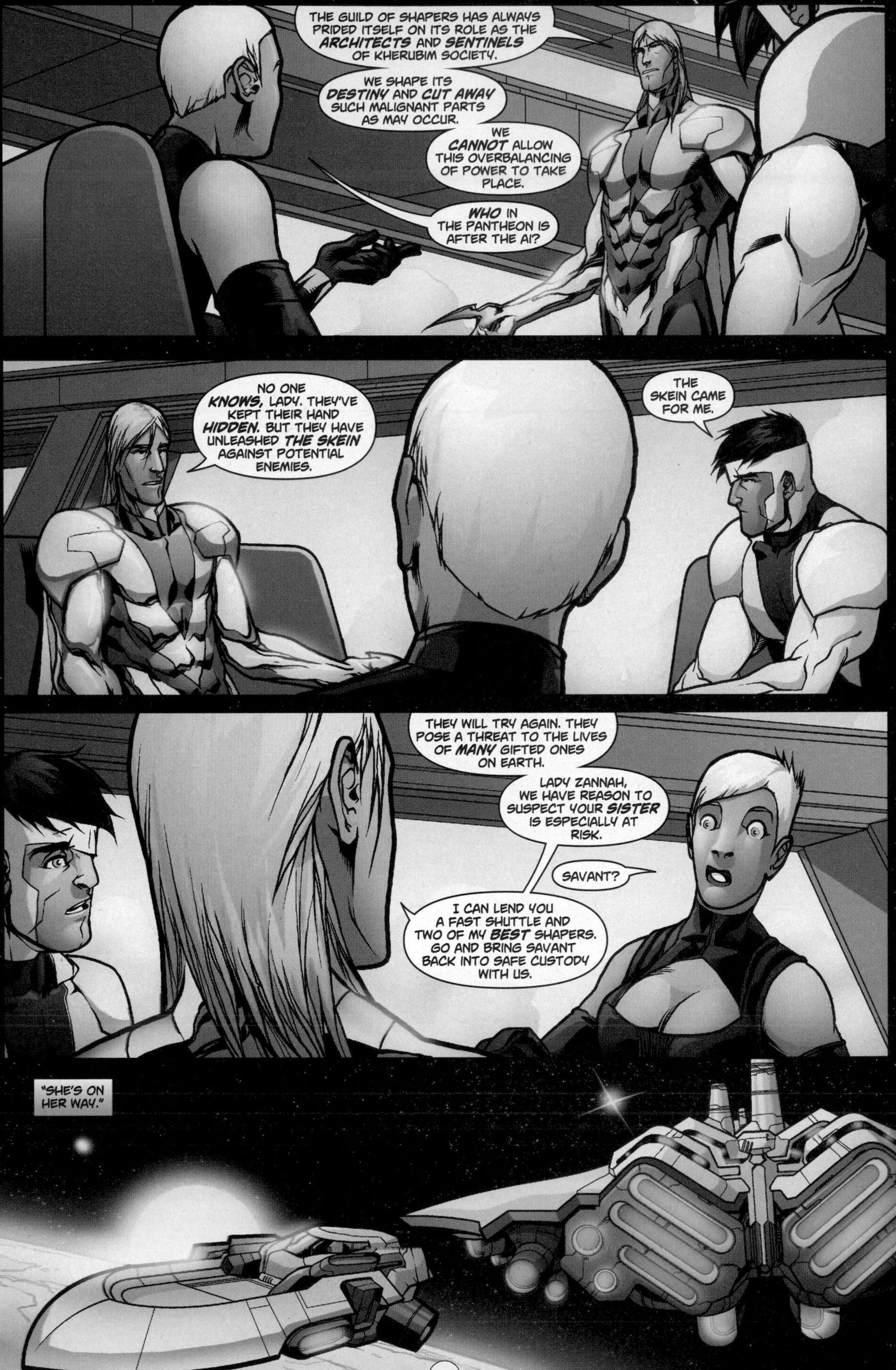
THE GUILD OF SHAPERS HAS ALWAYS PRIDED ITSELF ON ITS ROLE AS THE ARCHITECTS AND SENTINELS OF KHERUBIM SOCIETY.
WE SHAPE ITS DESTINY AND CUT AWAY SUCH MALIGNANT PARTS AS MAY OCCUR.
WE CANNOT ALLOW THIS OVERBALANCING OF POWER TO TAKE PLACE.
WHO IN THE PANTHEON IS AFTER THE AI?
NO ONE KNOWS, LADY. THEY'VE KEPT THEIR HAND HIDDEN. BUT THEY HAVE UNLEASHED THE SKEIN AGAINST POTENTIAL ENEMIES.
THE SKEIN CAME FOR ME.
THEY WILL TRY AGAIN. THEY POSE A THREAT TO THE LIVES OF MANY GIFTED ONES ON EARTH.
LADY ZANNAH, WE HAVE REASON TO SUSPECT YOUR SISTER IS ESPECIALLY AT RISK.
SAVANT?
I CAN LEND YOU A FAST SHUTTLE AND TWO OF MY BEST SHAPERS. GO AND BRING SAVANT BACK INTO SAFE CUSTODY WITH US.
"SHE'S ON HER WAY."

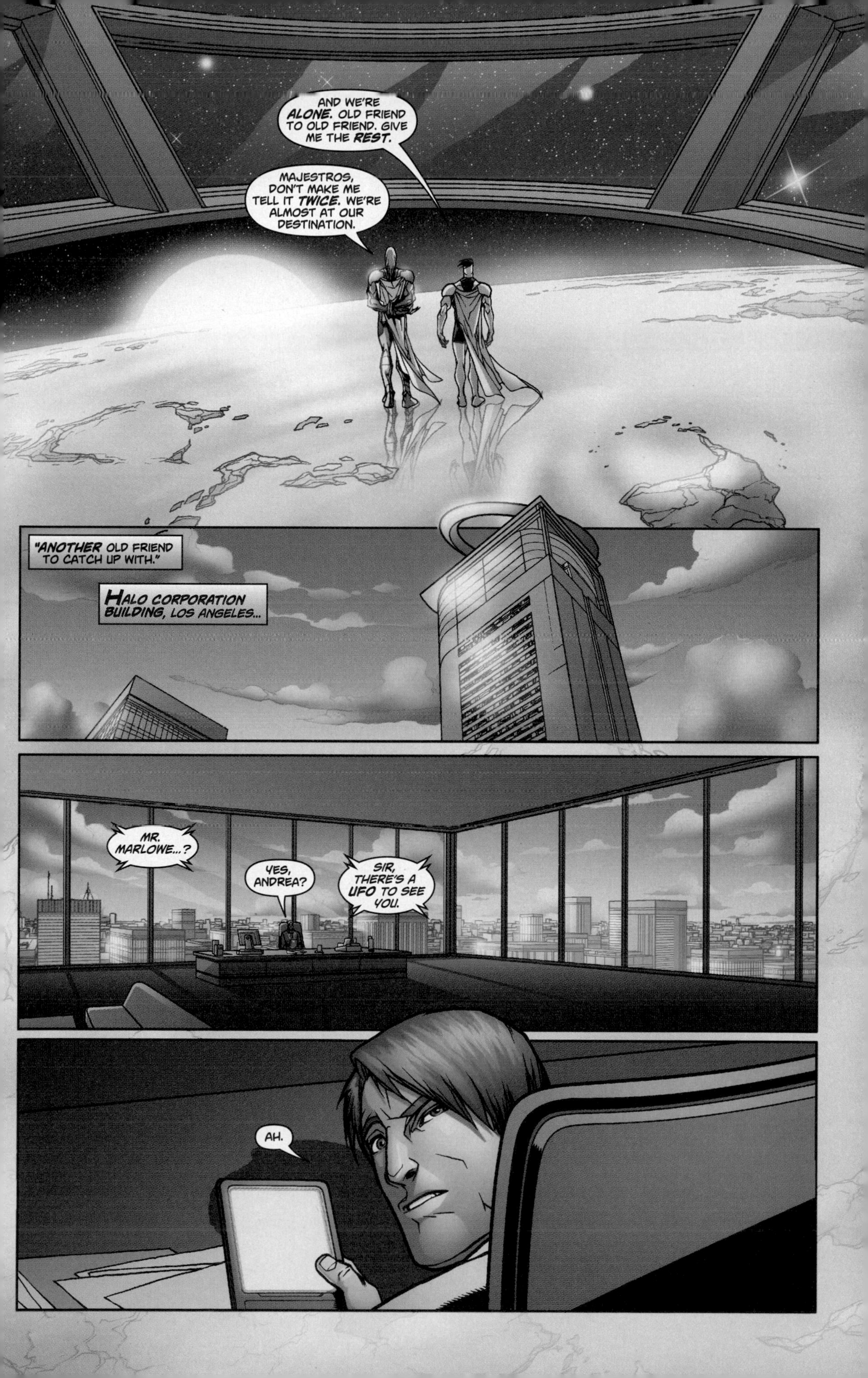
AND WE'RE ALONE. OLD FRIEND TO OLD FRIEND. GIVE ME THE REST.
MAJESTROS, DON'T MAKE ME TELL IT TWICE. WE'RE ALMOST AT OUR DESTINATION.
"ANOTHER OLD FRIEND TO CATCH UP WITH."
HALO CORPORATION BUILDING, LOS ANGELES...
MR. MARLOWE...?
YES, ANDREA?
SIR, THERE'S A UFO TO SEE YOU.
AH.

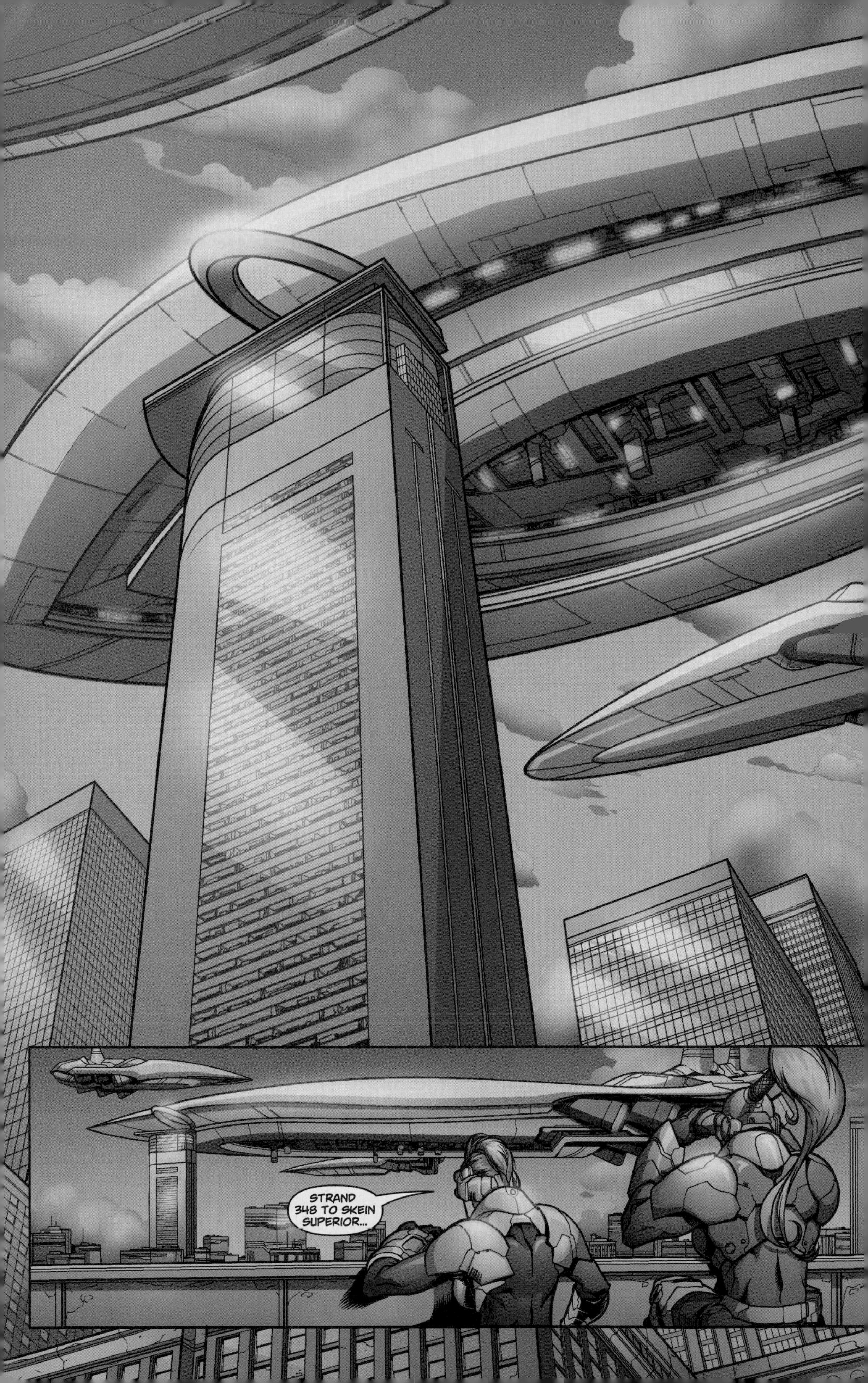
STRAND 348 TO SKEIN SUPERIOR...

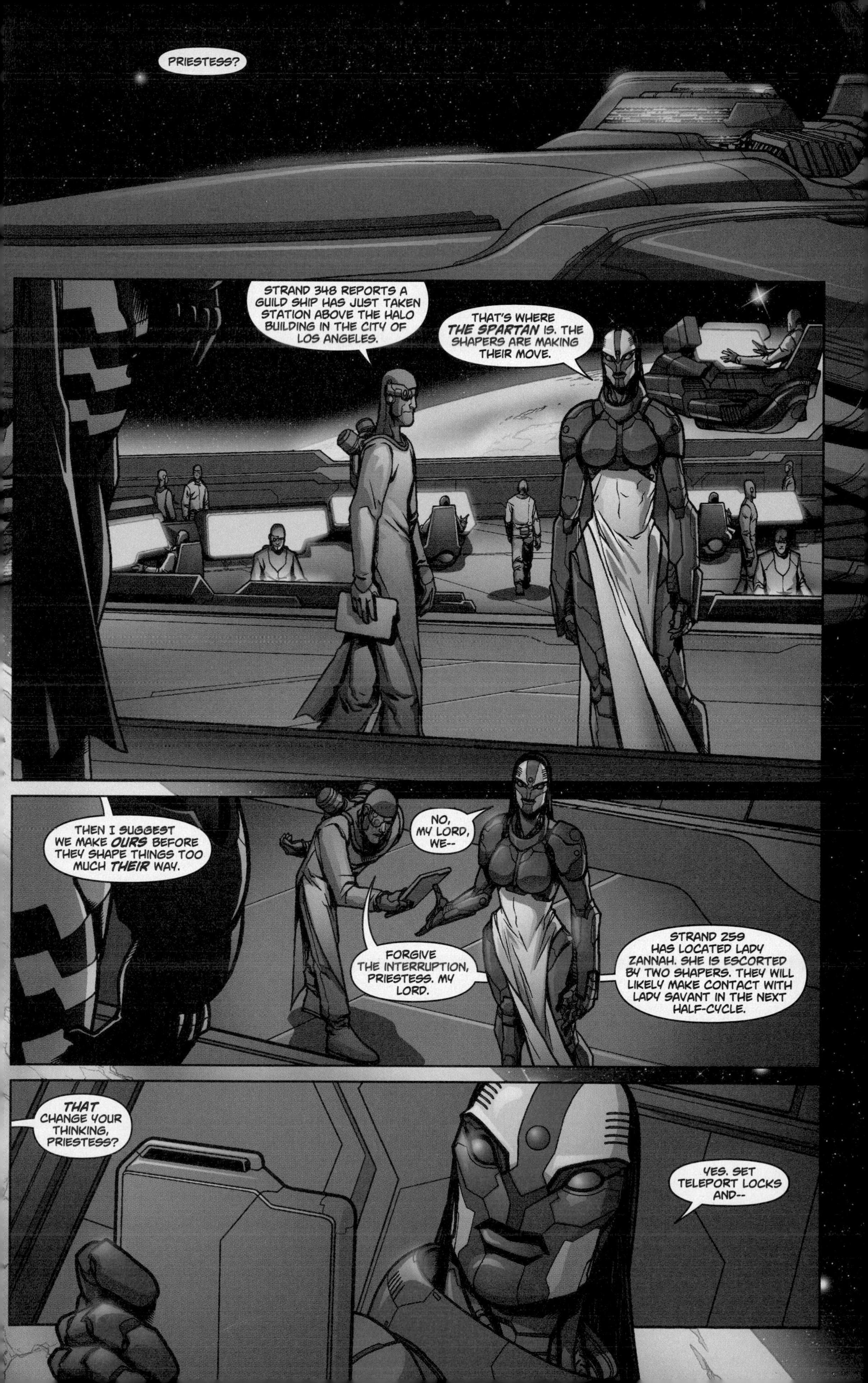
PRIESTESS?
STRAND 348 REPORTS A GUILD SHIP HAS JUST TAKEN STATION ABOVE THE HALO BUILDING IN THE CITY OF LOS ANGELES.
THAT'S WHERE *THE SPARTAN* IS. THE SHAPERS ARE MAKING THEIR MOVE.
THEN I SUGGEST WE MAKE *OURS* BEFORE THEY SHAPE THINGS TOO MUCH *THEIR* WAY.
NO, MY LORD, WE--
FORGIVE THE INTERRUPTION, PRIESTESS. MY LORD.
STRAND 259 HAS LOCATED LADY ZANNAH. SHE IS ESCORTED BY TWO SHAPERS. THEY WILL LIKELY MAKE CONTACT WITH LADY SAVANT IN THE NEXT HALF-CYCLE.
THAT CHANGE YOUR THINKING, PRIESTESS?
YES. SET TELEPORT LOCKS AND--

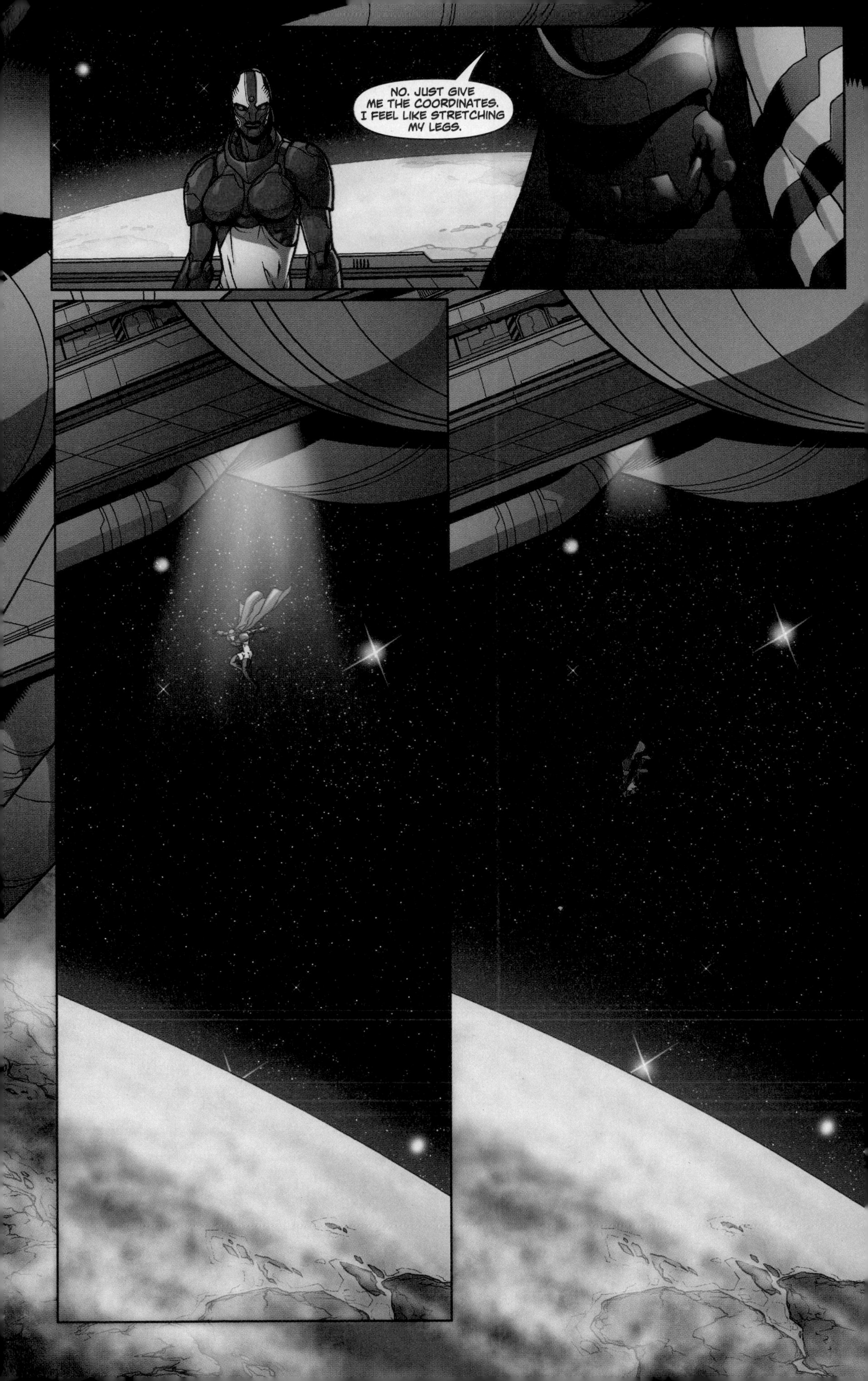
NO. JUST GIVE ME THE COORDINATES. I FEEL LIKE STRETCHING MY LEGS.

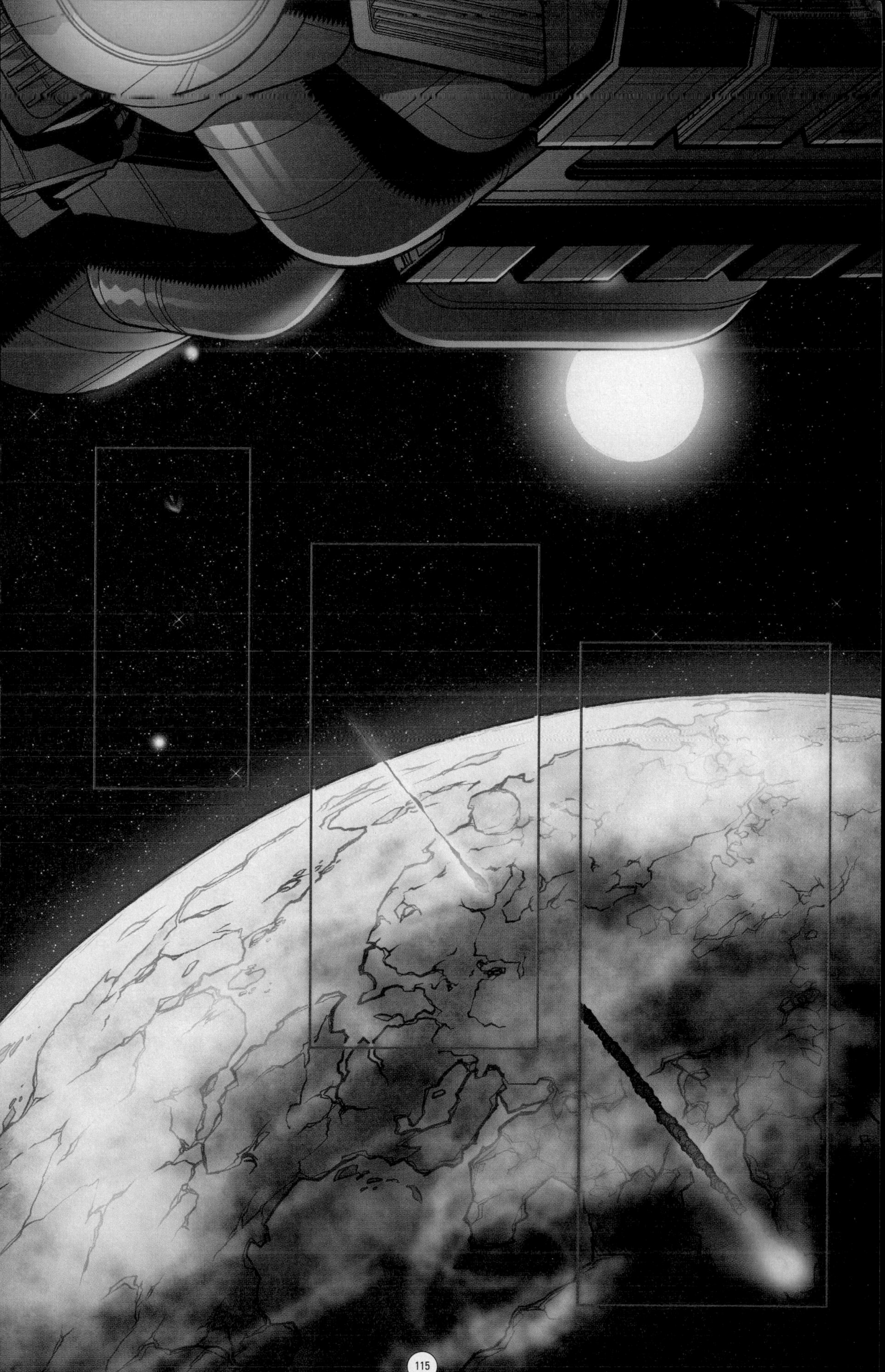

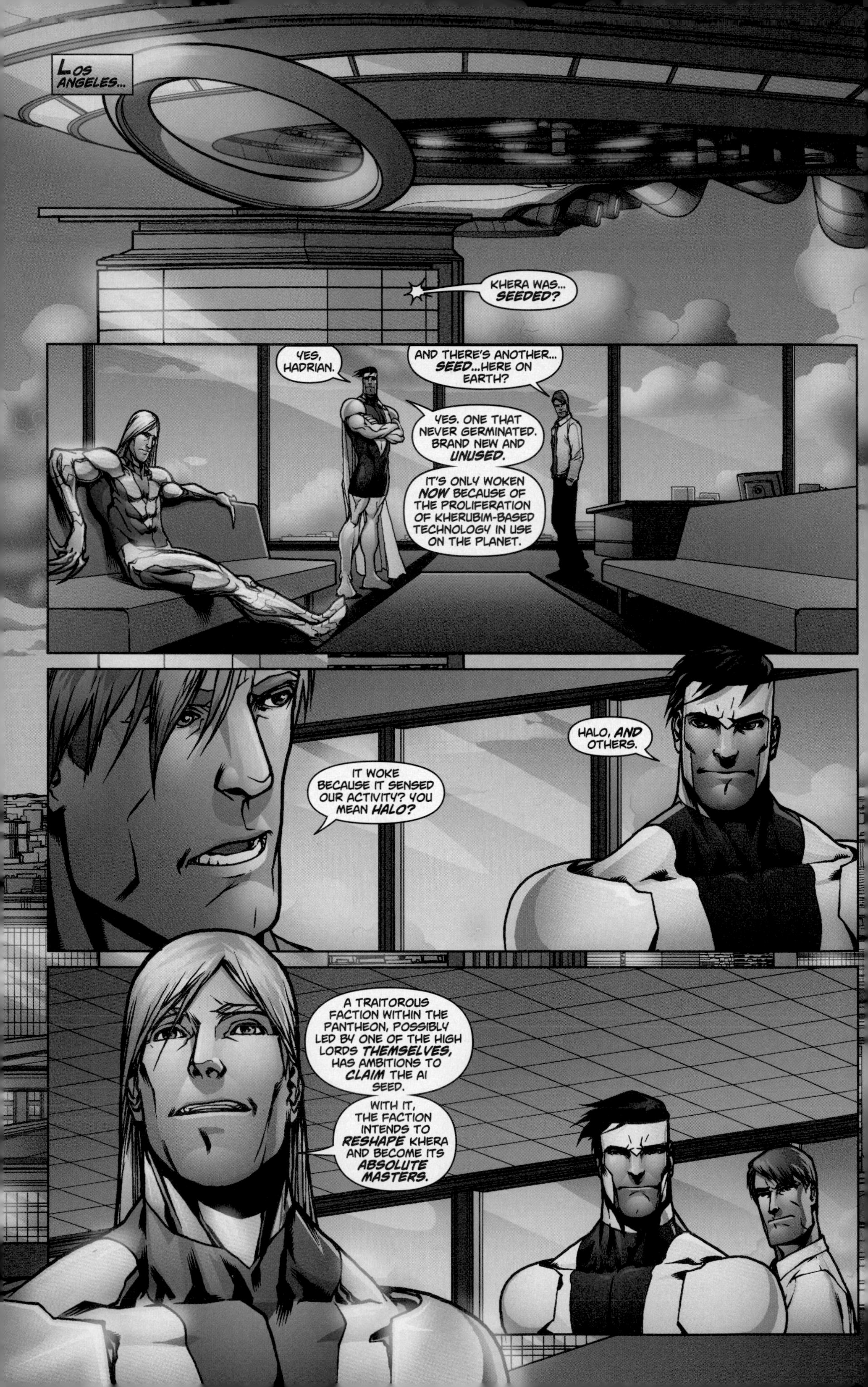
LOS ANGELES...
KHERA WAS... SEEDED?
YES, HADRIAN.
AND THERE'S ANOTHER... SEED...HERE ON EARTH?
YES. ONE THAT NEVER GERMINATED. BRAND NEW AND UNUSED.
IT'S ONLY WOKEN NOW BECAUSE OF THE PROLIFERATION OF KHERUBIM-BASED TECHNOLOGY IN USE ON THE PLANET.
IT WOKE BECAUSE IT SENSED OUR ACTIVITY? YOU MEAN HALO?
HALO, AND OTHERS.
A TRAITOROUS FACTION WITHIN THE PANTHEON, POSSIBLY LED BY ONE OF THE HIGH LORDS THEMSELVES, HAS AMBITIONS TO CLAIM THE AI SEED.
WITH IT, THE FACTION INTENDS TO RESHAPE KHERA AND BECOME ITS ABSOLUTE MASTERS.

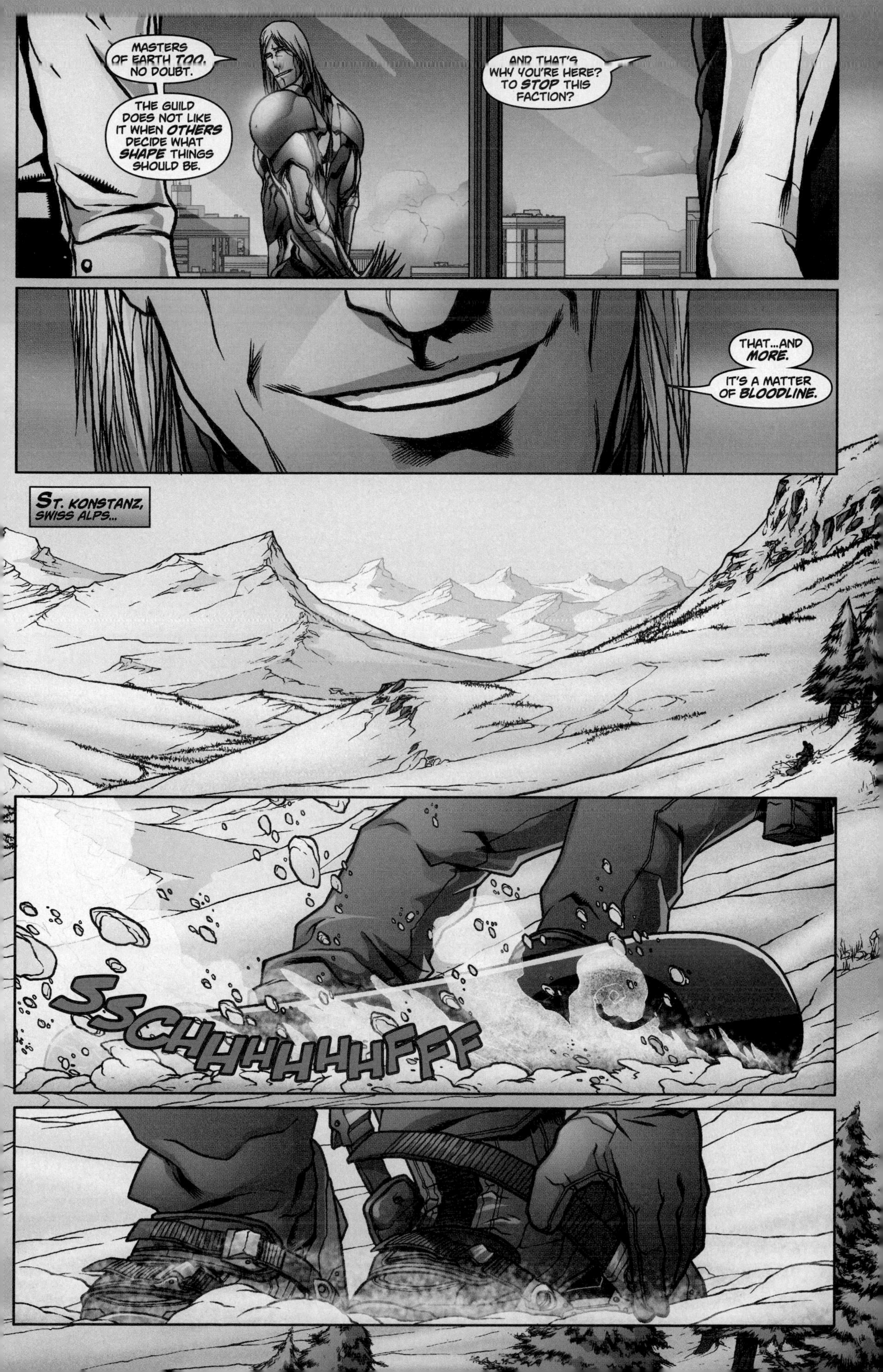
MASTERS OF EARTH TOO, NO DOUBT.
THE GUILD DOES NOT LIKE IT WHEN OTHERS DECIDE WHAT SHAPE THINGS SHOULD BE.
AND THAT'S WHY YOU'RE HERE? TO STOP THIS FACTION?
THAT...AND MORE.
IT'S A MATTER OF BLOODLINE.
ST. KONSTANZ, SWISS ALPS...
SSCHHHHHHHFFF

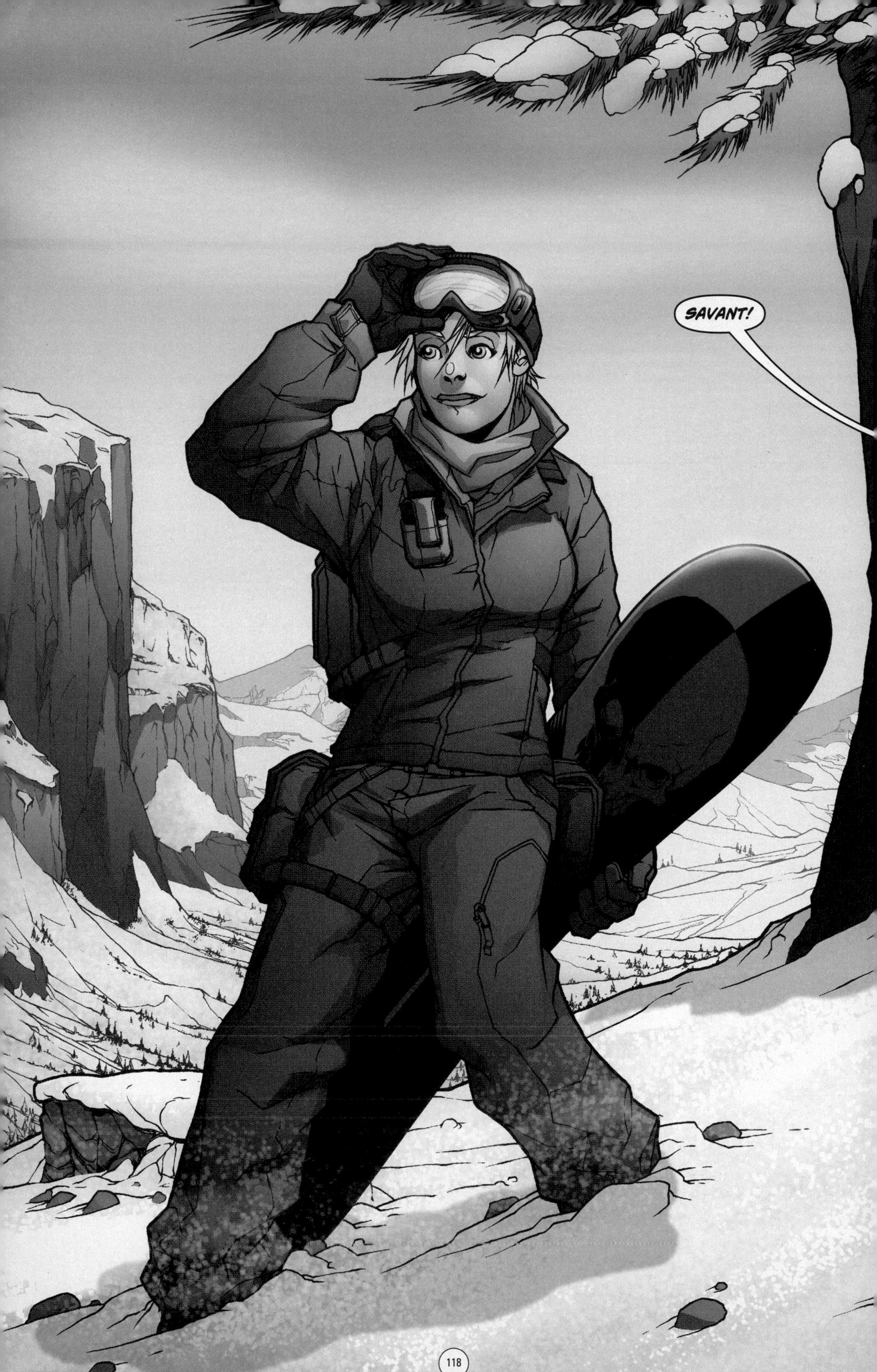
SAVANT!

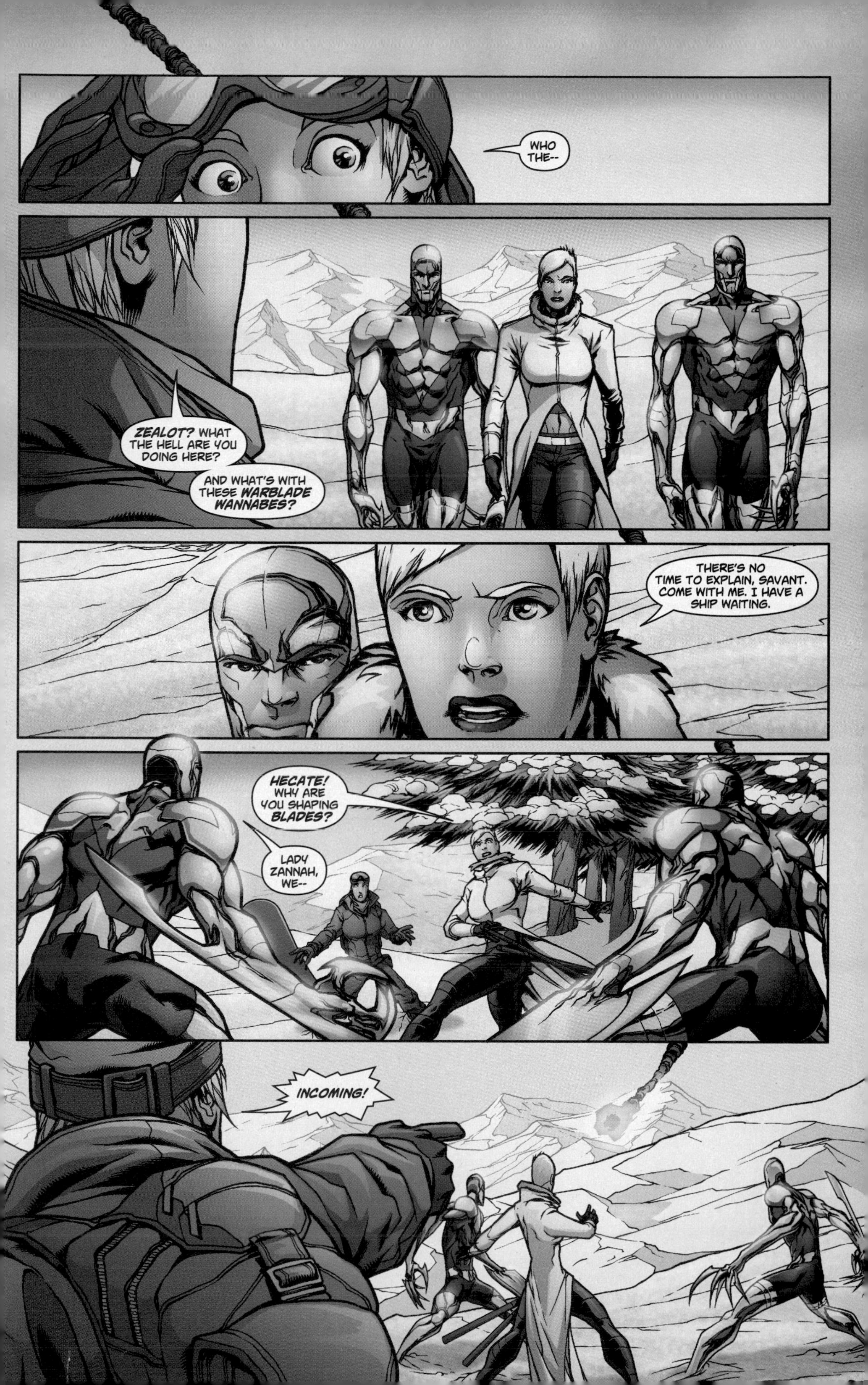
WHO THE--
ZEALOT? WHAT THE HELL ARE YOU DOING HERE?
AND WHAT'S WITH THESE WARBLADE WANNABES?
THERE'S NO TIME TO EXPLAIN, SAVANT. COME WITH ME. I HAVE A SHIP WAITING.
HECATE! WHY ARE YOU SHAPING BLADES?
LADY ZANNAH, WE--
INCOMING!

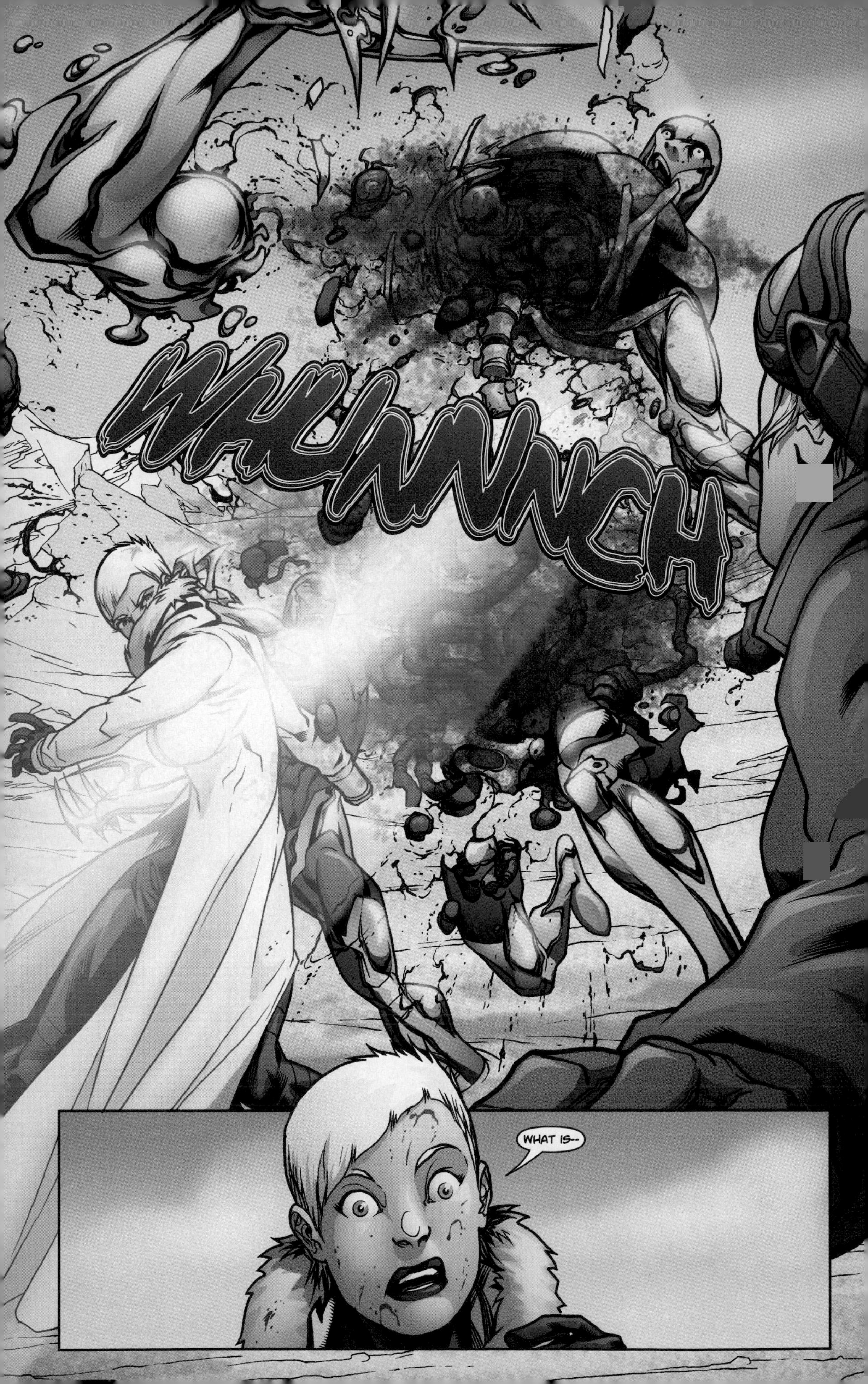
WHAT IS--

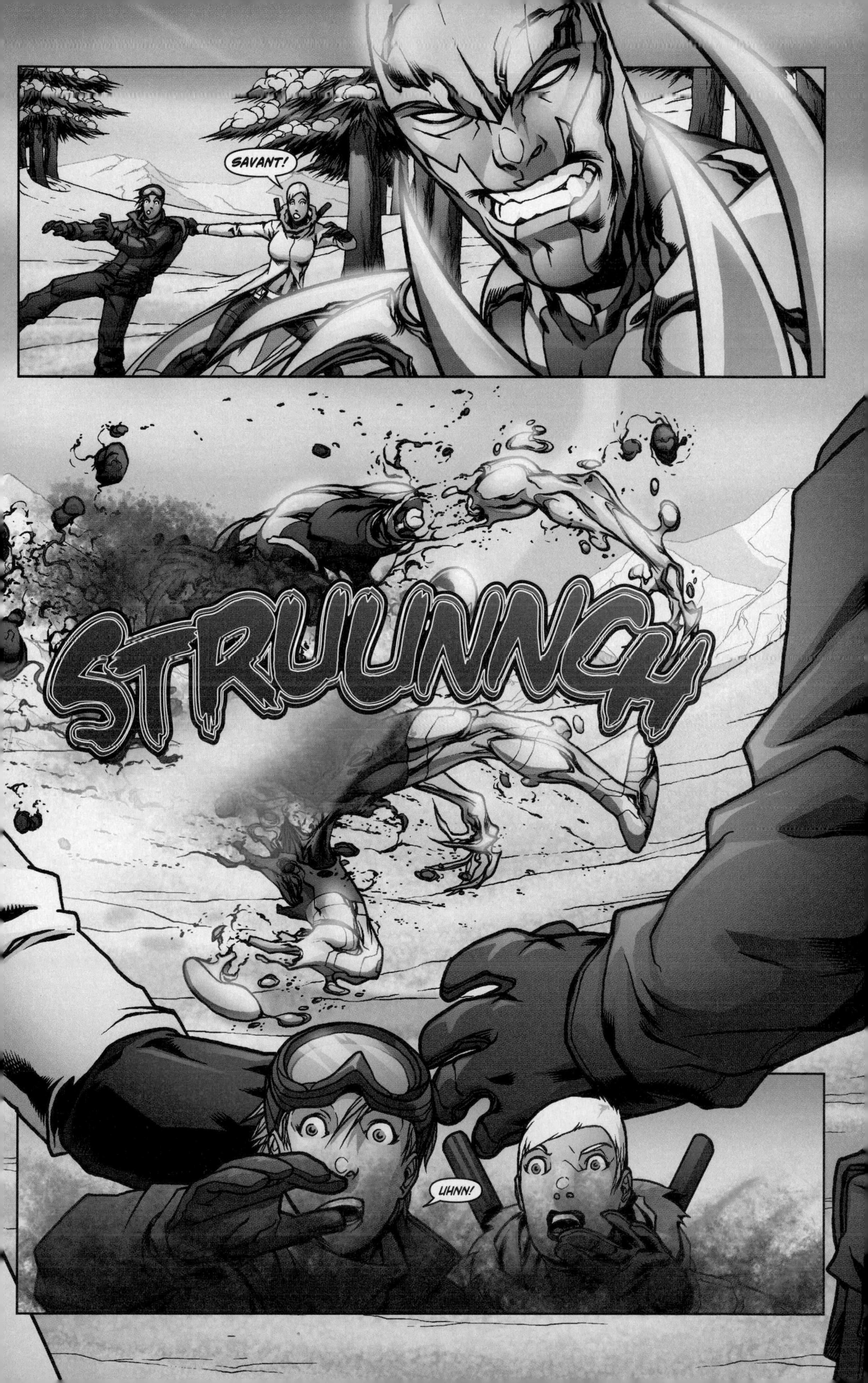
SAVANT!
STRUUNCH
UHNN!

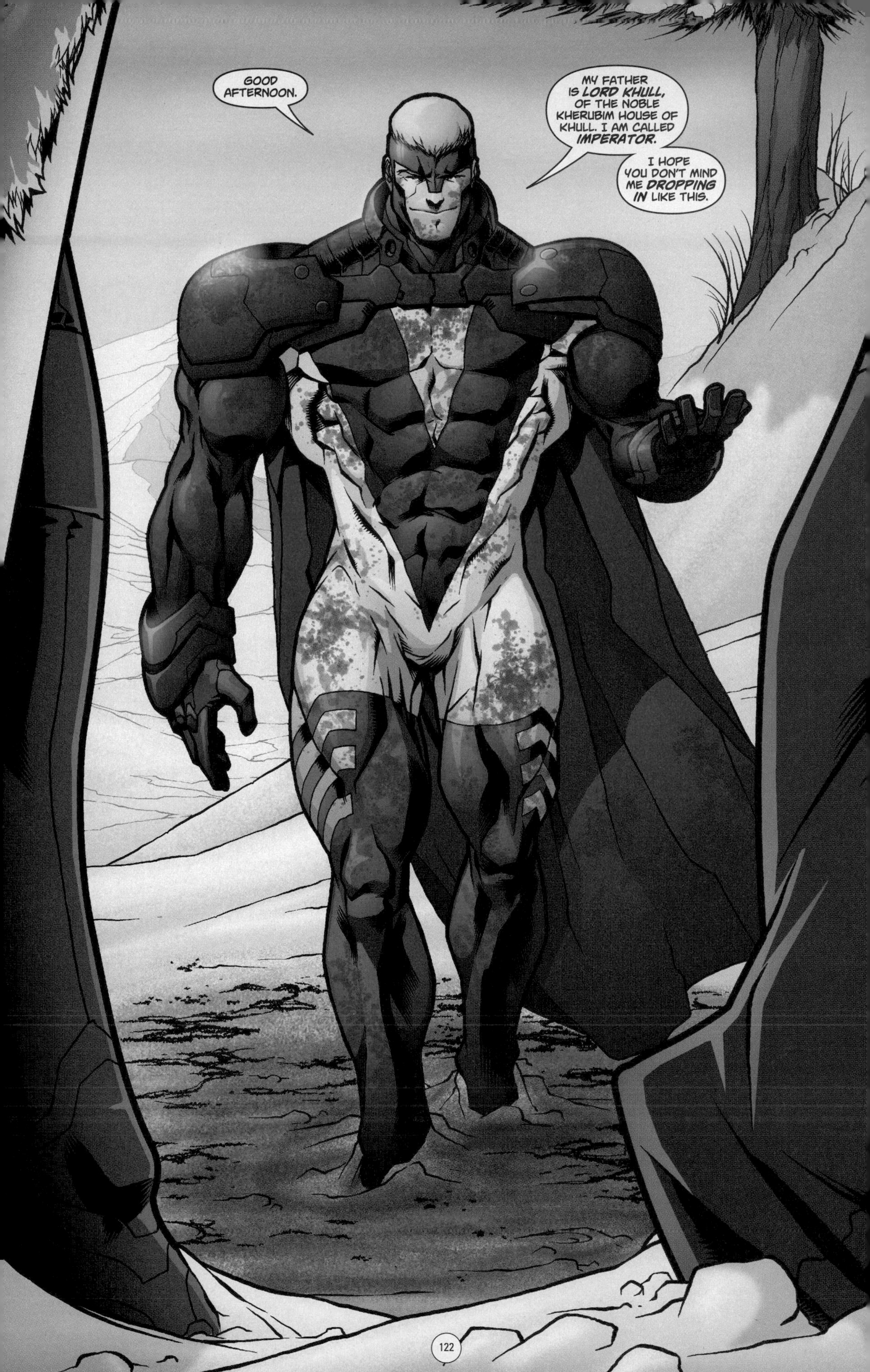
GOOD AFTERNOON.
MY FATHER IS **LORD KHULL**, OF THE NOBLE KHERUBIM HOUSE OF KHULL. I AM CALLED **IMPERATOR**.
I HOPE YOU DON'T MIND ME **DROPPING IN** LIKE THIS.

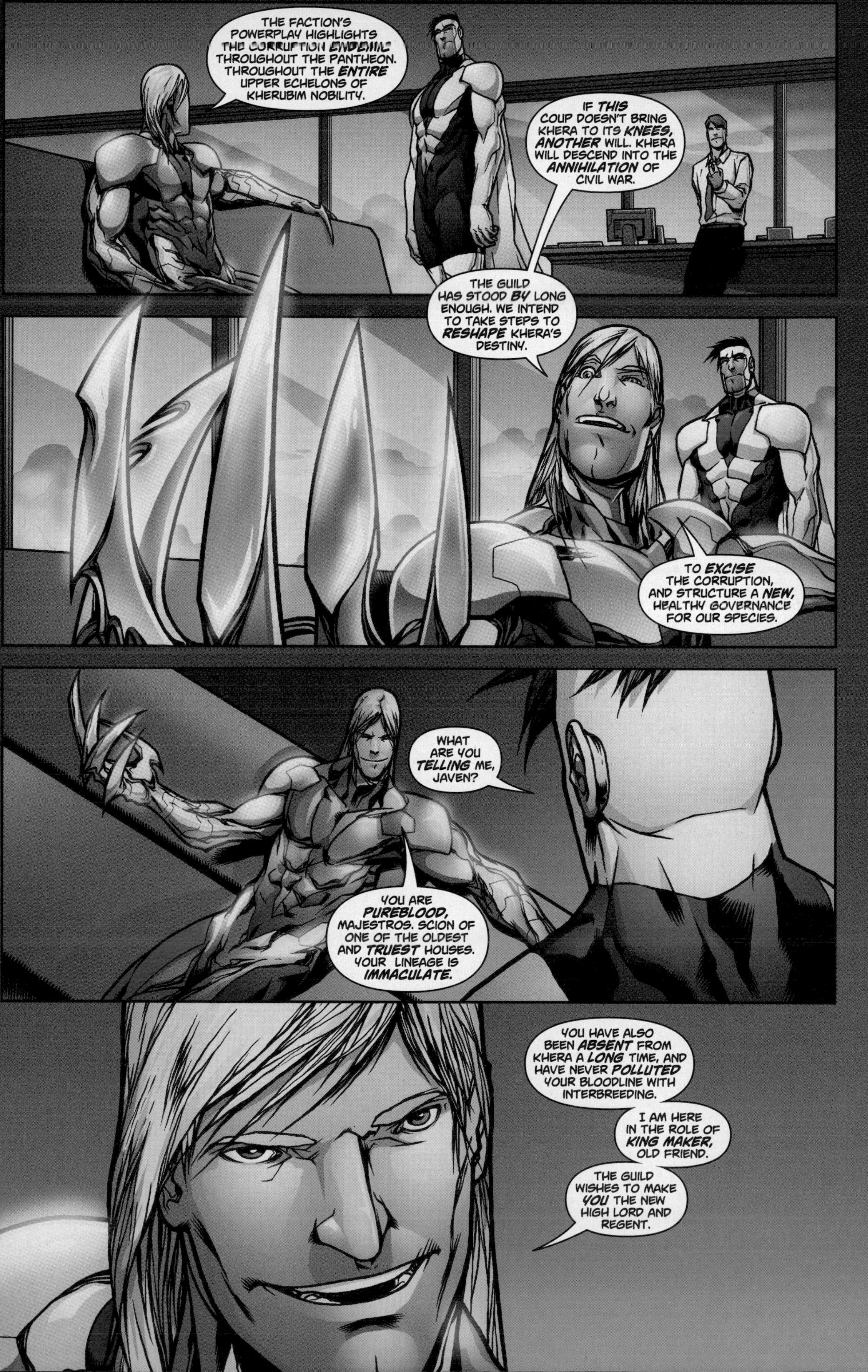
THE FACTION'S POWERPLAY HIGHLIGHTS THE CORRUPTION ENDEMIC THROUGHOUT THE PANTHEON. THROUGHOUT THE ENTIRE UPPER ECHELONS OF KHERUBIM NOBILITY.
IF THIS COUP DOESN'T BRING KHERA TO ITS KNEES, ANOTHER WILL. KHERA WILL DESCEND INTO THE ANNIHILATION OF CIVIL WAR.
THE GUILD HAS STOOD BY LONG ENOUGH. WE INTEND TO TAKE STEPS TO RESHAPE KHERA'S DESTINY.
TO EXCISE THE CORRUPTION, AND STRUCTURE A NEW, HEALTHY GOVERNANCE FOR OUR SPECIES.
WHAT ARE YOU TELLING ME, JAVEN?
YOU ARE PUREBLOOD, MAJESTROS. SCION OF ONE OF THE OLDEST AND TRUEST HOUSES. YOUR LINEAGE IS IMMACULATE.
YOU HAVE ALSO BEEN ABSENT FROM KHERA A LONG TIME, AND HAVE NEVER POLLUTED YOUR BLOODLINE WITH INTERBREEDING.
I AM HERE IN THE ROLE OF KING MAKER, OLD FRIEND.
THE GUILD WISHES TO MAKE YOU THE NEW HIGH LORD AND REGENT.

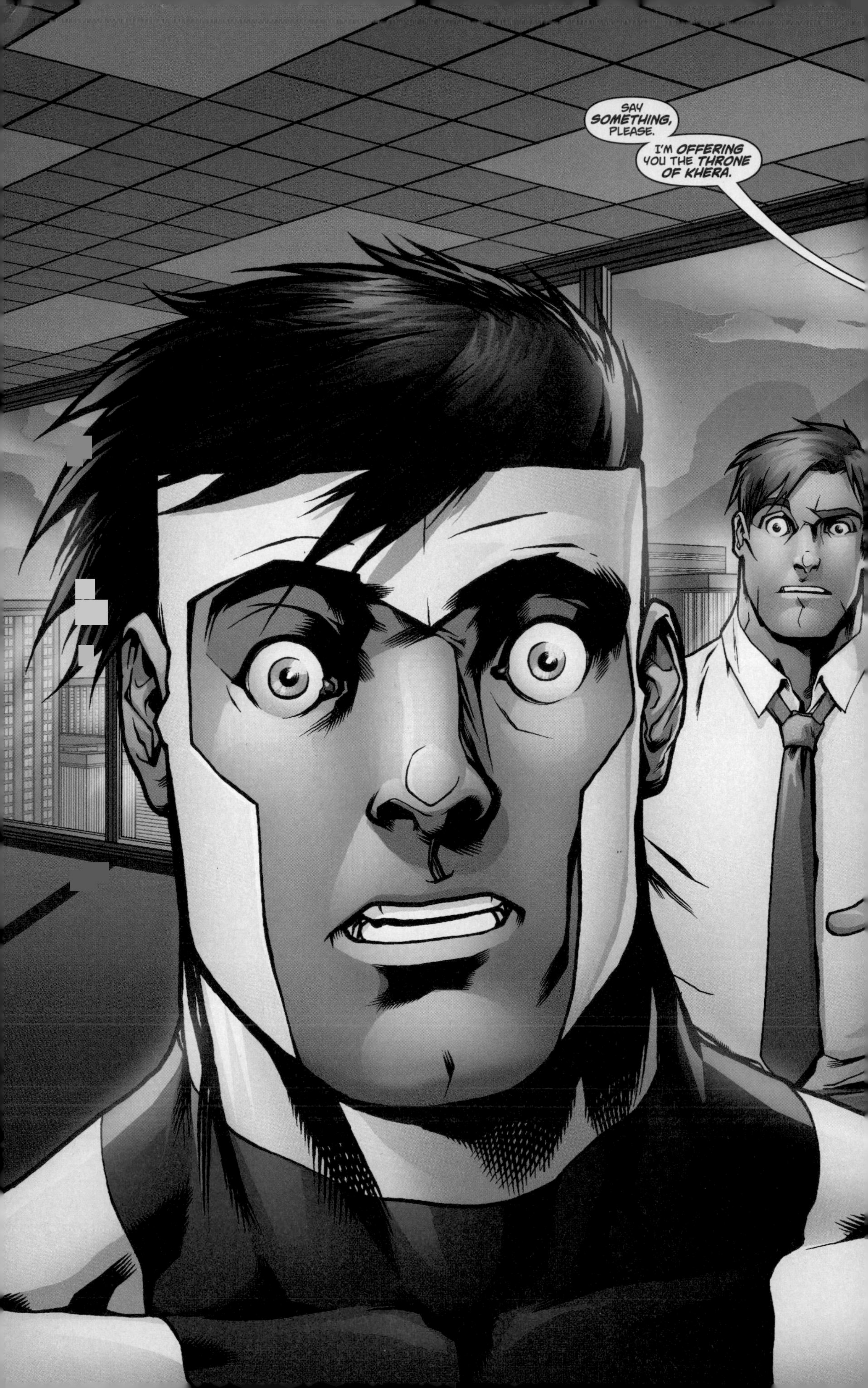
SAY SOMETHING, PLEASE.
I'M OFFERING YOU THE THRONE OF KHERA.

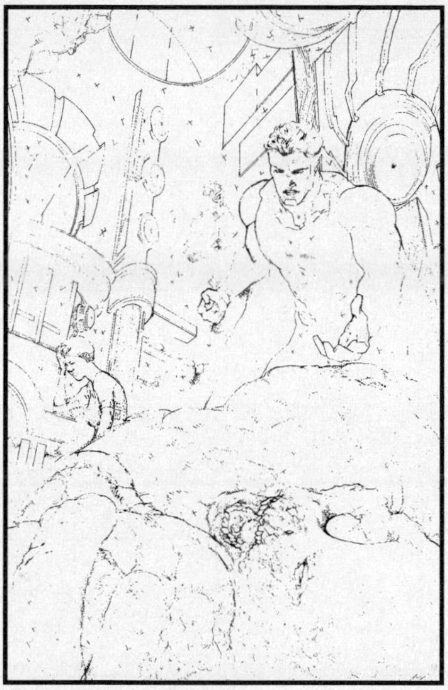

Pencils

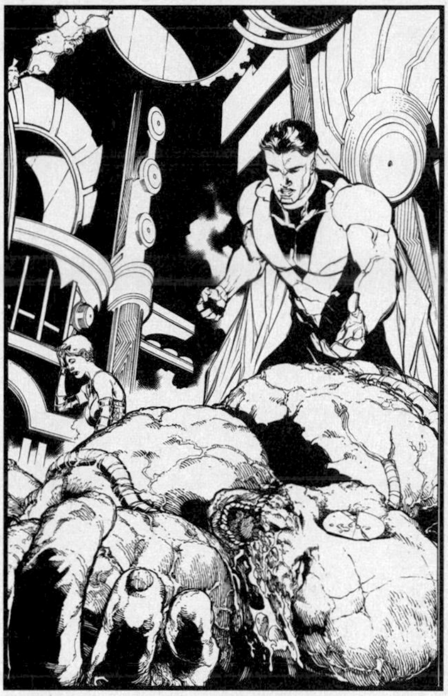

Inks

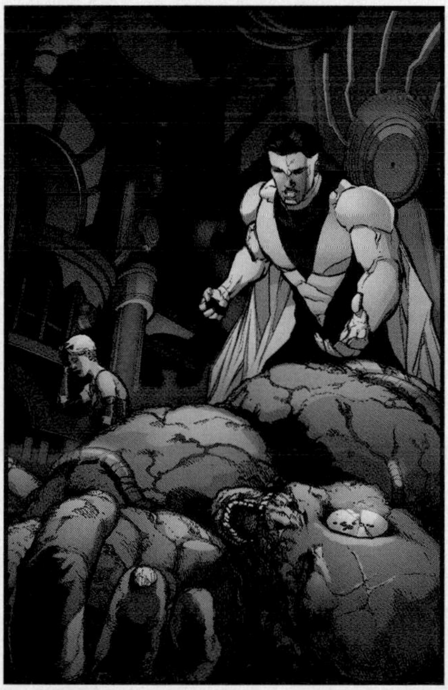

Colors

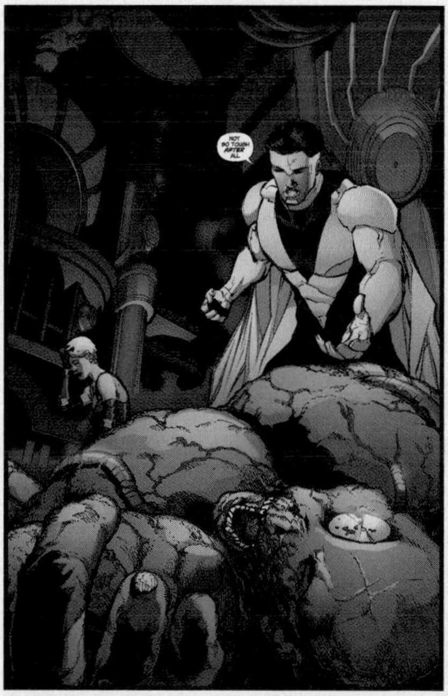
NOT SO TOUGH AFTER ALL.

Lettering

This page and the next give you a sampling of a comic book page's progression from pencils to inks, and then on to coloring and lettering.

Pencils

Inks

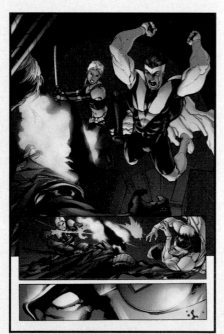

Colors

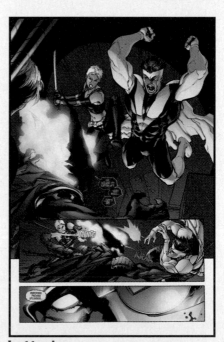

Lettering

CATCH ALL OF MAJESTIC'S ADVENTURES IN THESE COLLECTIONS:

MAJESTIC
WHILE YOU WERE OUT
ABNETT LANNING GOOGE SCOTT

When cosmic-level forces threaten Earth, people in the WildStorm Universe can count on one man to save them. Not that Majestros is an ordinary man–with the powers of a Kheran lord, the hardest part of defeating your enemies can be discovering them!

MAJESTIC: WHILE YOU WERE OUT brings our hero home, in a story by Dan Abnett and Andy Lanning, featuring art by Neil Googe, Juan Santacruz and Trevor Scott.

MAJESTIC: STRANGE NEW VISITOR

MAJESTIC
STRANGE NEW VISITOR
DAN ABNETT ANDY LANNING KARL KERSCHL

ABNETT/LANNING/KERSCHL

MR. MAJESTIC

MR MAJESTIC
Joe Casey
Brian Holguin
Alan Moore
Ed McGuinness
Carlos D'Anda

CASEY/HOLGUIN/MOORE McGUINNESS/D'ANDA

WILDC.A.T.S: HOMECOMING

WILDSTORM
BOOKS
HOMECOMING

MOORE/VARIOUS ARTISTS

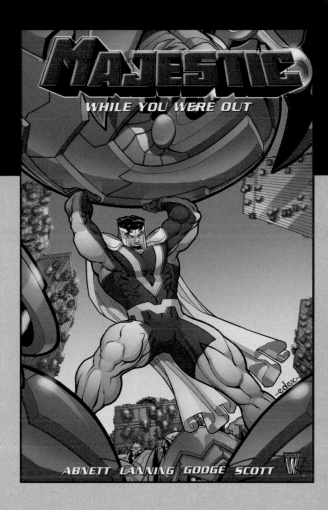

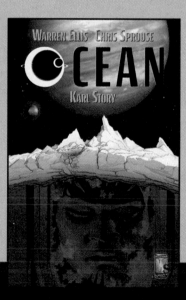
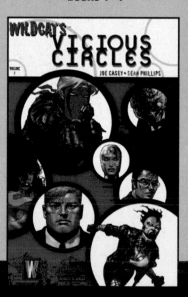